MW00613350

Savannah in the Time of Peter Tondee

Peter Tondee

Savannah
in the Time
of Peter Tondee

The Road to Revolution in Colonial Georgia

BY CARL SOLANA WEEKS

Carl Solana Weeks

Savannah

SUMMERHOUSE PRESS

COLUMBIA, SOUTH CAROLINA

Published in Columbia, South Carolina by Summerhouse Press
Copyright © 1997 by Carl Solana Weeks

Library of Congress Cataloging-in-Publication Data
Weeks, Carl Solana, 1948- Savannah in the time of Peter Tondee : the road to
revolution in colonial Georgia / by Carl Solana Weeks
       p. cm. Includes bibliographical references (p.   ) and Index.
   ISBN 1-887714-13-8 (alk. paper)
   1. Savannah (Ga.) - Social life and customs. 2. Tondee, Peter, ca.
1723-1775. 3. Savannah (Ga.) - Biography. 4. Working class-
-Georgia - Savannah - History - 18th century. 5. Georgia - History-
-Colonial period, ca. 1600-1775. I. Title.
   F294.S2W44   1997
975.8′72402 - dc21   97-18178
                                                                        CIP

10 9 8 7 6 5 4 3 2 1
First Edition

Contents

Illustrations

Maps

Acknowledgments

HAVING BROUGHT TO THE SUBJECT of colonial Savannah the expertise of an average native—that Oglethorpe was the founder; that the Battle of Bloody Marsh was a bloody battle fought in a marsh; and that if you walk around Tomochichi's grave three times and knock on the boulder, he'll say nothing—I feel justified in claiming more than an average debt of gratitude to the experts whose guidance made this book possible. They have been generous with suggestions and encouragement, and borne patiently the inconveniences of the novice.

Specifically, for their advice on genealogical research I wish to thank Kenneth H. Thomas, Jr.; Mary Bondurant Warren; and Diane Dieterle. For help with colonial maps I am grateful to Louis De Vorsey, Jr., of the University of Georgia; Tom Hardaway, of the University of Georgia Library Map Room; and John W. Reps. Larry E. Ivers and Virginia Steele Wood shared freely of their knowledge of military and naval affairs, and Preston Russell gave direction in researching the Siege of Savannah.

I am especially indebted to the librarians and staff members of the three depositories of records in Georgia where most of my research has been conducted. At the Georgia Department of Archives and History, Dale Couch has provided extensive knowledge and resourcefulness throughout this project. At the Hargrett Rare Book and Manuscript Library at the University of Georgia, the late Larry Gulley guided my first steps into the world of colonial Savannah, and Mary Ellen Brooks, Nelson Morgan, and Tom Deitz have facilitated the journey. To the librarians and staff of the Georgia Historical Society I owe the greatest thanks; their insightful suggestions and cheerful assistance have made working in Hodgson Hall a pleasure. Particularly I wish to acknowledge the help of Karen Osvald, Tony Dees, the late Lilla Mills Hawes, Bobbie Bennett, Anne P. Smith, Tracy Bearden, Eileen A. Ielmini, Jan Flores, Nancy Birkheimer, Carey Shellman, Kim Ball, and Frank Wheeler.

I would also like to express my appreciation to Joe Thompson of the Wormsloe Historic Site; Phil Noblitt of the Fort Frederica National Monument; Rabbi Saul Jacob Rubin; Marion L. Mendel; Carroll Greene; Harvey

H. Jackson; Robert Cooperman; Chuck and Nicki Moorer; Joyce T. Weeks; Clifton T. Cooper; James K. Creasy; Tim W. Forbes; Mike Bashlor; David A. Hammond; and Glenn Rivers.

Special thanks are due to Professor John D. Duncan for liberal loans from his collection of Georgia history and for continual guidance in research, and to both him and Virginia Duncan for years of patient support. To V. & J. Duncan Antique Maps and Prints I am indebted for three fifths of the illustrations in this volume.

For their enthusiastic aid in tracking the progeny of Peter and Lucy Tondee, I am obliged to the following descendants: W. L. Carpenter, the late Nina Usher, Donavon Tondee, Elizabeth Tondee Colvin, Martha A. McCorkle, Marion Praytor Colvin, Myra Willis Hargrove, Walter G. Basinger Wright, the late E. A. Mathis, and Barbara Ward Makris.

I wish also to honor the memory of three other descendants: Edith Doty Weeks, who told me as a boy about the bartender in the family; Edith Weeks Steele, who fostered all things creative and beautiful; and Anna Weeks Herrin, who first suggested this book thirty years ago.

Last, for their steadfast encouragement, wise counsel, and forbearance throughout this venture, I am deeply grateful to my parents, Stephen Elmo Weeks and Elizabeth Solana Weeks.

Prologue

ON A SATURDAY EVENING LATE in November of 1796, Savannah burned. The fire began around suppertime in a small bakehouse in Market Square, and by morning two thirds of the city smoldered in ruins. A cold northwest wind had whipped up the blaze, blowing embers into the night sky that arced like flaming arrows onto wooden shingle roofs parched by months of drought. Two hundred thirty houses were consumed, and four hundred families left destitute. It was the worst fire in Savannah's history.

Among the buildings lost were the two main churches—Christ Church Episcopal and Independent Presbyterian—the city market, the newspaper, all of the first ward of houses laid out at the founding of Savannah, and half each of four other wards. The two-story brick courthouse still stood, but unsteadily. Narrowly spared was a wooden structure called the silk filature, in which George Washington had attended a ball five years earlier; fire would not claim it for another forty-three years.

Also leveled was an old house at the corner of Broughton and Whitaker, a former tavern with an adjacent Long Room large enough to hold an assembly of a hundred. Once home to a family of nine, it was remembered too by veterans of the War of Independence as the birthplace of freedom in Georgia. There the Provincial Congress had convened to plan rebellion and to elect delegates to Philadelphia; there the Council of Safety had met to enforce rebel policies and to banish Tories; and before it the first Liberty Pole had been raised.

Even the British had met there when they occupied Savannah from late 1778 until the summer of 1782, when the rebel government resumed control and again took up its seat in the tavern, and unlike the Americans, the British had paid their bill.

One veteran in particular might have remembered the tavern fondly and mourned its loss. Noble Wimberly Jones had come to Georgia as a boy of ten on the first boat; had grown up in the new colony with the tavern's owner, Peter Tondee, who came on the second boat; and had led the cause of liberty during the final years of royal rule. But Jones had lost his own home in the fire that November night, and within two weeks the house of his son-in-law, in which his family had taken refuge, would also burn to the ground.

So along with most of eighteenth-century Savannah, Tondee's Tavern vanished into smoke and legend, leaving only the name to conjure visions of shirtsleeve patriots plotting liberty by candlelight.

In the Georgia Historical Society hangs an oil portrait of Peter Tondee painted by a descendant in the 1920s from a watercolor miniature passed down through generations. In the portrait Tondee resembles a melancholy Wordsworth, with gray eyes, a sensitive mouth, and soft waves of white hair. In the original miniature, however, he is a puckish Robbie Burns, his brown hair unkempt and streaked with gray, his deepset eyes peering coolly at the onlooker.

Like the painter of the portrait, posterity has viewed Tondee as a benevolent humanitarian, protecting orphans and promoting brotherhood, and without doubt he believed in the fraternity of man. Just the names Union Society and Unity Lodge, two groups he helped to found, profess his faith. But he was also capable, in his mid forties, of rousing the town at three in the morning to make a point.

This book grew out of a search for the real Peter Tondee. What little had been written about him outlined a life of dramatic twists, and I wanted to clear away the smoke and see the man in his time. I followed him from London to Port Royal to Savannah; through the sandy streets and squares of General Oglethorpe's little settlement; out to Henry Parker's plantation at the Isle of Hope and evangelist George Whitefield's orphanage Bethesda; through the rooms of the silk filature, the courthouse, the Commons House of Assembly, and the tavern. I came to know the families he lived with and his boyhood contemporaries, his friends and neighbors and in-laws, the prominent men who affected his life in Savannah and the common people who comprised his social circle. In short, I entered his world as completely as I could.

Only once, however, did I surprise Tondee himself. It was at the guardhouse late in December of 1769, and he was in the company of the Attorney General of the province. At the moment, though, neither man was in a mood for badinage, and Tondee's few comments were peevish and confrontational.

Otherwise, he has remained elusive, a shadow at the edge of the lamplight, receding after merely a glimpse. We can say where he was in any year, what land he owned and sold, what lawsuits and petitions he submitted and their outcomes, what public buildings he constructed, what offices he held and what acts performed in the discharge of his duties—all the kinds of records kept by an Empire remarkable for thoroughness. We have reliable reports in the colony's newspaper of many of the meetings and events that took place at the tavern. We have a brief description of Tondee at fifteen and, because he was too weak to sign his will legibly, an account of his death from the witnesses. But after all, he does not inhabit these pages so much as haunt them; and this was to be expected. For though records may provide extensive details about the lives of the great and powerful or the low and villainous, men of the common sort—and Tondee was the exemplar of the common man—often go unmentioned.

A curious change occurred, though, in the course of this search. The further I pursued Tondee through the streets and lanes of town, the more intimate I grew with colonial Savannah—his Savannah, peopled with blacksmiths and clerks and tailors as well as gentleman planters and members of the Governor's Council. Over time, his life became more the vehicle than the destination, and when the journey was done, it was not so much Tondee I missed as the young town on the bluff where I had sought him.

Peter's brother Charles, in his only application for land in Georgia, referred to himself as a "Child of the Province." His intent was to remind the Governor and Council that he had been raised as a ward of the Trust. The term applied equally to Peter, but before his death in October of 1775, at the twilight of the colonial era, Peter had also become, among legions of other carpenters and masons and shopkeepers, a father of the state. This narrative is an account of that voyage, both for him and for the colony of Georgia.

Part One
Child of the Province

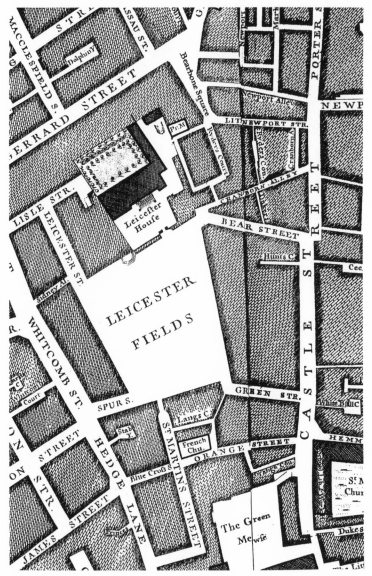

**Ryder's Court Chapel, where Peter's brother Charles was baptized, lies to the right of
Leicester House and is marked by "Pr M" for "Protestant Meetinghouse," or
Huguenot church. Detail from 1746 "Plan of the Cities of London
and Westminster, and Borough of Southwark," by John Rocque.**
(V. & J. Duncan, Antique Maps and Prints.)

London

PETER TONDEE GOT TO GEORGIA only through the dogged Huguenot tenacity of his father. Forty-eight at the time of the crossing, Pierre Tondu had known adversity from the first year of his life, and it challenged him up to his final few days in London before the ship set sail. His most valuable legacy to his two sons would be this tenacity, when soon after reaching Savannah he left them orphans.

Born in Chatillon-sur-Loire one year before Louis XIV opened season on Huguenots by revoking the Edict of Nantes, Tondu (the name means "shorn" or "tonsured") had made his way to London by the age of twenty-four and probably settled near Leicester Square, an area favored by French Protestants. He registered his faith in 1708 at a small Huguenot chapel in Ryder's Court, a block and a half from Leicester, and there he and his wife Jeanne had their younger son Charles baptized in January of 1728.

Five years later, just before Christmas of 1732, Tondu agreed to accompany a retired army ensign named Henry Pinkerton to the new colony as an indentured servant, one of three the ensign intended to bring. Pinkerton would pay the passage for Tondu and his sons—his wife is not mentioned— and provide for them in Georgia in exchange for labor, and at the end of his term Tondu would be granted twenty-five acres by the Trustees in London.

Pinkerton's grant of three hundred acres was approved and he paid the consideration fee, but a week before the ship was to sail, he reneged, citing land tenure restrictions, a common complaint from early colonists. In theory only the eldest male could inherit land, although in practice exceptions would be liberally allowed; but more worrisome, colonists did not have the right to sell their grant without permission from the Trustees.

As well as misgivings about the land policy, Pinkerton may have had second thoughts about the voyage itself. The weather had turned especially harsh just prior to his decision to decline. A storm called the worst in years had battered England, toppling chimneys and stripping tiles from roofs. Several boats on the Thames had sunk, and ships moored at Deal on the

Channel had been blown into each other or ashore—conditions not propitious for a sea voyage.

Somehow in the week between Pinkerton's withdrawal and the embarkation of the ship, Tondu scraped together the £7 6s. 8d. passage for himself and his sons Peter and Charles, aged ten and five, and they boarded the *James* at the Rotherhithe docks on January 24, 1733—eight days before the first colonists from the *Ann* would pitch their tents on the high bluff overlooking the Savannah River. Thomas Coram, one of the Trustees, came down for the mustering of passengers, but the ship initially got no farther than Deal, where it rode at anchor for two weeks, along with thirty other vessels, waiting for the gale to abate.

Almost certainly a carpenter by trade, Tondu joined seven other carpenters on the *James*, described in London as "miserable objects" and sent as a kind of afterthought to the original one hundred and fourteen colonists on the *Ann*. The Trustees had apparently realized that the half-dozen carpenters

**Captain Thomas Coram, one of the first Georgia Trustees, attended the muster
on board the *James* when the Tondees embarked at London.**
(V. & J. Duncan, Antique Maps and Prints.)

in the first landing would not be enough to build a town. The cargo in the hold of the *James*—a ship with roughly half the capacity of the *Ann*—included eight casks of nails and spikes and several more of gunpowder flasks, cartridge boxes, and bayonets.

The Tondus' fellow passengers were a motley company. Besides the carpenters, the Trustees had sent a blacksmith; a tailor, who would serve briefly as a magistrate but resign from a feeling of inadequacy since he could not read; and a last-minute addition named Botham Squires, who brought with him a letter of introduction from the Trustees to founder James Oglethorpe. Of the carpenters, one—Robert Hows—would become a devout follower of the Reverends John Wesley and George Whitefield, while another—Paul Cheeswright—would contribute generously to the moral turpitude of the colony. Among the carpenter's wives, two were pregnant during the voyage, and the tailor's daughter would marry in July. Hows's eight-year-old girl Mary, one of the two other children on board besides Peter and Charles, would die five years later, while her father was in England with Wesley, under rigorous discipline from her Moravian guardians; and Cheeswright's wife Rebecca, two years after arriving, would incur sixty lashes for "barbarously cutting an infant down the back with a knife." In cramped quarters with these companions, the Tondus passed the ten weeks of the voyage, sailing to a wilderness and leaving behind a life in the burgeoning hub of the Empire, a city bristling with extremes.

This was the London of Christopher Wren, of Handel and Hogarth, Fielding and Swift. Where one worshipped in the morning at the new and magnificent St. Paul's, and wagered at night on the cockfights in Covent Garden. Where the *Water Music* wafted over the Thames to the ears of George I, while the cries of fishwives and flower-girls rang in the streets. Where a young rake could attend the court of St. James on Christmas Eve, and find himself chained to a cot in Bedlam come Twelfth Night; and tales of a shipwrecked Englishman named Gulliver mocked mankind from both ends of the telescope.

On their way to board the *James* at Rotherhithe, the travelers would have crossed the old London Bridge, with houses four stories high from bank to bank; and from the deck of the ship as they cast off, they could have seen the Tower on the north shore, its pennant fluttering in the wind.

Along with all this, they were leaving also the teeming squalor of life on the streets, the chronic poverty and despair that drove men to gin houses and crime. They might have recalled an account ten days earlier in the *Weekly Miscellany* of a boy in Lincolnshire who had been sent by his grandfather to fetch a horse and chaise and was discovered on the carriage seat with his head almost cut off and the horse stolen. Or another story in the same issue about the post-boy of Ancaster who was found murdered—along with his horse—on the high road. And some might have joined the mob that so severely beat Bartholomew Harnett, a perjurer in pillory, that he had to be carried back to Newgate in a cart.

But it is certain that whatever their lot in England, whatever hardships they had endured, the passengers had given up a life which they knew for one which they did not. And somewhere between London and Georgia, Pierre Tondu gave up his French name for Peter Tondee.

Port Royal

THE VOYAGE OF THE *JAMES* ended with a flourish of weird luck. On the evening before the ship made landfall, Charles Town, sixty miles to the north, had been pelted by hail the size of pullets' eggs. Entering Port Royal Sound the next day, the *James* by chance encountered the cutter of Squire Oglethorpe on the way from Savannah to Charles Town. With him was Tomochichi, the old chief of the Yamacraw who had welcomed the English, and his nephew and heir Tooanahowi, a boy roughly Peter's age. In Charles Town they would talk treaties and prepare for a general council of chiefs to convene in Savannah after their return. But first the cutter escorted the *James* to the southeast point of Port Royal Island, where stood a half-finished enclosure of tabby walls named Fort Frederick, and there on May 2 the *James's* passengers finally touched American soil.

That night in the barracks at Port Royal, Oglethorpe contracted with the captain, James Yoakley, for the ship to sail up the Savannah River to the settlement on the bluff. The first contingent of colonists on the *Ann* had stopped at Fort Frederick also, but they had transferred to smaller coastal vessels for the final leg of the journey, down the inland waterway and upriver to the site. The Savannah River was rumored to be unnavigable, with its constantly shifting bars, and it is a measure of the significance Oglethorpe attached to establishing that ships could reach the new town that he promised the captain a bonus of £100 for proving it. Possibly not everyone was pleased with the arrangement.

Early the next morning Oglethorpe continued to Charles Town, and for five days the *James's* passengers rested at Port Royal and readied themselves for the trip to Savannah. They may have been visited by gentlemen from Beaufort, a town three miles away—the colonists on the *Ann* had received calls and gifts from several of them—but the impression the passengers from the *James* might have made is dubious. In any case, on the morning of May 8, the ship set sail for Savannah.

The ensuing mutiny must have occurred almost immediately. Led by a former pirate who had been freed by the Act of Grace on the accession of George II, the foremast-men had threatened to run away with the ship. Notice was somehow given to the garrison at Fort Frederick, and a scout boat commanded by Lieutenant James Watts rowed out and subdued the sailors, taking away the ringleader in irons. Possibly the mutineers had heard the rumors about the Savannah River and wanted none of it.

The *James* was six days in passage, dropping anchor safely below the bluff of the new town in about fifteen feet of water. The channel up the river was pronounced good, and larger shipping invited.

At that point, the little settlement was a thoroughly modest sight. With many of their tools destroyed in a fire soon after the landing, the colonists had built barely a dozen small houses. They were living in four large tents on the bluff, and with the stress of constant communal dwelling and hard labor in the hot Georgia sun, the first grumbles of discontent were growing audible.

Founded in the optimistic spirit of the Enlightenment, Georgia was truly an experiment in social engineering, from its idealistic premises about governing a society to its policies on slavery and the equal distribution of

Tabby ruins of Fort Frederick, Port Royal Island. Colonists on both the *Ann* **and the** *James* **landed here before proceeding to Savannah.**
(1904 photograph by Leigh Richmond Miner. From the Penn School Collection. Permission granted by Penn Center, Inc., St. Helena Island, South Carolina.)

land. Even the layout of Savannah—a felicitous gridwork of streets and squares—sprang from the Age of Reason.

Just as integral to the project, and typical of the age, was the philanthropic nature of Georgia's Board of Trustees, whose motto read "Not for Themselves, but for Others." James Oglethorpe's personal impetus for promoting Georgia had been to give debtors an alternative to jail—he had lost a friend to smallpox in Fleet Prison—and though ultimately few actual debtors were sent, the colony did offer a chance of betterment to England's "worthy poor."

Of course, there were also more practical motives for founding Georgia. Primarily, it would provide a buffer between the English Carolinas and Spanish Florida, at a time when the two nations were steering a course toward war. And with its mild climate, the region could be expected to produce silk and wine, freeing England from dependence on other countries.

Lamentably, reason and reality seldom agree. Land distributed equally on a map did not distinguish between fertile soil and sandy pine barrens or swamp bottoms; important issues of government decided in London were often obsolete by the time they reached Georgia; and neither weather nor the laws of economics paid any heed to high expectations.

Perhaps most unreasonable, ironically, was the Trustees' method of choosing colonists. For while it was laudable to offer a chance for a new life to London's poor, the candidates considered were already established failures. Indeed, one criterion stipulated that those sent should pose no economic loss to the homeland, and many were turned away as not being hopeless enough.

On arriving in the wilderness, the colonists had faced unwonted physical challenges. Praised as *The Most Delightful Country of the Universe* fifteen years earlier in a tract that compared the territory to Eden—at least the two shared the same latitude—Georgia had revealed, with the advent of spring, not only a fiercely hot climate but a proliferation of biting, sucking, and stinging insects. Alligators sunned on the riverbank opposite the town; snakes moved into the houses along with the colonists.

So the *James* arrived at the beginning of the end of the honeymoon. Among the passengers on the *Ann*, the high morale and first flush of success were giving way to a creeping disillusionment in the Squire's version of utopia. Admittedly, he shared their hardship, living in his tent as though on campaign even after they had built a house for him. But the colonists were growing weary with the strain. Indefatigable he might be, but they were not. Though great hardship can bring out heroism in mediocre men, it also brings out a great deal of mediocrity. By midsummer they had ceased calling him Father Oglethorpe.

But in May most hearts were still stout. Only the physician Doctor Cox had died since the founding. With the help of black sawyers lent by South Carolina—Georgia's Trustees prohibited owning slaves—the building of the town went forward daily, and in the evening there was rum punch just up the river at the trading post of Mary Musgrove, the Yamacraw interpreter. The real unrest would not come until the black sawyers left and the water went bad and lead-poisoned rum killed half a dozen carpenters.

Savannah

AROUND THE TIME OF THE *James*'s arrival, delegations of Indians were converging on Savannah to meet with Oglethorpe, and by his return four days later the chiefs of eight Creek tribes had assembled with their war captains and attendant braves, over fifty in all. For the English, the sight of the Squire's cutter approaching the bluff surely came none too soon. That afternoon he received the delegations in one of the new houses that stood conveniently close to the battery of six cannon on the Strand, which he hoped they would notice.

To the Creeks, the meeting was a momentous event—the contingent from Coweta had traveled for twenty-five days to reach Savannah—and they behaved with dignity and decorum. First to speak was a chief called by the English "The Long King." He rose, and with broad, graceful gestures and sonorous words declared that the Great Power which dwelt in Heaven and all around and which gave Breath to All Men had sent the English to instruct them and their wives and children, and therefore they gave up freely their rights to all the land they did not themselves use, for as long as the sun shines and the waters run. That amounted to a thirty-mile-wide strip of coastland, from the Savannah River south to the Altamaha, and for three decades it would be enough. The eight tribes also presented Squire Oglethorpe with eight bundles of buckskins, their best and given with a good heart.

That night they feasted and danced at Tomochichi's settlement up the bluff. On Monday the treaty was signed, and the Squire distributed to each of the chiefs a laced coat, a laced hat, and a shirt; to each warrior a gun and a duffel cloak; to the attendants coarse cloth; and to each tribe a barrel of gunpowder, bullets, rum, Irish linen, and eight belts and cutlasses with gilt handles. The Indians were delighted.

By evening Oglethorpe had placed the colony in the care of two Carolina gentlemen and boarded his cutter again for Charles Town to raise more money. When he returned a month later, he would not be pleased with what he found.

Meanwhile the clapboard houses went up steadily, though not fast enough for most colonists. Children worked too, at tasks within their scope, and at ten years old Peter sweated alongside boys of similar age, most nota-

Tomochichi and his nephew Tooanahowi.
(V. & J. Duncan, Antique Maps and Prints.)

bly Noble Wimberly Jones and the two Milledge boys, John and Richard, who would figure prominently in his life and in that of the colony. As well, there was Marmaduke Cannon—who went predictably by Duke; William Cox, the son of the late physician; John Wright, Sam Parker, James Thibaut, John Goddard, and Charles Clark. Of these, half would lose their fathers before Christmas.

Besides lead poisoning from tainted rum, the colonists were afflicted with the "bloody flux," or dysentery, from drinking river water, and with the ague, a fever that was probably malaria, borne by the ubiquitous mosquitoes. Within a month after the death of Doctor Cox, the Reverend Henry Herbert retreated to Charles Town to recover his health, but died of a bloody flux en route to London, leaving Savannah with neither a physical nor a spiritual minister.

When James Oglethorpe returned to the town in June, he promptly traced the cause of the rampant sickness to rum. Rum had made the colonists impatient of discipline, and rum would reduce them, as had the gin houses in London, to objects of charity, sotted and idle. To remedy drunkenness he ordered every keg in town staved; to remedy idleness he sent the black sawyers back to South Carolina. If the men worked as he did, they would have no time to drink; and without rum, they would surely regain their health. The illness was only a symptom. That small children, who drank no rum, suffered in equal numbers puzzled him little: once established, the disease had simply grown contagious. By midsummer nearly half the colony was sick, and half of those did not get well.

For the funeral of Doctor Cox, to signify that his life had been given for England, Oglethorpe had commanded full military honors, with cannon fired from the guardhouse and three volleys of small arms over the grave. Later, in the funerals that followed, the tradition of military honors was upheld, even for the funerals of women. But as the deaths came faster, the frequent firing of the cannon and small arms served only to terrify the sick and disconcert the healthy, so Oglethorpe ordered the practice dropped.

John Goddard's father died on the first of July, his mother by the end of the month. Sam Parker's father, installed as constable in the first civic ceremony on July 7, did not live to see jury duty three weeks later.

On the morning of that ceremony, when Squire Oglethorpe named the streets and swore in the bailiffs and constables, the colonists had met at dawn on the bluff for prayers of thanksgiving and then walked to Johnson Square, named for the governor of South Carolina, to hear the speeches and receive their lot assignments. Thomas Milledge, whom Oglethorpe called "our best carpenter," made the presentation of the twenty-one finished houses on behalf of all the carpenters, who had agreed to take empty lots for the time being so that those less able might move into homes at once. The gesture was especially magnanimous for Milledge's wife, who was eight months pregnant. The town celebrated with a dinner, and the arrival of thirty more colonists from the *Pearl* seemed to crown the day with providential approval.

Much more providential—if perturbing to Oglethorpe—was the unexpected appearance four days later of the *William and Sarah*, with forty-two colonists, all Jews. One of them was a doctor.

Orphans

ALTHOUGH THE CHARTER OF THE colony expressly prohibited admitting Catholics—England wanted no souls sympathetic to Spain or France in this buffer zone—the Honorable Trustees had faced a delicate dilemma regarding Jews. The issue had been considered and discussed and tabled, but not determined. For though the Trustees had commissioned three highly respected Jews in London to raise money for Georgia, they hardly expected them to contribute colonists as well.

Oglethorpe guessed correctly that the Trustees would demur against admitting them, but most of the passengers were strong, healthy men, and several had skills badly needed in the new town. The leader, Doctor Samuel Nunez, had formerly held the post of personal physician to the Grand Inquisitor in Lisbon, despite Portugal's persecution of Jews. So the Squire counselled with some South Carolina lawyers, assessed his situation, and after keeping the passengers waiting on board for a day, agreed to grant them lots. The Jews disembarked, and Doctor Nunez set to work, for free.

After the death of Doctor Cox, Noble Jones—Wimberly's father—who brought with him a smattering of medical knowledge, had treated the sick with doses of rhubarb and tincture of opium and the Indian root diascordium, but these had little effect, and eventually Jones himself fell ill. Doctor Nunez used instead cold baths and cooling drinks, and his success won Oglethorpe entirely.

Writing in August to his fellow Trustees, he claimed that under the care of Nunez the sick had wonderfully recovered, and none had been lost who followed his prescriptions. Second only to the doctor's skill in restoring the health of the colonists, he concluded, was his own prohibition of rum.

The sanguinity of Oglethorpe's claims, however, was not entirely warranted. Two days after he wrote this letter, Botham Squires, a passenger on the *James*, fled the sick town for South Carolina. Those who subsequently died—apparently not having followed the doctor's prescriptions—included

"A View of Savannah as it stood the 29th of March, 1734." Presented and dedicated to the Trustees by Peter Gordon, the plat for this map was drawn in **Georgia by Noble Jones.** *(V. & J. Duncan, Antique Maps and Prints.)*

Thomas Cornwall, Richard Hodges, William Little, John Warren, Duke Cannon's mother Mary, and several others, among them carpenters Thomas Milledge and Peter Tondee. But Oglethorpe may have hoped to dispel growing skepticism about the colony and to defend his decision to admit the Jews.

During the year after the death of their father, the whereabouts of the Tondee boys is unclear. They show up early in 1735 in the household of Paul Amatis, the Italian silk expert sent on the *Ann* to direct silk production. But Amatis lived in Charles Town until September of 1734, propagating grapevines and fruit trees and mulberries for the silkworms, and it is unlikely that the Tondees were sent to him there.

In Savannah, the placement of orphans in foster homes followed a pattern: since the constable of the ward in which the orphan lived had the responsibility of finding the child an acceptable home, he often took under his own roof as servants any who were old enough to contribute labor; and those too young to work might have been hard to place anywhere else. So the Tondees may well have lived for a while with the family of Joseph Coles, the constable of Decker Ward, where the Tondee lot was located.

A miller and baker in England, Coles had come to Georgia on the *Ann* with his wife and daughter and one servant. During the voyage he had suffered the ignominy of being beaten by his wife in a bout of skimmingtons, a game played with padded cudgels. But by March of 1735 he too was dead.

With the high mortality rate the first year and the resulting orphans, a committee of trustees for the orphans' affairs was appointed, among whom one, Edward Jenkins, took his duties quite seriously. He first mentioned the Tondee boys in January of 1735 in a letter to Oglethorpe, then in London, relaying Amatis's wish that the Tondees be taken off his hands. In another letter several months later, he fretted that the Tondees were not being properly cared for, Amatis having taken "a scandalous wench to himself instead of a wife." The Italian married the wench, however, and Catherine Amatis gave birth to Paul junior six months later.

Life with Amatis was not uneventful, but his treatment of Peter and Charles likely amounted to little more than indifference. Elsewhere he had duties and distractions enough to demand his full attention. When he was not at Purrysburg or Charles Town, the moody Piedmontese (he spoke and wrote in French, one reason for the Tondees to be placed with him) was constantly embroiled in disputes with Joseph Fitzwalter about what to plant in the public garden and with Thomas Causton about the use of the public servants there.

Fueling these disagreements was the issue of respect. Unlike almost all the other colonists, Amatis came from an ancient family, perhaps not revered as aristocracy but certainly esteemed as masters of the mysteries of silk. He expected deference as only his due, and his pique flared if his judgment were even questioned. Sometimes his brother Nicholas joined the fray, but Amatis argued with him too, and eventually fired him. To assist in the silk culture, the Trustees had sent within the first year another family of French named Camuse, and in the wife Mary, Amatis found a worthy adversary. Their impassioned volleys, though largely unintelligible to the English, were full of color and high drama.

But despite his feisty pride, Amatis must have cut a lonely figure, belonging to no clubs, attending no parties (he did not dance). He deeply resented the Freemasons, and his claims that he was thwarted by the town's leaders—Thomas Causton, Henry Parker, Thomas Christie—were probably in part justified.

With all Amatis's preoccupations, the Tondee boys likely had a great deal of time to themselves. There was no formal school in Savannah—the teacher sent on the *Ann* had proved a drunkard and left the colony—and until the Wesleys came in 1736 no attempt was made to conduct lessons. At twelve years old, Peter surely had chores, and maybe seven-year-old Charles too, but with the silk man out of town for long periods, there were ample hours to roam the streets.

In the spring of 1735, the streets they roamed did not range far. Only four wards had been laid out, each with a cleared square in the center for use as a market or as a place of refuge for outlying settlers in case of attack. To the north of the square were two tythings—blocks of ten sixty-by-ninety-foot house lots—and to the south were two more, or four per ward. The double lots east and west of the square were intended for public buildings, like the Trust storehouse, the oven, and the House for Strangers, where visiting Indians could stay.

At this time only Derby Ward, the first established, boasted a full complement of forty houses. These were pine bungalows twenty-four feet long, sixteen feet deep, and eight feet high, with a pitched roof. Half the house was usually given to one larger room, and the other half split into two smaller ones, with a loft or garret above. The walls were unplaned featheredged boards, the roofs tarred wooden shingles, and the plank floor was raised two and a half feet off the ground on log foundations. Soon after the colonists completed each house, the termites began on it.

The only trees left standing in Savannah were the four tall pines in

Johnson Square, at the center of Derby Ward, so the general appearance of the town was simply open space, dotted with dwellings or overgrown with weeds and briars. With no shade, the sun beat fiercely on fair summer days, and after a rain the sandy streets melted into quagmires.

The forty-foot bluff where the first tents had been pitched looked out over a low island across the river, with pastures cleared for cattle. Beyond this stretched a wide plain of marsh and serpentine creeks and scattered blue hammocks of oak and palmetto and red cedar, growing darker in the distance until they formed a solid olive silhouette on the horizon. At the west end of the bluff lived the Yamacraw; at the east end was the ten-acre public garden. Both east and west the land beyond the bluff sloped down to swampy bottoms, futile to farm and thick with insects.

Later, as elder son, Peter would inherit, in addition to the house lot in Decker Ward, a five-acre garden lot in the nearby swamp east of town and a forty-five-acre farm lot in the farther swamp west of town.

The Silk Man

SIX WEEKS AFTER HIS REQUEST to be quit of the Tondee boys, Amatis reached his peak of paranoia, colliding ultimately with gardener Joseph Fitzwalter, a man who was his virtual antithesis. Their conflict was the coda to an episode known as the Red String Plot, which by its end had brought out the worst in almost everyone involved.

The thirty-three-year-old Fitzwalter loved to hunt and fish, and his letters to the Trustees catalogue the bounty of game in the woods and rivers around Savannah. He claimed to have shot six wild turkeys in one day and to have caught a three-hundred-pound sturgeon, and from the abundance of deer and boar, wood pigeons and ducks, salmon, trout, and bass, he had concluded, "In a word, I take our settlement to be the promised land." It was probably his penchant for rambling in the woods that provoked Edward Jenkins, in the same letter that branded Amatis's wife a scandalous wench, to condemn Fitzwalter as a ruinous guardian. His ward John Goddard, a year younger than Peter, would later be called an idle rambler as well after running away from his master, a shipwright in Charles Town, with three years left to his apprenticeship.

Fitzwalter's affinity with nature also drew him close to the Indians, so close in fact that in April of that year, 1735, he married Molly, the eldest daughter of Tuscany, one of Tomochichi's captains. The aged chief gave the bride away—as the first marriage between a colonist and an Indian, the event took on diplomatic overtones—and both the Indians and the townspeople, if not the Trustees, thought it a politic union. But time failed to wear the bride of her savage way of living, as Fitzwalter had hoped; and possibly her opinion of the match had never been asked. In any case, Molly ran away from him.

The incident of the Red String Plot erupted on a Sunday evening early in March, 1735, the same week that Joseph Coles died. One of the constables sounded the town alarm, and within fifteen minutes nearly fifty freeholders had mustered at the guardhouse on the Strand. Word was that the

Irish transport servants—in league with disgruntled Indians led by John Musgrove, Mary's half-English husband—were planning to burn the town and murder the inhabitants.

The Irish transports had been blown to Georgia by a truly ill wind. Around the first Christmas in the colony, bad weather and dwindling provisions had forced their ship to put in at Savannah, and because of their desperate condition, some already having died of starvation, Oglethorpe thought it an act of charity to take in the remaining forty and purchase their indentures for £5 each, as a boon to all the new widows and busy magistrates. The widows and magistrates would later trace the beginning of many grievances to the day those servants set foot in Georgia, but at the time the prospect of laborers seemed a godsend.

While the constable took some men to search Musgrove's trading post, Joseph Fitzwalter went to fetch Thomas Causton from Skidaway Island, south of town, and someone went for Henry Parker, the third magistrate. In the meantime, Thomas Christie, court recorder and by default the highest-ranking official in town at that instant, learned that the sign of recognition among the conspirators was to be a red ribbon worn on the wrist.

Immediately Christie sent out armed parties to examine the wrists of all servants and any well-known malcontents among the colonists. Three were discovered at once, and as darkness fell, Christie had his men drag several cannon out to flank the Strand, posted guards around the magazine, and chose twenty able men to patrol the streets all night.

No attack came; the alarm bell seemed to have scattered the cabal. Early Monday morning the magistrates convened in the courthouse, a small structure on the lot behind the house built for Oglethorpe, to question the parties involved. At first no freeholders were incriminated; then it was one of the original colonists from the *Ann* who had hatched the plan, aided by Thomas Tibbut, who came over on the *James*.

Later, Thomas Causton concluded that there were probably two plots: the Irish transports had hidden guns and ammunition in the woods, and meant to murder the men, take the women, and burn the town; and several freeholders who had run into debt—their common resolve bolstered by rum—meant to desert the colony during the ensuing chaos. Musgrove and the Indians were exonerated, and one freeholder and two servants were convicted and given sixty lashes each.

But the affair was not entirely over. In a fit of intuition, Amatis perceived that his enemies were using the Red String Plot as a means to harass him by whipping one of his servants, who was summoned from the garden for questioning. At first he aimed his ire at Causton, charging that the magistrate had no business whatsoever to examine any of his servants for any reason. But he soon turned his invective against Fitzwalter as well, damning him and Causton and ending with a warning that he would shoot Fitzwalter if he saw him in the garden again.

The gardener returned to work as usual early the next morning to give the servants orders for the day, and Amatis appeared around nine waving a gun and sputtering threats. Fitzwalter promptly swore out a warrant against him to appear in court and promise peaceful behavior, and Amatis, raging at this summons by a subordinate, vowed to remove him.

Aside from the opposite natures of these two men, the friction between them was due in large part to the ambiguity of their positions. Put simply, Amatis was the silk man, Fitzwalter the gardener. But in Charles Town Amatis had planted an extensive garden of thousands of mulberries for the silkworms, and grapevines, and scores of orange, peach, apple, and plum trees, so considered himself the proper gardener. Meanwhile, in Savannah Fitzwalter had labored to clear the land for the public garden, while Amatis enjoyed the civilized comfort of Charles Town, and had begun growing plants for kitchen and medicinal use (writing with a brogue of his "Baby nussery of plants"), so considered himself the proper gardener.

Unfortunately, neither the Trustees nor Oglethorpe had anticipated any conflict in these roles, and no hierarchy had been established. The magistrates and the recorder knew little about the Trustees' intentions and less about the law—in London Thomas Causton had been a calico printer, Henry Parker a linen maker, and Thomas Christie a merchant—so they could offer no help without further instructions.

To the dismay of Fitzwalter and the magistrates, however, the Trustees sided with Amatis. The Italian grew irrepressible, and by autumn Fitzwalter had left for South Carolina.

A year later Charles Wesley praised the abundance of cucumbers, melons, and vegetables in the garden, but observed that the nurseries of trees had been poorly managed by the previous gardener, Amatis, whom Oglethorpe had eventually removed.

Joseph Fitzwalter returned to the garden at the end of 1737, restored it to order within a few weeks, and married the Widow Wright. The silk man had been dead then for over a year.

Long before that, though, the Tondee boys had moved in with the new second magistrate, Henry Parker.

The Parkers

WHEN HENRY PARKER TOOK IN the Tondees, he had already proved himself an able administrator and an upstanding colonist. While they lived with him, he would also emerge as one of the gamer men in town, subject to flaws but generally liked and trusted.

From the moment he arrived in Georgia until his death, Parker remained—except for a brief hiatus—a public servant. Appointed constable en route to Savannah on the *Georgia Pink* during the first summer, he had risen to third magistrate in little more than a year, and to second magistrate in less. By the time the Trustees surrendered their charter for Georgia to the Crown, he would be President of the Colony.

One of his early adventures that caught the Trustees' attention occurred in the autumn of 1734. Henry and his brother William, who came to the colony with him, were working with Edward Jenkins on his garden lot southwest of town to repay him for some work he had done them, when one of Jenkins's servants announced, "Yonder goes a man very fast." As Jenkins related it, he looked up and saw the man and said, "I believe it's White that broke out of prison. If it is him let us go and take him." The Parkers agreed, and with two hooks and an axe, the three followed to within twenty yards of him.

As soon as the fugitive turned and saw them, Jenkins asserted, "Your name is White, it's in vain to escape." The hapless prisoner fell to his knees and beat his breast, and as they led him to town he begged for his life. When told he would only perish in the woods if they set him free, he declared it would be joyful to perish in the woods rather than die on the gallows.

Richard White had been condemned to hang for the murder of old William Wise, a man of reduced circumstances and a bit of a lecher, having tried to pass off as his daughter a London streetwalker he wished to bring to Georgia. Old Wise had settled on Hutchinson's Island, directly across the river from town, to tend the Trust's cattle put out to pasture there. But he had fallen ill soon after his arrival, so the magistrates placed with him White and Alice Riley, two of the Irish transports, to care for his needs and keep the cattle till he could recover. Each morning Wise made it his habit to call for a bucket of water to wash, and then to lie with his head at the edge of the bed so that White could comb his long hair, in which he took great pride. But one morning in March, White had slipped his fists around Wise's neckerchief and twisted it tight, while Alice Riley, to be thorough, pushed his head into the bucket of water. Joseph Fitzwalter had led the pursuit, and White and Riley were caught and sentenced to hang. Before the execution could be carried out, though, the pair had escaped.

On the way to town—flanked by Henry Parker and Edward Jenkins, with William Parker behind—Richard White had offered to lead them to Alice Riley, who he said was hiding nearby, or to testify under oath against the other Irish transports, who were planning to break into the Trust's store. None of this was judged to have much import by Jenkins or the Parkers, though, and White was led immediately to the gallows and hanged.

Alice Riley was taken not long after, but on examination she was found to be pregnant, so her execution was delayed until she gave birth. Her son James was born just before Christmas, and Riley was hanged two months later, protesting her innocence to the last. The baby survived his mother by only a few weeks.

At the end of this tragedy, Henry Parker found himself £16 13s. 4d. richer, having split with his brother and Jenkins the £50 reward for the recapture of White and Riley. The cash, however, did not reach Savannah until late July of 1735, the same week in which the magistrates sentenced Rebecca Cheeswright to sixty lashes for cutting an infant down the back with a knife.

The Parker family was then living on the corner of Bryan Street and Drayton in a house rented from the Widow Cooper; Henry's house at York and Bull was rented by his brother William. Within a year, however, Henry took possession of a five-hundred-acre tract southeast of town, one third of an island Noble Jones named the Isle of Hope, and increasingly it became his main residence.

When Peter and Charles joined the Parkers, the family was growing again, after an initial setback. Henry and Anne Parker had lost two small sons within a month after landing in Savannah, but another son, Henry William, had been born a year later, and a daughter would arrive in the spring of 1736.

The Tondee boys, at thirteen and eight, finally belonged to a stable household. Parker's prospects looked bright: as the protégé of Thomas Causton—first magistrate and keeper of the Trust's store—he had ample provisions and occasional use of the Trust's servants. And Anne Parker would prove a strong-willed and ardent mother, defending her young like a lioness.

The Wesleys

IN FEBRUARY OF 1736, AT THE OUTSET of Georgia's fourth year, Oglethorpe returned from London with two shiploads of colonists, two hundred fifty-seven in all, known as the Great Embarkation. Among them were sixty Germans, the last of three contingents of Salzburger refugees who settled up the Savannah River. Hardworking and devout, they had already shown themselves model colonists, and in future years the Tondee boys would come to know some of them well. Oglethorpe brought also the new preacher, John Wesley, and his brother Charles, and with them a new schoolteacher, Charles Delamotte.

The Wesleys applied themselves at once to preaching and praying, and Mr. Delamotte opened school. For the first time since coming to Savannah, Peter and Charles Tondee sat in a classroom, along with Richard Milledge, John Goddard, James Thibaut, and even Duke Cannon, who had moved in with the Caustons after his father died. More recent faces filled out the roll, and for two years Delamotte—a close friend of the Wesleys and a practitioner of their strict and serious method of living—drilled the children in letters and numbers and religion. Brief as it was, his tenure in Georgia would outlast the new preacher's.

John Wesley had found a warm welcome in Savannah, which had lacked a real spiritual leader since the founding of the colony. The Reverend Henry Herbert had fallen ill the first spring, left for England, and died at sea; and his successor, Samuel Quincy, spent so much time away from his parish duties that for a period of six months services had been read and the dead buried by one of the freeholders. Having already decided to dismiss Quincy, the Trustees accepted his resignation with equanimity.

So Savannahians initially embraced Wesley, this energetic Oxford graduate who wished most to teach and convert the Indians, and through their simplicity and innocence to attain a state of pure faith. Wesley's commission as minister of the colony left little time for saving the natives, though, and the English soon grew restive under his critiques of parishioners from the pulpit and his strict adherence to church canon.

One of the first clashes involved the Parkers. On a Wednesday evening early in May, three months after his arrival, Wesley was asked to baptize their baby Anne. He had begun practicing Trine Immersion—submerging the recipient three times—as a revival of the ancient custom of the apostles. In February he had dipped a girl of eleven days, who was ill at the time, and claimed that she had recovered from that instant.

Anne Parker, however, preferred the more common method of

The Reverend John Wesley. *(V. & J. Duncan, Antique Maps and Prints.)*

sprinkling for baptism, and informed Wesley that neither she nor Mr. Parker would consent to the baby's being dipped. Here the preacher's inexperience may have misled him, for in an effort to oblige, he suggested that if the Parkers would certify that the baby was weak, church law would permit him to sprinkle it.

With the indignation of impugned motherhood, Anne Parker replied, "Nay, the child is not weak; but I am resolved it shall not be dipped."

Faced with this impasse, Wesley conceded that he could not help them and left the Parkers, and the baby was baptized by someone else. But this early skirmish portended the eventual open warfare that ceased only when Wesley slipped out of town under cover of darkness.

With the exception of one notable lapse—in a matter of romance regarding Causton's niece—Wesley's intentions were generally lofty and admirable; it was in the mundane application of them that he sometimes lost perspective. Believing that God ordained each event in life, no matter how trivial or unfathomable, he would observe in his journal in the autumn of that year, after conducting the funeral of Mary Musgrove's fourth and last son, that the bereaved mother "would probably have been quite lost in grief, but that God diverted her from it by the pain of a violent rheumatism."

Since the ministry of the two Wesleys ranged over the entire colony, they occasionally visited the outlying settlements, like Hampstead and Highgate, five miles south of town. Soon after arriving, they traveled down the inland waterway to St. Simons Island, where that spring Oglethorpe's regiment and a growing body of colonists had begun building and fortifying the town of Frederica. Neither of the Wesleys was well received by the rough-hewn congregation there, though, and after his life was threatened during one visitation, John did not go back. Charles's stay in Georgia lasted less than six months.

The inland water route to Frederica wound past several outposts which Oglethorpe intended as defensive buffers, able to give early warning to Savannah of spy boats or parties of Spanish Indians. The settlements at Thunderbolt and Skidaway he established within the first year, and less than a decade later Noble Jones's plantation at the south end of the Isle of Hope would serve as the base for a company of marines.

Returning from Frederica on a Sunday in May of 1736, Charles Wesley stopped at the home of Thomas and Lucy Mouse on the north end of Skidaway Island. Having failed at raising food for his family on the sandy soil of the island, Mouse had requested and received a license to run a tavern—many boats anchored at that bend of the river to wait for high tide before heading down the Narrows. Wesley dined at Mrs. Mouse's, rounded up some colonists for prayers, and preached to almost a dozen in the guard-house. Around four that afternoon, he continued to Thunderbolt by boat, and from there walked the five miles to Savannah.

When Charles Wesley passed the Parkers' bluff at the Isle of Hope, likely no one was there to hail him. Not until later did the Parkers spend most of their time at their country home. But Peter would soon grow used to the sight of scout boats going and coming, and he would get to know Thomas Mouse's daughters well, especially the youngest, Lucy.

The Isle of Hope

THE INDIANS HAD NEVER NAMED the Isle of Hope; it was simply a place from which to get to Skidaway, one of their favorite deer-hunting grounds. Noble Jones's choice of a name for it may have been influenced by a horseshoe bend of the Thames called Stanford le Hope, which the Skidaway River resembles as it loops wide within the bluff of the island; but more likely Jones was expressing the hopes for prosperity of the three men who settled it: himself on the southern third, Henry Parker on the northern, and John Fallowfield, who became a magistrate but later abandoned the colony, on the middle tract.

The Parkers' house overlooked the river to the south, open to the morning sun and prevailing southeastern breezes and sheltered from the northwestern winter winds. Standing on the bluff, Peter could see Skidaway Island in the distance to the east, with cabbage palms rising at the edge of the bank. Burnt Pot Island lay closer, almost surrounded by marsh; and to the west the river made a sweeping curve against the bluff, meandered south between blue hammocks of cedar and pine and spreading live oak, then forked at Long Island and vanished into the Narrows.

It was a spot for glorious sunsets and plentiful seafood. Shrimp teemed in the creeks, oysters bristled on the mud bars, blue crabs clambered in the shallows for a scrap of offal, and trout, croaker, bass, and flounder vied to take a hook. Schools of traveling porpoises puffed in the channel, or splashed as they fed on mullet near shore; and brown pelicans dived with abandon, their wings folding akimbo, into shoals of menhaden. At dusk a family of otters or a mink would tour the bank, and across the river the marsh hens clattered raucously as they settled in for the night. Then the possums and raccoons rustled out from the underbrush, and through the still dark air would echo the hoarse *cronk!* of a heron.

It might have been Eden indeed, except for the bugs. They were not always oppressive, long dry seasons were almost free of them, but at times

Bluff of the Isle of Hope. *(V. & J. Duncan, Antique Maps and Prints.)*

they emerged in torturous profusion. Deerflies and horseflies, mosquitoes, sand flies—all would bite, with varying degrees of sting, and there was little protection from them short of a stiff breeze or standing in a billow of smoke. Worst were the smallest and least visible, the sand flies, which swarmed at twilight and during muggy calms, invading eyes and ears and noses and driving folks to frenzy.

Upriver from the Isle of Hope and around two bends, on a bluff of Skidaway Island facing north, was the home of the Mouses, barely half an hour's row from the Parkers'. Thomas and Lucy and the five girls had been among the first colonists placed on the island and would be the last family to abandon it six years later. At the end of the first year, Thomas Mouse had written to Oglethorpe, then in London, detailing the improvements he had made on his lot and thanking the Trustees for allowing the settlers on Skidaway another year's provisions. A diligent worker—truly the kind of colonist for whom the Trustees intended Georgia—Mouse had built a dwelling of the same dimensions used in town and a smaller storehouse for making bread and raising chickens, and he had surrounded it all with a palisade of upright logs. At that time his optimism about farming had not yet waned, and he listed peas, potatoes, and Indian corn as coming up in abundance. He closed the letter with the news that his wife was expecting and had gone to Savannah to deliver, though apparently the child did not survive.

All was not praise and gratitude, however. Mouse earnestly requested that Oglethorpe send more families to the island, since guard duty for those few men who remained fell more and more frequently. He had been tied neck and heels by the tythingman, William Dalmas, for refusing to stand guard one night. Though he declared that he liked Skidaway better than any other place in Georgia, he asked that he be permitted to return to England if this treatment were to persist.

But Dalmas, who had been sick since he came to Georgia, would be dead before the letter reached Oglethorpe.

Lucy Mouse also incurred the censure of the authorities, for an offense involving the operation of the tavern. During July of 1737—the summer Henry Parker planted his first four acres at the Isle of Hope—a Yamacraw woman complained to Thomas Causton that Mrs. Mouse's daughters had beaten her. Causton's investigation disclosed that the Indians often bartered with Lucy Mouse for small items, but on this occasion the squaw had received strong liquor. How this led to the beating is not explained, but after a severe reprimand from Causton for dealing with the Indians at all—much less supplying them with rum—Mrs. Mouse promised to be more careful in the future.

The trouble between Causton and John Wesley began that summer as well. Soon after his arrival, Wesley had gathered around him a select group of the faithful, whom he termed Serious, for study and prayer and rigorous self-examination. Among them was Causton's eighteen-year-old niece Sophie Hopkey, who in addition to joining the group in praying and weeping, received from Wesley instruction in French. The Serious met often, and for a while Thomas and Martha Causton had good reason to believe the thirty-three-year-old parson a likely match for their ward.

But youth is impatient, and a year later, while Wesley still anguished over the state of his soul, Miss Hopkey ran off with a clerk in the Trust's store named William Williamson. They were married in Purrysburg, just up the Savannah River in South Carolina, and on her return Mrs. Williamson no longer met with the Serious.

The Caustons had been somewhat disappointed—they rather liked Wesley despite his piety—but not nearly so disappointed as Wesley himself. He made no public comment about the sudden marriage, but he began relaying to Causton the complaints of his parishioners about short measures at the Trust's store, deliberate delays in issuing supplies, and the rumor of several Deists in town. Causton assured his distraught friend that the charges were groundless, and reminded him that on several occasions he had defended Wesley against Savannah gossip, the only commodity not rare in the young colony. And as for Deists, Causton had no doubt that Wesley would set them straight.

The parson, however, was more intent on setting Mrs. Williamson straight, and one Sunday early in August he denied her communion at the altar. Savannah buzzed, Causton fumed, and on Monday morning William Williamson swore out a warrant against Wesley, demanding £1,000 sterling in damages for defaming his wife's character.

Constable Noble Jones served the warrant and conducted Wesley to a hearing, where Henry Parker and Recorder Thomas Christie considered the charge. Wesley denied that the civil authorities had any power to question him on ecclesiastical matters such as communion, but Parker determined that, regardless, Wesley would have to appear at the next court held in Savannah. At Williamson's urging that he provide bail, Parker replied brusquely, "Sir, Mr. Wesley's word is sufficient for the court."

Guided by Causton, a grand jury indicted Wesley on ten counts, which included dividing the morning service on Sundays and refusing to baptize Parker's baby except by dipping. But none of the charges were ever decided. Court after court Wesley attended, and time and again the case was deferred. The spirit that in August had moved warmly among the Serious, by December had cooled through tedious inconvenience.

Hearing daily of new plots against him, Wesley posted in Johnson Square his intention to leave the colony, and when the magistrates issued an order to all tythingmen and constables to detain him, he took a boat to Purrysburg, just after evening prayers.

Rum

ALMOST EVERYONE IN GEORGIA at some time ran afoul of the Trustees, even fellow Trustee James Oglethorpe. Communication was painfully slow, and decisions made in the heat of a crisis in the colony—by those of sound judgment and good intentions—might appear hasty and ill-informed three months later to those in the chambers of Old Palace Yard. Conversely, instructions sent from London were often outdated or inappropriate by the time they reached officials in Georgia.

So it is not surprising that Henry Parker too, despite his early successes, fell under the displeasure of the Trustees. One general cause for this shift was his close association with Thomas Causton, whom they had grown to distrust thoroughly and who was gradually coming to resemble the despot his enemies described. His bald vindictiveness in the Wesley dispute had made even his staunchest supporters squirm.

But a quite specific flaw in Parker also soured the Trustees: a fondness for rum.

Like many commodities prohibited but widely consumed, rum was bought in quantity by anyone who had the opportunity and the capital to buy it. Oglethorpe disapproved; the Trustees forbade it. Yet no one felt especially hypocritical about it. Rum was simply a matter of business, an investment that readily converted into cash and returned high profits. Recorder Thomas Christie had sent the Trust's own dinghy to plantations up the river to vend his "Bottled Beef," and even Amatis had peddled a few gallons when the chance arose. Surely Lucy Mouse's promise to be more careful, when admonished by Causton for selling rum to the Indian squaw, meant exactly that—next time she would be more careful.

Parker himself was never accused of selling it, but he drank it in quantity and often. Eventually almost everyone in town knew at least one story of Henry Parker drunk, and several got back to London.

But for a while, Parker continued to rise. He made a favorable impression on William Stephens, a gentleman of sixty-six whom the Trustees had sent to Georgia in the ambiguous position of Secretary. Primarily they wished Stephens to write regular reports of events in the colony, ensuring at least one disinterested and consistent point of view, and since he arrived at the peak of the Wesley-Causton conflict, there was already much to write.

After about a month in Savannah, Stephens recorded in his journal his opinion of Parker as "an honest, plain, well-meaning Man, and one who I apprehended had as good a Share of Common Understanding as most of his Neighbors." Stephens remarked on Parker's forbearance under hardship, and was particularly moved by his chagrin at having nothing to wear but rags beneath the purple gown edged with fur which the Trustees had sent to the magistrates to boost the dignity of their office. Filial at heart, this early bond between the two men would survive Parker's brief fall from grace and endure Stephens's last years, when Henry was the only official who could deal with the infirm and embittered seventy-five-year-old President.

The final days of 1737 brought calamity to the Isle of Hope, and the new year resurrected dreams of prosperity for the Parkers. Within a week after Christmas, John Fallowfield's house burned to the ground. Mrs. Fallowfield had left only the faintest spark in the chimney and walked out to meet her husband, coming back from town with fresh provisions, but in minutes the house and everything inside—stores, furniture, linen, bedding— had gone up in flames.

In January, Thomas Causton gave Parker, for four years, an indentured servant and his wife, John and Janet Kemp. Both thirty, they would help with the farming at the Isle of Hope, since Henry spent more time than ever on court business. The Kemps had come to Georgia expecting to pay their passage with an indenture contract on arriving, but no one in town had wanted to buy them, so Causton had charged them to the Trust and placed them with Henry.

Three months later, in the middle of April, the Isle of Hope had what the colonists called a Spanish Alarm. Everyone was in town except for John Kemp, who had stayed at the Parkers' alone, but who showed up in Savannah late one evening with a report of four strange men, all foreigners, who had threatened but spared his life. On the way to alert the authorities, he had encountered Thomas Causton, who listened briefly to his story and, not spurred to urgency, sent him on to William Stephens.

Under examination by Stephens and Parker and Thomas Christie, John Kemp had recounted this episode: Around ten in the morning, four foreigners had come upon him, and at first one of them drew his sword with intent to kill him, but another, who was the only person among them who had a little broken English, interposed and spared his life; after which they all went into the hut nearby, where they sat down and rested themselves about an hour and a half, without offering further violence of any kind. Kemp was, however, obliged to stand at the door and watch so that nobody could surprise them. Then they walked away into the country by a path which showed that they knew their way, after first making him swear he would not discover what he had seen. They were all swarthy men, he said, with black hair braided and brought up from behind their hats, every one in black or dark-colored clothes, and each armed with a sword, gun, and pistol.

The next morning Parker rode out to meet Causton at the Isle of Hope with Captain Aeneas McIntosh and two of his rangers from Fort Palachocolas, a garrison up the Savannah River on the Carolina side. They returned that night with no news of strange Indians, and though Parker resolutely vouched for the veracity of his man, Stephens and most others concluded that Kemp had simply missed company and cooked up this story to come to town with the rest of the family.

Whatever the case, other Spanish Alarms would be serious enough. Two years later a servant at Fort Argyle would lose his head.

Whitefield and Habersham

EARLY IN MAY, THREE WEEKS after the Spanish Alarm at Bailiff Parker's, the new preacher George Whitefield arrived to fill the pulpit Mr. Wesley had vacated, bringing with him a new schoolmaster, James Habersham. In time both would exert a major influence on the life of the colony as a whole, and on Peter and Charles Tondee specifically.

Zeal incarnate, Whitefield with his phenomenal voice could move mountains. That he sometimes placed them in the paths of others was only to be expected. Pious at a tender age, he had practiced reading prayers aloud as a boy and acted in dramas; and work in his mother's inn, the Bell—his father had died when George was two—had convinced him of the wretched sinfulness of mankind in general and of himself in particular. Familiar with the black hearts of children, he would later found an orphanage in Savannah, where he could help them root out their own wickedness. It would be his greatest inspiration, securing both an independent base from which to launch his preaching tours and a first-rate fund-raising cause.

His preaching tours, mainly to the northern colonies, would succeed resoundingly, reaping big donations for the waifs and renown for Whitefield. He often preached outdoors to throngs on hillsides, both because he could reach more ears and pockets that way and because many churches were closed to him. He was prone to attack his fellow clergymen as "slothful shepherds" and "dumb dogs," and he charged that the author of *The Whole Duty of Man*—a religious volume of which the Trustees had sent fifty-nine copies with the first colonists on the *Ann*—had sent thousands to hell.

Both the persuasive power of his oratory and the sheer volume of his voice were confirmed by Benjamin Franklin in his *Autobiography*. While listening to Whitefield deliver a sermon from the courthouse steps in Philadelphia, Franklin undertook to gauge empirically the distance that the preacher's voice would carry. After backing away from the edge of the crowd to the

The Reverend George Whitefield. *(V. & J. Duncan, Antique Maps and Prints.)*

point where Whitefield's words became indistinct, he calculated the area of the semicircle and determined that the evangelist could be heard by thirty thousand souls at once.

Regarding the preacher's oratorical prowess, the eminently frugal Franklin offered this illustration: He had suggested to Whitefield that the orphanage be built in Pennsylvania, where the material and the workmen were, and that the orphans be brought there, rather than the reverse; but finding his advice rejected, Franklin had resolved to contribute nothing. "I happened soon after to attend one of his sermons," he recalled, "in the course of which I perceived he intended to finish with a collection. I had in my pocket a handful of copper money, three or four silver dollars, and five pistoles in gold. As he proceeded I began to soften, and concluded to give the coppers. Another stroke of his oratory made me ashamed of that, and determined me to give the silver; and he finished so admirably that I emptied my pocket wholly into the collector's dish, gold and all."

Whitefield's impact on Georgia would always be more economic than spiritual. He brought back money from old and New England, created jobs for sawyers and carpenters and brickmasons, and early on, bought and outfitted a sloop for the business of the orphanage.

It was there, in the realm of business, that his friend James Habersham excelled. He managed the affairs of the orphanage like a thriving plantation, and in the economic wasteland that was Georgia in the 1740s, he came to be regarded as a kind of Midas; everything he touched turned to copper. Rising steadily as a planter and merchant throughout the colonial period, he would serve as President of the Governor's Council during the royal era and as acting governor for two turbulent years before the Revolution, when Governor James Wright was in England arranging for another large cession of land from the Creeks.

A loyal King's man, Habersham would write to a friend in London on the eve of the war that he could not "think of the event but with horror and grief—father against son, and son against father, and the nearest relatives and friends combating with each other." Nowhere would this be truer than in forty-two-year-old Georgia, where many of the colonists had grown up in England and remembered the homeland dearly; and no one at that time understood better than Habersham the rifts that rebellion would rend in families. His middle son Joe was already leading the charge against English tyranny, and Jemme and John would join their brother soon.

But when Whitefield and Habersham arrived in Georgia that May of 1738, both were young—twenty-four and twenty-six—and just beginning their long careers. As yet only a deacon, Whitefield would have to return to

England for ordination before he could celebrate communion; and Habersham would teach for almost two years before surrendering the classroom to another of Whitefield's followers.

From the beginning of his ministry in Savannah, Whitefield drew large crowds to church. After his second service, William Stephens reported in his journal that it was "the most thronged Congregation I had ever seen here." Aisles were packed and the doorway spilled over with worshippers. So popular indeed was Whitefield that he presumed Savannahians' devotion to him had prompted their extensive efforts to find James Habersham's brother Joseph when he got lost in a swamp.

The crux of Joseph Habersham's plight had been mud—marsh mud, the color of lead sinkers, slick as oil, and soft as grits. One step plunged a man thigh-deep, and the next sucked off his shoe. Early in August, Joseph had ridden south with Mr. Whitefield to the Vernon River, where the Reverend had met a boat for Fort Frederica to exhort the troops there. The young Habersham was to return with the horses, but he missed the path and wandered onto the fringe of a marsh. When the horse he was leading balked at stepping into the mud, he tied it to a tree and continued on his own mount to Savannah, arriving in the morning after wandering most of the night.

Later that day he set out with two townsmen to retrieve the abandoned horse. They split up in the woods to cover a wider area, but in the evening when the townsmen came home, Joseph Habersham did not.

William Stephens sent for Parker—they passed many hours together now in conference, viewing settlements up the river or walking through the Trust's garden—and Henry rounded up some freeholders to search for Habersham and several Indians to track him. A cannon was fired at intervals to guide him to town, and the searchers shot pistols into the air and called out continually. But after two days, hope had dimmed.

So the circumstances that led to his discovery seemed all the more miraculous; even William Stephens deemed it Providence. One of the French colonists at the little settlement of Hampstead south of town, who had been searching for Habersham, dreamed about him, and in the morning went out again and fired his musket. Having lain down to die, Habersham answered faintly, but the Frenchman heard him and carried him to his hut, gave him milk and what food he had, and came to town with the joyful news.

On his return from Frederica, Whitefield thanked his parishioners profusely, both individually and from the pulpit, for "the late Instance of their sincere Affection." He refrained from taking credit for the miracle, however, having been out of town.

At the end of the summer, Whitefield sailed for England to be ordained, but several days before embarking, he found occasion to interrupt a funeral he had refused to conduct. The deceased, William Aglionby, had been a confessed Deist and a "smatterer in the law"—equally contemptible terms in Georgia—and moreover had resisted the Reverend's attempts to convert him.

After the burial office had been read by one of the indentured servants and the body had been interred, Whitefield, who was waiting nearby, suddenly approached the grave. Before the mourners could disperse, he harangued them on the dangers of temptation and the wages of sin, pointing to the depraved life of this heretic and his certain damnation.

The Reverend did not see Georgia again for a year and a half. In the interim, England declared war on Spain, the old chief Tomochichi died and was given the colony's first grand funeral, Henry Parker's fortune rose and fell, and James Habersham secured a grant of five hundred acres for the orphan-house, not far from the swamp where his brother got lost.

His brother Joseph, however, died at Frederica soon after Christmas.

Keeper of the Store

FOR THE DURATION OF THE TRUSTEESHIP, poverty found a home in Georgia. Whatever the freeholders had been in England—carpenters, cordwainers, blacksmiths, linen drapers—most of them had been poor. "Unfortunate poor," meaning that it was not entirely their fault, but poor nonetheless. Poverty had united them: brought them to the Georgia Offices in Old Palace Yard; led them to the wharves at Deptford or Rotherhithe; moved Henry Parker to leave Fleet Street and James Papot his Hog Lane home in Soho for a place none of them had seen.

They had followed Squire Oglethorpe as the Hebrews Moses, and now in the promised land were land-poor, with the Squire gone off to Charles Town or St. Simons. He had never been intended to govern Georgia, anyway, and with power shared equally by three magistrates and a recorder, conflict inevitably erupted. Success fell, predictably, to the man with the keys to the store, Thomas Causton. An ocean away from the Trustees, the storekeeper could reward or punish, with fresh meat or spoiled, wholesome grain or mildewed, extended credit or demands for back payment.

At first Causton had tried to deal fairly, always keeping in mind unforeseen circumstances, like a man's losing his stores by flood or fire, or missing the spring planting through sickness. There were many exceptions which forced him to consider the general good of the colony, even if that required neglecting accounts in regard to particulars. But of course, he also understood that the Trustees' largesse was not limitless, and there were times when duty obliged him to draw the line, offend whom he might.

In five years he had acquired a comfortable estate and a fine plantation east of town which he named Oxstead. His friends did not want for beef or corn, he was generous to a fault with the Trust's servants' labor, and an invitation for Christmas at Oxstead promised a spread so grand it was scandalous.

So his friends doubtless heard with apprehension—not to mention Causton himself—the news that the Trust's store would soon undergo some shifts in policy. A clerk, one Thomas Jones, had been sent from London to assist in preparing the books and had accompanied Oglethorpe, now a general, to Frederica. With roughly £11,000 of the Trust's money unaccounted for, Causton began laying up provisions for the future, and true to his wont, he looked out for Parker as well.

Late in the summer of 1738, around the time that Whitefield left for England, Causton purchased from South Carolina one hundred steers for the colony and had them delivered to Parker's plantation at the Isle of Hope. Joined to the mainland by only a narrow strip of sandy marsh—dry at low tide and easily fenced—the island seemed a convenient place for the cattle to range. Within six months, though, most of the steers had wandered back to the mainland, and many wound up on the plates of freeholders and their families.

When a year later a cow and a heifer of Parker's were found axed through the spine and half-dead, William Stephens attributed the vandalism to some villain who bore a grudge about a court case. But it may well have been jealousy that Parker had care of so much while others had so little, or simply the presumption that the owner of chronic strays eventually forfeits possession.

Even before the steers were bought, Parker's hogs had been the object of seizure. They tended to frequent the area near Thunderbolt—Parker had retrieved them once from that neighborhood—and at least a dozen had finally been slaughtered and salted and barreled by the settlers there. The hogs were known to be Parker's, though for the record a head with notched ears was brought into court for him to identify. The perpetrators seemed to have no particular rancor toward him, at least no more than they had toward the rest of the magistrates and authority in general. In the same case two of them were convicted as well of killing a steer which was not Parker's.

In the middle of September, Thomas Causton learned in a letter from the Trustees that he had one month to prepare the accounts of the Trust's store for review. The next day he ordered the Trust's servants to load a barge with barrels of beef for Oxstead; and around two in the morning of the following night, several barrels of beef and flour made their way to Parker's house on Bryan Street, less than a block from the store.

General Oglethorpe came up from Frederica in early October, and a week later he assembled the colonists at the courthouse. In an impassioned speech, he decried the ruinous state of the Trust's finances and laid the blame at Causton's feet, and the next day he demanded bond from the erstwhile storekeeper to cover the Trust's losses. Since there was not enough money in the entire town at the moment to cover those losses, the General accepted instead assignment of everything Causton owned, including Oxstead, until the accounts could be settled. When two weeks later rumor spread that Causton might leave the colony, Parker had to stand bail for his appearance in court.

The Trustees in London were fed up with Causton; the new storekeeper Thomas Jones—a fractious, conniving man sent to audit the books and dole out the remaining provisions—emulated the General in his ardor to prosecute his predecessor; and Oglethorpe himself, recently shot at by one of his own men in the south, was not in a mood for clemency.

Along with Causton, Joseph Fitzwalter was removed as gardener to save expenses; and Noble Jones, because he spent so much time at his plantation Wormslow, was discharged as surveyor and first constable. To succeed Henry Parker as second bailiff, the Trustees appointed Robert Gilbert, the illiterate tailor who came to Georgia with the Tondees on the *James*. And Parker, ironically, found himself promoted to first bailiff, in Causton's place.

Also that autumn, Anne Mouse—whose mother Lucy would later appear on the civil payroll as midwife—gave birth to twins. She had married one of the first settlers on Skidaway, Francis Brooks, who gave up farming to follow the General, first as a servant and then as master of a scout boat. The twins, James and John, would be one and a half years old when Brooks, against orders, put ashore with his men to pick oranges on the bank of the Altamaha River and took a Spanish musketball in the back of his head.

Parker's Fall

AFTER THE TRUST'S STORE CLOSED, the few ships that had been braving the Savannah River stopped coming altogether. The freeholders felt abandoned and oppressed, and early in December a petition to the Trustees was circulated, requesting—for the economic survival of the colony—free title to the land and legalization of slaves. Without free title the colonists had no collateral on which to borrow when crops were poor, and nothing to offer London importers for security in starting their own businesses in Savannah. And without slave labor Georgians believed they could not compete with South Carolina in exporting anything at all.

One hundred twenty-one freeholders signed the petition, including John Fallowfield, Joseph Fitzwalter, James Papot, Edward Jenkins, Robert Hows, Henry Parker's brother William, and Francis Brooks. Henry Parker's name headed the list, followed by Robert Gilbert's mark and Thomas Christie's signature, so that all three current civil officers lent their weight to the document. The Trustees could not simply ignore this plea, as they had previous ones.

Christmas in town that year, 1738, was described by William Stephens as "a festival without any feasting." News from Oxstead, however, suggested a somewhat merrier holiday there. If Causton suffered under the Trustees' displeasure, he bore it well. His success as a host could be measured by the degree of resentment shown by Thomas Jones, one of those not invited to the celebration. On learning that his assistant, a former clerk in the store, *had* attended, Jones summarily assumed that he must be a spy for Causton, fired him the next day, and sent him and his wife and two daughters out of the colony.

Jones was also prompt in reporting to the Trustees an incident at Jenkins's tavern which presented Henry Parker in a posture less than magisterial. On a Monday evening in the middle of February, an already wobbly

Parker had agreed, for a bowl of rum punch, to entertain the company by trading places with Edward Jenkins for the night: Parker would be the tavernkeeper and Jenkins the magistrate.

Accordingly, they stripped and exchanged clothes, but when Parker called for the bowl, Jenkins exercised his new authority with the same sobriety he brought to the orphans' affairs. He lashed out at Parker for a drunken swab, chastised him for debasing the office of magistrate, and threw him down, though in truth Parker's legs may have folded under pressure. In any event, no bowl was produced.

William Stephens described the episode to the Trustees as a "foolish Frolick," which he deemed "too mean and ridiculous to relate," and chalked the whole thing up to Parker's "taking a Cup too freely." He was quick to point out that Parker rarely went to Jenkins's—twice a year at most—and that only mirth, not mischief, had resulted from the prank, though he conceded it might appear indecorous to "strict Moralists."

Whether or not Stephens truly believed that Parker seldom patronized the tavern, he trusted the man's integrity. Only two weeks before, Stephens had turned over an unruly young servant to him to rehabilitate, and Parker had sent the boy to work in the fields alongside Peter and the Kemps at the Isle of Hope. The boy, Tommy Roberts, had been assigned by the Trustees to Stephens, but had run away just before Christmas. After a few days, the old secretary had judged that no one would be more apt to find the truant than other boys his age, so he applied to the schoolmaster for assistance. James Habersham spoke to several of his students, and within a few hours Roberts was returned. After the second time he ran away, Stephens asked the magistrates to lock him in the log house; and when that produced no change, he declared the boy incorrigible and gave him to Parker. Roberts did not last long at the Isle of Hope either, but he did finally reform at the garrison up the Savannah River at Augusta, becoming one of the best drummers in the Regiment and eventually enlisting.

Meanwhile, in London the Reverend Whitefield and his followers were making headlines. The *Weekly Miscellany* of February 10 carried the story of their antics at St. Margaret's in Westminster when the regular priest was out of town. Whitefield's disciples had asked permission for him to preach during this absence, and when the request was denied by the officially appointed substitute, they locked the man in the minister's pew and guarded the steps to the altar while Whitefield harangued.

In March the General appeared on the bluff unexpectedly, bent on settling the store accounts once and for all and ending the feud between Thomas Jones and Causton. He left for Port Royal less than a week later, having accomplished neither. The accounts remained Gordian, and by April the magistrates were united in their opposition to Jones.

The tension between him and Parker fulminated at William Stephens' house. It had been a spring of hot, dry wind and a summer of wet, green rot. Fears in early May of another drought had turned by July into prophecies of another Flood. The sandy streets in town softened into mudbogs, weeds bloomed shoulder-high in the squares, and for the second year in a row crops were ruined. The closing of the Trust's store the previous autumn had only compounded the freeholders' hardships at a time when many were already destitute.

On a Saturday afternoon late in August, Jones was visiting Stephens and expounding on some points in the church service when Parker dropped by, with Causton in tow. Talk soon turned to the Trust's store, and Parker complained about problems he had encountered in getting provisions delivered to his family, particularly once when his wife Ann was expecting at any moment. Though the magistrates were still supplied by the store, Jones had refused the request unless the goods were paid for with cash. Parker now observed that this was a ready way to make servants thieves, to pilfer their master's goods to make money, and straightway both men grew vehement.

Parker, when wrought, had a habit of "throwing his arm to and fro," and at this gesture Jones jumped up and dared him to strike. For a while they shook their fists at each other, exchanged foul epithets, and offered "scurvy reflexions on one another's former courses of life, before they came here." Eventually the two cooled enough for Parker to take his leave in a civil manner—Causton had vanished at the height of the dispute—and events of the next couple of months eclipsed their animosity.

Two Saturdays later news reached Savannah that England had declared war against Spain. Whimsically dubbed the War of Jenkins's Ear after the event which precipitated it—the docking of an English trader's ear by the Spanish coast guard for illegally trafficking with the Spanish colonies—the conflict, though long anticipated, still would not touch Georgia soil for over two years. But the bare fact of it threw the freeholders into a state of alarm, and not without reason.

Less than a week had passed before, inspired by the news, a hundred slaves on a plantation near Stono, between Port Royal and Charles Town, murdered the owner and his family and ravaged the countryside, taking the heads of whites and torching farms in their path. Though crushed in five days by the Carolina militia, the uprising, as Savannahians feared, had been working south in a line for St. Augustine.

Early in October Tomochichi died, reputedly three years shy of one hundred, and was given as impressive a military funeral as could be assembled on short notice. The old chief was buried in the center of the courthouse square, with General Oglethorpe, Colonel William Stephens, and four other military officers as pallbearers. Cannon boomed each minute as the body was interred, and forty guns fired three volleys over the grave.

The smoke had hardly cleared when word reached Oglethorpe of a ship off Tybee Island with a packet on board containing instructions from the Trustees. That night the General sent William Stephens to retrieve it, and two days later learned that Thomas Christie was to replace Henry Parker as first magistrate.

Orphans Again

HENRY PARKER'S REMOVAL AS FIRST magistrate could not have come at a worse time for the Tondees. His loss of power and prestige put him in a weak position to protect them from Whitefield several months later, though his arguments were sound and both the General and the Trustees would support him. But as in many cases, that support would come too late to matter.

What Oglethorpe and William Stephens found most appalling in the Trustees' instructions, at least ostensibly, was that Thomas Christie, a malcontent and open adulterer, had been chosen to replace Parker. Without countermanding their orders—in fact, adhering to them fastidiously—the General insisted that Christie complete and submit all court records up to the present before assuming office, and since that task was considered herculean, if not impossible, Oglethorpe suggested that Parker remain on the bench until the Trustees' further pleasure could be known.

So in less than a week, Henry Parker had been condemned and reprieved. It was a sobering victory. The General would write to the Trustees at this time that Parker "now behaved well" and "had entirely left off drinking." Oglethorpe meant drinking rum, specifically; beer was not frowned upon. The General himself provided a cask of beer and another of bread for breakfast for the townsmen on the Wednesday following Parker's reinstatement.

Chagrined by the overgrown state of the town common and the squares, which Tomochichi's funeral had made obvious, he summoned all the men of Savannah to a civic work day. Included were servants and boys old enough to wield a hoe, which encompassed sixteen-year-old Peter and probably eleven-year-old Charles. They began at dawn, broke for breakfast, and continued until dusk, when the General brought out more casks of beer and bread. Oglethorpe had toiled alongside them, and in this mutual labor the freeholders felt an unaccustomed unity.

On Christmas Eve, Robert Hows, a fellow passenger of the Tondees on the *James* and a follower of Whitefield, returned from Philadelphia in the sloop that the Reverend had bought and filled with provisions for the proposed orphanage, to be called Bethesda, or "House of Mercy." James Habersham had already been granted five hundred acres for the orphan-house, though Whitefield on his return would insist that the grant be transferred to his own name. At present the town had no need of an orphanage—most of the children had been placed with families for some time—but the prospect of new construction meant jobs, and a sloop based in Savannah meant commerce.

Just before Christmas, Habersham took in the first orphan. Abandoned by his parents over two years earlier, eleven-year-old John Cundall answered the Reverend's needs exactly. Before deserting Savannah and their son, John senior had been fined a hefty sum for scandal, and his wife Elizabeth had been brought before the magistrates for stealing fowls, the property of Edward Jenkins, her next-door neighbor. When the court had passed sentence—standing at the whipping post for two hours with the label "Thief" pinned to her—she had confessed her crime so earnestly and promised such full compensation that the magistrates had suspended the punishment altogether.

The Reverend Whitefield returned early in January, rented for an exorbitant sum a large house across Drayton from the Parkers' town residence to serve as a temporary orphanage, and hired almost every sawyer, carpenter, and bricklayer in Savannah to work at the orphan-house construction site. He then took in Richard and Elizabeth Warren, aged twelve and ten, from the household of Sarah Goldwire, who would place her own son in the orphanage in April. And the following day he seized Richard and Frances Milledge from their brother John, who would by April succeed in restoring them to their home despite Whitefield's adamant opposition.

The Tondee boys he claimed early in February at a meeting with the magistrates and Edward Jenkins at William Stephens's house. Having asked repeatedly to be relieved of the orphans' affairs, Jenkins had opened the conference by dumping the whole business into Whitefield's lap. He promised to deliver the orphans' accounts the next day, and the Reverend assured him that his troubles in that regard were over.

Parker demurred strongly, though, against giving up the Tondees, especially Peter, whom Stephens described as a "well-grown Lad of fifteen or sixteen years." Parker reasoned that "it would be a great Hardship to have that Boy taken from him now he is grown capable of doing him some Service, after living so long with him when he could do him none."

Whitefield countered that "the Boy would be so much the better for him and his Purpose, as he could be employed for the Benefit of the other Orphans." For the Reverend, Peter conveniently served two ends, not only to populate the orphanage but to provide free labor for it as well.

Parker protested—with a little too much warmth, according to Stephens—that in a case like this, "where the Child was taken Care of as he ought, by a good Master (which the Magistrates might judge of) and without any Charge to the Trust," the child ought not to be reckoned an orphan to which Mr. Whitefield was entitled.

At that the Reverend produced his commission from the Trustees, and when no exceptions could be found to his authority, the Tondees were relinquished, although they would not move across Drayton to the orphanage for another few days.

Egregiously omitted in the entire debate is the question of whether Peter, at sixteen, should have been considered an orphan at all. He was already standing guard duty regularly, as heir to his father's lot in Heathcote Tything, and at fifteen boys were often apprenticed. Both men clearly wanted Peter in their household, though, and in this interview neither asked his preference.

William Stephens closed his journal entry with the observation that this was the first time he had seen Whitefield's commission, though his own name was mentioned in it for various purposes. Whitefield rarely felt any urgency to share instructions from the Trustees with others involved; he would not find occasion to mention their order to return Peter to Henry Parker until after the orphan-house had been built.

Charles, though, not named in that order, would ultimately have to take his freedom upon himself.

Bethesda

IN HIS MEETING WITH THE MAGISTRATES, Whitefield did not specify how he intended to use Peter for the benefit of the other orphans. But in a letter to the Trustees one month later defending his action, he claimed that Bethesda had a greater claim to the work of the older ones than any private person, having been intended as a "Publick Nursery for Planters & Mechanicks [craftsmen]." Since no planting or building was taking place at the orphanage in town, he likely meant for Peter to join the rest of the town's labor force at the construction site, and just as likely he sent him there as soon as possible.

Nothing else in Georgia could have been more auspicious for his training as a carpenter. Up to the last few years of the colonial era, the orphanhouse would reign as one of the most impressive buildings in the province; and though Peter would not be officially placed out with a master carpenter until Christmas, the Great House at Bethesda may well have been his primer.

In any case, the daily regimen followed by his brother Charles and the other orphans in town was rigorous. Roused at five for private prayer, they were taken to church at six, brought back for breakfast at seven, with hymns before or after or both, and given exhortations while they ate. From eight to ten there were chores—carding, picking cotton or wool, spinning, sewing; chopping wood, fetching water, cleaning house—and from ten to twelve was school, in the form of scripture study. Dinner was at noon, and until two "everyone is employed in something useful, but no time is allowed for idleness or play, which are Satan's darling hours." School again from two to four, work again from four to six, and church again until eight, after which the Reverend catechized the orphans: "His main business is to ground the children in their belief of original sin, and to make them sensible of their damnable state by nature . . . ." Then the orphans were sent to bed, after prayers. On Sundays they went to church four times.

The stewards of Bethesda sent an account of the schedule to the Trustees in London to reassure them that it "obviates idle pretenses for what is called innocent (though in reality damnable) recreations." The description proudly pointed out that, though the Family at the orphanage in town numbered seventy souls altogether, the house was an exceptionally quiet place.

On reading the orphans' agenda, the Earl of Egmont, the most faithful Trustee in London, entered into his journal the observation that "Not a moment of innocent recreation tho necessary to the health & strengthening of growing children is allow'd in the whole day . . . . The whole discipline appears too strict." Two days later he wrote, "Mr. Whitefield's purpose in erecting the Orphan house was, as since appear'd, to establish a school or seminary to breed up those of his sect in, for which end he proposed to be absolute independent of the Trustees as to this Orphan house . . . ." Having achieved independence, Whitefield resigned his post as parish priest at the end of 1740, after serving for less than two years, largely out of town.

Before work began at the construction site, Peter got to know thirteen-year-old Lachlan McIntosh, one of four Scottish children Whitefield had brought back in late February from a trip south to Darien and Fort Frederica. Most of the Scottish men of Darien were off with Oglethorpe fighting the Spaniards near St. Augustine, where McIntosh's father John, chief of the Scots, would be taken prisoner in June during a bloody Spanish raid against a small fort named Mosa. He would spend two years in a prison in Spain before seeing his home and family again. Lachlan himself, at fifteen, would join Oglethorpe's troops at Frederica for the Battle of Bloody Marsh, and decades later would serve as Brigadier General of the Georgia Continental Brigade during the Revolution. He would endure with Washington the brutal winter at Valley Forge; and in Georgia's most famous duel, he would kill Button Gwinnett, one of the state's three signers of the Declaration of Independence.

Even as Whitefield gathered fresh recruits for Bethesda, though, Oglethorpe was writing to secure the release of the Milledge children, expressing confidence that the Reverend, once he had considered the young Milledge family's progress and re-examined his commission from the Trustees, would be well satisfied to return Richard and Frances to their brother John.

"It is most certain," the General had reasoned, "that Orphans are human Creatures & neither Cattel nor any other kind of Chattels, therefore cannot be granted." What *had* been granted, he emphasized, was the *care* of the orphans, and—for Whitefield's purposes the most important provision—the right to collect money for them. But where the orphans were cared for already, or were self-sufficient, there was of course no power granted to seize them. It was the same argument Henry Parker had used about the Tondees.

To be sure that his orders were followed, the General sent a copy to William Stephens, who advised John Milledge to call on Reverend Whitefield and inform him of Oglethorpe's directive. This John did on the twenty-fifth of March, after the Reverend had returned from laying the first brick in the foundation of the Great House, but Whitefield told him curtly at the door that his brother and sister were now in their proper home, he knew of no other home they had to go to, and John could tell that to the General if he pleased.

Undeterred, John had simply waited. The Reverend left for England a week later, the General arrived in town three days after that, and within several more Richard and Frances were back with their family.

When he learned of the Milledges' success, Whitefield wrote the Trustees threatening to move his orphan-house to Pennsylvania if he were not obeyed, but Richard and Frances stayed with John, and construction went on nonetheless. In June the Trustees instructed Whitefield also to return Peter to Henry Parker, but the Reverend would defer sharing this letter with the magistrates until the end of the year, after the Great House had been built and the Family had moved in, and then Peter would be officially apprenticed to James Papot, one of the leading carpenters in town, who had worked on Bethesda.

The Great House

NOT LONG AFTER NEWS REACHED town of the stunning loss of Fort Mosa, the workmen at the Bethesda site had a Spanish Alarm of their own. The site was then the southernmost settlement in the vicinity of Savannah—except for Bewlie, William Stephens's nearby plantation on the Vernon River—and a small army of laborers had assembled there.

In March, Thomas Mouse, one of the last two hold-outs on Skidaway, had given up farming, placed his daughters Mary and Catherine and Lucy in the orphanage in town, and joined Bethesda's work force. The widowed Anne Mouse Brooks eked out a living for herself and the twins from what sewing she could find, and Mrs. Mouse moved in with her and practiced midwifery.

In May, Duke Cannon, who had been taken in by Causton five years earlier, was found in town in rags and brought before the magistrates. The only orphan not surrendered to Whitefield, he had been working at Oxstead, east of Savannah, and though Cannon was too cowed to complain, witnesses alleged that Causton's wife Martha "tyrannized over him with great Cruelty." William Stephens, who was present at the meeting, instructed the sixteen-year-old to return that night with his gun—at Oglethorpe's direction Stephens had issued a "light Indian Gun" to each of the orphans capable of handling one. Cannon stood guard that night with the other freeholders whose turn it was, and the next morning after guard duty, he declared his wish to leave the Caustons and move into the orphanage.

Concerning the general exodus from Savannah to the future Bethesda, Stephens recorded that "the Work at the Orphan-House seemed to be the great Gulph which swallowed up most of our common People, whether Artificers, Labourers, or Planters, . . . which made the Town become thin indeed." But Stephens admired the results, describing the Great House in late July as a "grand Edifice," and the construction so advanced "as to be ready for raising the Roof this Week."

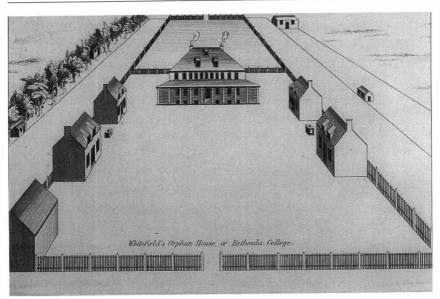

Whitefield's Orphan House, or Bethesda College.

The Great House and outbuildings at Bethesda, drawn by Noble Jones.
(V. & J. Duncan, Antique Maps and Prints.)

The Spanish Alarm at Bethesda had occurred earlier that month, and it showed the skittishness among the workmen after the fall of Fort Mosa. Stephens had been awakened at two in the morning by a party of eight or nine workers, warning of two boatloads of Spanish Indians approaching from the south. He notified the guard on duty, roused the constables and magistrates, and mustered out the town militia by beat of drum. In fifteen minutes thirty-five freeholders had assembled, seriously shaken by this new rumor, and Stephens sent out two patrols to reconnoiter the outskirts of Savannah.

Meanwhile the magistrates—who were all in town, court having sat the previous day—interrogated the "two Lads" who had seen the Indians. The evening before, the boys had been fetching oyster shells in a boat, to be burned into lime for mortar. Shells were commonly gathered from ancient Indian middens along the riverbank, and a large one edges Skidaway Island down the Narrows from the Isle of Hope. After spotting the Indians, and believing themselves pursued, the lads had got back ashore and scrambled to the work site. Under examination, they stuck to their story, but by ten that morning reports from Thunderbolt and Skidaway revealed that these were in fact friendly Indians come to hunt deer on the islands, as was their custom.

In mid July rumors spread from the south that the General had withdrawn his siege of St. Augustine, and by August he had returned with his troops to Fort Frederica, seriously ill. For the rest of the summer, Georgians debated whether the fault lay more with the South Carolina troops or the South Carolina warships.

The August sun burned hot and dry through September, then seared on into October. An outbeak of the intermittent fever—alternate wracking chills and drenching sweat—infected the town and carried off Thomas Causton's only son; a week later his wife Martha died of a convulsion. The former storekeeper, still harried by the Trustees' accounts and in bad health himself, had sunk so low that even his critics viewed him with pity.

But at the Great House, October was a hectic time. Those of the Family who had not yet moved out to the worksite were growing impatient, and midway through the month—though the Reverend was away on tour in New England—they began to talk of the move as imminent. On All-Hallow's Eve, the weather turned abruptly cold, "with smart Frost" in the mornings, and the Great House was still unfinished when the Family journeyed out three days later in wagons, on horseback, and on foot.

The magnitude of the building, as the caravan drew close, was like nothing the orphans had seen in Georgia: three stories high, sixty feet across by forty deep, a ten-foot-wide porch all around the main floor, with ten columns front and back and ten on either side. The approach to the House crossed a cleared commons flanked by six outbuildings: a carthouse and a distillery, a wash house and a kitchen, a workhouse and an infirmary. In these quarters the Family would lodge until the interior of the Great House could be finished. Beyond, the land sloped down to the marsh, with an earthen causeway to a deepwater creek and a wharf for the Reverend's sloop.

A week after the Family moved, a boat passed the wharf carrying the body of a hanged murderer. Oglethorpe had ordered the corpse to be chained to a gibbet on a marsh point near the mouth of the Ogeechee River, at a stretch of the inland waterway now called Hell's Gate, where the shoals shift treacherously. Aided by a Spanish accomplice, William Shannon had hacked off the head of John Smyth, a servant at Fort Argyle originally assigned to Thomas Mouse, who had dismissed him. The two had thrown Smyth's body into the river, and then carried into the woods his wife, whom they later killed. So barbarous was the crime that the old secretary William Stephens had suggested to the General that Shannon's body be displayed as a deterrent. Though the display could not have stood long, the site was known for fifty years afterward as Shannon's Point.

On the last Tuesday in November, the orphans woke to a strange vision: before dawn, snow had begun to fall, and by ten o'clock four or five inches blanketed the ground. It had all melted by early afternoon, but for a while Peter and Charles had a brief reminder of London, and Lachlan McIntosh the Scottish Highlands.

When the Reverend Whitefield finally returned in mid December, he brought with him from Rhode Island a Presbyterian minister named Jonathan Barber, who would oversee the orphans' spiritual development as Mr. Habersham oversaw the temporal, or monetary, affairs of the orphanage. In a meeting with the magistrates a few days later, the Reverend found occasion at last to produce the Trustees' instructions to him regarding the orphans, and Peter was promptly apprenticed to James Papot. Henry Parker and John Fallowfield signed the indenture.

Papot also took on Richard Milledge as an apprentice; but still at Bethesda, Charles Tondee late in May felt the fires of enthusiasm rage out of control.

House of Mercy

THE ARGUMENT THAT RELIGIOUS ZEAL spawned the carnage of the Crusades is a patent oversimplification. Historians have long recognized that secular motives, like greed and lust for glory, figured prominently as well. Soldiers of the Cross expected rich booty from the pagan East, and the kind of fame earned only by great prowess in battle. Uneasy monarchs, too, seized the chance to send off idle knights to bash the heads of other peasants than their own. But allowing all these, the fact remains that for the truly cathartic bloodbath, nothing worked like holy fervor. It brought out the virtue in a man; inspired him to deeds beyond the normal pale.

The Reverend Jonathan Barber was possessed of just such enthusiasm, and under his tutelage the orphans grew ardent for Christ's mercy. More ardent indeed than ever they had been in town. They learned the vileness of their sinful hearts, saw Satan's snares all around them, and cried out for salvation. They took to praying clamorously, anywhere: in a classroom, picking seeds from cotton, one would fall to his knees with the spirit, and the rest would drop in droves.

With spring the frenzy peaked, and late in March the orphans were moved en masse to write the Reverend Whitefield in England, testifying to the marvelous change wrought in their black hearts. That their redemption had been a genuine, common experience was confirmed by their common turns of phrase.

Most of the children craved both a thorough and a sound conversion, though several seemed ready to settle for one or the other. Rebecca Bolton, a child of ten whose seventeen-year-old sister Mary had become Mrs. James Habersham the day after Christmas, was filled with Wonder and Amazement that God had not cut her off long ago and sent her to Hell; whereas sixteen-year-old Elizabeth Pitts and another girl of twelve, perhaps due to their maturity, were filled with only Wonder and Admiration at the same phenomenon.

John Riley and Jeremiah Jones depicted the Devil as a roaring Lion going about seeking whose Soul he may devour, and John, with a keen eye for an image, concurred with Lachlan McIntosh both that the Lord was knocking at the Door of his Heart and that the Lord was Stirring among the dry Bones there. He wished too, along with William Bradley, that the Lord would search his Heart and try his Reins, and at twelve years old John already feared spiritual Lethargy and a reprobate Mind. It was not his wont to wax overpoetical, though, so his letter did not echo the pleas of his younger cohorts that the Lord not quench the smoking Flax and break the bruised Reed, nor that they might never return with that Dog to his Vomit nor with the Sow that was washed to her Wallowing in the Mire. Simplicity, for John, was the heart of the metaphor.

The only sentiment universally shared was a protest of unworthiness—your dutiful and unworthy Child, your unworthy Boy, your unworthy Servant—and William Bradley flirted perilously with pride by declaring himself the Unworthiest. The most significant clause common to most of the letters, however, was a request that Whitefield remember them at the Throne of Grace. For an Anglican flock in a staunchly anti-Papist colony, this prayer for intercession rang remarkably like a Hail Mary. To whatever genius informed the orphans' letters, at least, Whitefield had achieved canonization on earth.

The letters were sent off to the Reverend, along with more articulate descriptions by Habersham and Barber of the revelations of grace at Bethesda, and published that same year in Glasgow under the title *Orphan-Letters to the Reverend Mr. Whitefield*. Touring England to raise money for the orphanage, the Reverend had in the slim volume a welcome wedge to pry open the hearts of the parsimonious.

There was among the letters to Whitefield, however, none from thirteen-year-old Charles Tondee. He had written instead, several weeks later, to Henry Parker, complaining of "severe usage." Parker paid no attention to the letter, claiming in June that he had thought it just "the common Case of many School-Boys under the Chastisement of a Rod."

But Barber learned of the letter and took it quite seriously. He fashioned a rod and lashed Charles from his shoulders to his knees. Then he ordered the boy to write Parker again and contradict all he had said before or the beating would be renewed. Charles promised compliance, and ran away to Parker at the Isle of Hope.

From William Stephens's description of Charles's wounds two weeks later—Parker was ill at the time of the incident and could not bring the boy to town at once—Barber's zeal was ferocious: ". . . the Boy being now present, and stripp'd, it is yet too visible from Scars and Wounds not yet healed, that great Cruelty had been used: . . . the boy was made naked to the Waist, after the Manner of common Malefactors, and lashed with five strong Twigs tied together, as long as they would hold, whereby his whole Back, Shoulders, Loins, Flank and Belly were in a dreadful Condition." Both the distribution of stripes and the reference to the manner of whipping common malefactors suggest that Charles's arms were bound above his head.

The magistrates summoned Barber to town and reprimanded him—Thomas Jones absented, being a friend of the accused—but the defiant Barber challenged their authority to meddle at all in the affairs of Bethesda. They assured him warmly that they would convince him of that authority very soon, when they visited the orphan-house to investigate matters there. But in truth nothing material was accomplished. It would be another eight months before the magistrates officially inspected the orphanage, and that visit would be occasioned by a further outburst of zeal, directed against the new minister in Savannah, Whitefield's replacement.

Charles they apprenticed to Thomas Bailey, a blacksmith in town whose forge across the lane from the Milledges' house had burned in April and taken an entire block with it. Later events would cast doubt on whether the move was in fact any improvement for Charles, but for Bailey it meant a servant.

Beyond doubt, the Reverend could not have selected more wisely for his flock than orphans. Few objects of charity arouse more pathos, and it was only natural for them to accept that their fallen state resulted from some dire transgression, some unfathomable flaw; their abandonment confirmed it daily.

Bloody Marsh

GEORGIA'S BAPTISM BY FIRE CAME less than a decade after its founding, and most of the able men in the colony in the summer of 1742 took part. Stung by the failure of his siege of St. Augustine in 1740, Oglethorpe had withdrawn his men to St. Simons Island to strengthen Fort Frederica for the Spanish counteroffensive, which he knew must follow. In June two years later it did.

With about two thousand men and fifty-two ships, ranging from men-of-war to small support craft, Governor Montiano sailed from St. Augustine with the intention of taking first Fort St. Simons, on the southern tip of the island, and then Fort Frederica, the main bastion, on a western bluff overlooking the Frederica River. No other line of defense lay between them and the rest of the Georgia coast. The plan was to pillage and burn Savannah and the outlying settlements and plantations, then return to Florida. That he retreated to St. Augustine by late July—leaving the outgunned and outmanned British in possession of St. Simons and the colony safe from further Spanish assault—came to pass from the happy coincidence of fickle weather, fierce determination, and a strategic ploy by Oglethorpe that only desperation could have inspired.

For nineteen-year-old Peter Tondee, most likely at Frederica that summer as a volunteer with one of the provincial units, this would be his only experience with open warfare.

The first word of the impending invasion reached Savannah early in June. The General had learned that a convoy of Spanish ships from Cuba had arrived at St. Augustine, and immediately he began marshaling his forces. British-allied Chickasaws came down from near Augusta, and Yamacraws and Creeks joined them at St. Simons. Urgent requests for ships and men were sent repeatedly to South Carolina, and over the next month contingents of Savannahians headed either south to join the war or north to escape it. Early in July, James Habersham took the Bethesda Family to a plantation in South Carolina, bringing on his way the news of the fall of Fort St. Simons. And by mid July, when Oglethorpe sent John Milledge to Savannah to gather whatever men and horses remained, the town was so deserted that William Stephens described these late recruits as "the last Gleanings," with "most of our Young People being already gone thither," and "Scarce any body being left but Masters of Families."

A cadet in the regiment, Lachlan McIntosh had reported to Frederica as early as April. Noble Wimberly Jones had been a cadet in the regiment in 1740, but since his father commanded the Northern Company of Marines, stationed at Wormslow, and captained the scout boat *Savannah*, one of two in the company, Noble Wimberly may have been among the marines. John Milledge, at twenty-one recently made quartermaster of the rangers at Fort

General James Edward Oglethorpe. Copperplate engraving, c. 1745, no known previous publication in the United States. *(V. & J. Duncan, Antique Maps and Prints.)*

Argyle, was the General's main courier between the south and Savannah.

From the outset, storms had delayed the Spanish fleet and prolonged its voyage, and high winds and surf thwarted its landings. But even more crucial to the British, the constant threat of truly bad weather persistently harried Montiano and his officers, who were acutely aware that as the summer heightened, so did the hurricane season.

The initial two encounters between the armies, after the Spanish had landed and occupied the abandoned Fort St. Simons, proved pivotal. The first skirmish erupted when five rangers on patrol suddenly confronted a Spanish reconnaissance party of over a hundred on a narrow trail, only a mile and a half from Fort Frederica. One ranger was killed, but the other four rushed back to the fort, and in moments Oglethorpe, on horseback, led the available units—Highlanders, rangers, and Indians—in a frenzied charge out the east gate and about a mile to the Spanish party, which the General had assumed to be Montiano's main force. Though on foot, most of the Indians and half a dozen Highlanders had kept up with the mounted vanguard. Roughly a third of the Spanish were killed or captured, and the rest straggled back to camp at Fort St. Simons with terrified accounts of wild-eyed, skirted men who ran through the woods as fast as cavalry and murderous Indians whom bullets would not stop. Leading the Yamacraw, Tooanahowi—Tomochichi's heir—had been wounded in his right arm, but drew a pistol with his left hand and killed the Spanish officer attacking him.

Another encounter in the afternoon, at a stretch of savanna later dubbed Bloody Marsh, yielded only a standoff, and compared to the morning's fierce charge, little bloodshed. But for the British forces merely to hold out—against superior numbers and notably without the General, who was then drawing up the rest of the regiment at Frederica—bolstered the troops like a sweeping victory. Under a fine sprinkle, the blue gunsmoke had blanketed the marsh, so when for lack of ammunition the Spanish captain withdrew, he had no idea how few of the enemy he had faced.

That evening Oglethorpe marched the rangers, most of the Indians, and half the regiment to within a mile and a half of Fort St. Simons, where they spent the night, the Spanish having retreated into the fort. Three days later a Spanish galley and two smaller vessels rowed up the Frederica River on reconnaissance, but were met by cannonfire and mortar bombs from the fort and made a hasty escape, with the General giving chase in one of several scout boats.

The next evening Oglethorpe took five hundred men back to the south end to attempt a night raid on Fort St. Simons. At two o'clock, as they waited silently in the dark for scouts to reconnoiter the fort a mile and a half away, the musket of a French seaman went off and he bolted into the woods. Deliberate or not, the shot destroyed the element of surprise, and the Frenchman chose to join the Spanish rather than face the fury of the English. The General resigned himself to half an hour of drumming to disconcert the enemy, then took his men back to Frederica.

But there was still the matter of the Frenchman, who knew the size of the British forces and the defenses of Frederica. In a shrewd gamble, Oglethorpe wrote a letter to the Frenchman—in French, as though from a confederate—and convinced a Spanish prisoner, for his freedom and some cash, to deliver it secretly. The letter expressed satisfaction with their plan, urged the Frenchman to stress the weakness of the English resistance, and promised to double his reward if he could persuade Montiano to attempt a naval assault on the fort from the Frederica River, directly under British guns. On arriving at Fort St. Simons, the Spanish prisoner was greeted with suspicion and searched, as the General had hoped, and the letter reached Montiano straightway.

By a stroke of astounding luck, at about the same time five ships from South Carolina materialized briefly on the northern horizon. Montiano presumed they were the first of the British fleet and promptly ordered a total withdrawal from the island. By sundown they had razed the fort, packed up, and headed south.

Two weeks later the South Carolina fleet did finally arrive, but because of contrary winds and the fear that the Spanish would attack South Carolina, they left after four days.

The Spanish would not return, though, and one year later, in July of 1743, General Oglethorpe sailed for London to answer accusations of fraud by one of his lieutenants and to seek compensation for the £60,000 he had spent on the war. Welcomed as a hero, he was acquitted of all charges and reimbursed fully, and came to Georgia no more.

Apprentices

VOLUNTEERS RETURNING FROM ST. SIMONS faced another peril in Savannah. As well as hurricanes, the summer months in the low country brought sickness. By late July, few families in town remained untouched by a violent fever, probably malaria, which attacked suddenly and periodically, reducing victims to mortal exhaustion. The new minister, who had arrived the preceding December, succumbed in middle August; Thomas Mouse died a week later, and his daughter Elizabeth, married only the previous winter, followed in October, one day after Joseph Fitzwalter. The only effective treatment was quinine, an extract of the bark of the cinchona tree, grown in Spanish Peru and not sold to English physicians.

A more chronic malady in Georgia during the 1740s, and one which affected almost everyone, was economic stagnation. When the decade commenced, the phrase "poor as a Georgian" was already common currency in South Carolina, and in Savannah the many vacant lots in the six wards stayed vacant. Hardened by repeated disappointments from their labor, by continually lowered expectations, and the indifference of Trustees an ocean away, Savannahians acquired a grim fatalism, based largely on the disbelief that things could get any worse.

Stasis reigned incarnate in the antique person of William Stephens. The old secretary had been appointed, at seventy, President of the Colony, and from the autumn of 1741 he ruled for ten years with an inert hand. In the restructured civil government, the former magistrates had become Assistants to the President, and as Stephens's senility calcified over the Forties, Henry Parker assumed most of his official duties. Finally, in 1750, to avoid embarrassing the old gentleman, the Trustees created the office of Vice President and appointed Parker to it.

When at eighty Stephens himself recognized his incapacity and retired to his plantation at Bewlie, Parker succeeded him as President. By the summer of 1752, however, the Trustees had surrendered the charter of Georgia to the Crown—at their final meeting only four of twenty-one members attended—and until Governor John Reynolds arrived in 1754, the colony coasted in limbo.

For a few years after the Battle of Bloody Marsh, the town of Frederica continued to thrive. With the Spanish threat checked, colonists felt safe on St. Simons, and the army payroll gave Frederica an economic base to attract trade and labor. James Papot had worked at Frederica before Bloody Marsh, and in the years between the completion of Bethesda and the start of work on the church in Savannah, he may have taken his two apprentices back there to build clapboard huts for the soldiers or houses for civilians. But four years later a hundred of the huts would go up in flames, and not long afterward the Regiment would be disbanded. Within two decades the pines and oaks and palmettos would efface the town.

As Thomas Bailey's apprentice, Charles Tondee saw little improvement in his fortune. For a while he had earned 10s. per quarter from the President and Assistants for setting the tune in church. Parish clerk Thomas Lee, whose duties included leading hymns, had gone to Frederica to replace the General's secretary soon after Bloody Marsh, and at first Charles had carried out the task without promise of payment. Then in February of 1743, the President and Assistants took note in their regular meeting that Charles had "so behaved as to be well approved of" and ordered that "ten shillings a Quarter be allowed him for his Encouragement."

A year later, though, Thomas Bailey notified them that unless his apprentice were paid the full salary of £5 annually, he would have to withdraw the boy's services. Observing both that Bailey's request was outlandish and that none of the 10s. previously allowed had ever reached the boy's hands anyway, William Stephens rehired Thomas Lee, who had since returned to Savannah.

Early in the spring of 1744, the masons laid the cornerstone for the church on the Trust lot beside the store, facing Johnson Square, and for the last three years of their apprenticeship and three more as journeymen, Peter Tondee and Richard Milledge worked with Papot and the other town carpenters—whenever Georgia had money to pay them—on that building. By the time parishioners could worship in it, a decade would have passed since the Reverend Whitefield had first bought the stones for the foundation.

About a year after construction began on the church, Papot had the misfortune to be standing below some scaffolding when a pine plank fell. The board broke his leg, but the bone was set immediately, and Stephens expressed confidence that Papot, "one of our best reputed Carpenters," would mend.

Another event, initiated by the carpenters, had a strong impact on Tondee and Milledge, and the ramifications pervaded colonial Georgia up to the Revolution and beyond. In August of 1746, several carpenters posted notice around town that they would not work for less than a fixed rate, effectively proposing a labor union. It was a futile gesture, since Parliament forbade collective bargaining, but more to the point, at that time so little construction took place that those few who could find work accepted whatever wages were offered. Four years later, though, Papot's two protégés would revive the idea—as artisans in their own right—and by then the threat of impending slave craftsmen would unite the "mechanicks" solidly.

Savannahians during the Forties were not preoccupied exclusively with economic hardship, however. They had the occasional diversion of Indian unrest as well. In her third husband, a former clerk to William Stephens and a sometime clergyman, Mary Musgrove Matthews Bosomworth had found a champion for her claim to the islands of Ossabaw, St. Catherine's, and Sapelo, plus £1,200 for past services as interpreter and Indian agent. The Reverend Thomas Bosomworth compiled affidavits, drew up deeds, and sent the evidence to London. When response from the Trustees was slow in coming, as it always was, Mary marched to Savannah with her cousin Malatchee, who had a tenuous claim to the title King of the Creeks, and met there two hundred chiefs and warriors to discuss the issue with President Stephens and the Assistants. For nearly a month, the town slept lightly, if at all.

For group encounters, Noble Jones's militia was drawn up, but John Milledge's troop of horse rangers formed the first line of intimidation against the Indians, and patrolling day and night, were the most visible authority in town. So visible was John himself that Malatchee, when he finally left, made a stop at John's plantation on the Ogeechee River, ransacked the house, and slaughtered six steers.

The Bosomworths' tactics were bluff and bluster. Calling herself Cousaponakeesa, her Indian name, Mary would concoct an injury to her dignity—or to Malatchee's, or to the Creeks' in general—throw herself into a rage, and eventually require restraint. At this the Indians would rise in arms, and Captain Noble Jones would confront them with the militia and order their arms put down. The misunderstanding would soon be explained, regrets extended, and William Stephens would declare a feast to celebrate the reconciliation.

But fresh rumors flared daily: a warrior overheard that Mary would be sent to England in chains, and the Indians revolted; a freeholder bruited that William Stephens's head had been cut off, and the townsmen mobbed.

Central on this seesaw, Malatchee vacillated, tipping his warriors one way, then the other until, weary and exasperated, the chiefs accepted gifts without him and went home. Over a decade would pass before the Bosomworths' suit was finally settled, for the most part in their favor.

But Mary was not the only volatile Indian. Visiting warriors brought their tribal vendettas to town and took revenge whenever the chance arose. One afternoon a party of Creeks, reeling down Bull Street in search of more rum, came upon a lone enemy, beat him to death with fists and clubs, and threw his mangled body off the bluff, while whites looked on. Even the heroic Tooanahowi, with a little liquor, was moved to shoot an unarmed Cherokee in the House for Strangers, aiming his rifle between the cracks of the boards.

As the Forties closed, though, there were glimmers of hope for the Fifties. For the first time Savannah enjoyed a competent and trusted minister in Bartholomew Zouberbuhler, a native Swiss raised in Carolina, whose voyage from England aboard the *Loyal Judith* presaged his pastorate in the colony. Mid-ocean the crew and passengers were stricken by an outbreak of spotted fever which killed the captain and twelve others—among them Thomas Causton, returning from defending himself before the Trustees—and the Reverend Zouberbuhler had taken charge of the ship until the navigator recovered. His ministry would span twenty years and provide the only stable Anglican leadership in colonial Georgia.

And at least one Savannah firm made headway in business. In the middle Forties, James Habersham had formed a partnership with Francis Harris, previously a clerk in the Trust's store, and by the end of the decade the two had built a wharf and opened an import-export house. Only through commerce could the little settlement realize its purpose as a seaport, which was after all Oglethorpe's intention in placing the town on Yamacraw Bluff and his point in awarding James Yoakley £100 to sail the *James* up the Savannah River in May of 1733.

For amusement there was cricket in Johnson Square on holidays, and in the evening there was backgammon and cards and quoits in the taverns. The King's birthday and Oglethorpe's birthday and a few special saints' days furnished cause for festivities, and marriage celebrations and funerals brought the colonists together. When Mary Musgrove Matthews married Thomas Bosomworth in the summer of 1744, before the land claims and Indian showdowns and histrionics, the whole town came to the reception. William Stephens offered his house for the occasion, three long tables with benches were set up, and guests dined on "a Cold Repast of all such kind of provisions as this place could afford, boyled, Roasted and Baked, brought ready dressed." Well-wishers drank wine and rum punch and danced to a fiddle, "8 or 10 Couple at a time," until the late hours.

It would be another decade before change managed to breathe new life into the province, but one innovation was imminent—the introduction of slavery—and as the 1750s dawned, Peter Tondee and Richard Milledge prepared for it.

Part Two
House Carpenter

Changing Times

THE COLONISTS OF GEORGIA HAD been requesting the legalization of slavery almost from the moment of its founding. Now as the goal
approached, the artisans of Savannah took steps to protect themselves from
it. Though clearly a benefit to planters—and deemed indispensible for rice
cultivation—slave labor posed a threat to men whose livelihood depended
on a skilled trade. Aware of this dilemma, the Trustees stipulated when they
voted to approve slavery in August of 1750 that it would be limited primarily to agriculture. But already in April of that year, Peter Tondee, Richard
Milledge, and Benjamin Sheftall had formed the Union Society with the
same object in mind.

They met on the twenty-third of April, St. George's Day, festival of the
patron saint of England and slayer of the dragon. It became their annual
celebration date, in addition to quarterly meetings and others called "for
particular business," especially in the years just before the Revolution. Their
concerns later embraced the welfare of widows and orphans, but their initial
purpose was to protect their own interests as mechanicks: carpenters, masons, blacksmiths, saddlers, tailors.

As membership grew, the club included men of other vocations and
some gentlemen of the upper class. Even among the founders, one was not
an artisan but a shopkeeper already along in years. Fifty-eight at the inception of the Union Society, Benjamin Sheftall was the patriarch of one of two
families of German Jews—the rest were Portuguese—who came with Doctor
Nunez during the first summer. The Sheftalls lived across the lane from the
Tondees and one lot west, on Duke Street. During the 1750s Benjamin rose
to the status of a successful merchant, and two decades later his sons Mordecai
and Levi would emerge as leaders among the Liberty Boys.

Change came rapidly to Peter Tondee's life during the early Fifties. The
two men who had been most like fathers to him—Henry Parker and James

Papot—died in 1752, Parker having been appointed president of the colony only a year earlier. The former president William Stephens had retired to Bewlie and died at eighty-one the year after Parker, leaving his estate to his youngest son Newdigate, who married John Milledge's sister Frances.

Also in 1752 Peter began to acquire land. He had already sold to John Milledge, shortly before the founding of the Union Society, his five-acre garden lot in the swamp east of town. The purchase price of only 10s. reflects Peter's opinion of the property, but John was anticipating the advent of slavery and intended it for rice cultivation. He paid the same price to tavernkeeper John Penrose for a contiguous garden lot, both of which he later sold in a larger parcel to James Wright, the last royal governor of Georgia, for rice fields.

On December 7, 1752, the last "land day" of that year—when the President and Assistants met to read petitions and award grants—Peter requested and received one hundred and twenty acres three miles west of town, adjoining a tract belonging to the church, the "glebe land." The amount of acreage is somewhat puzzling. As the head of a household, Tondee would have been entitled to only one hundred acres; for each additional member of that household—meaning a wife, child, or slave—he qualified for fifty more. But the twenty-nine-year-old Tondee mentioned no wife in his petition to justify the extra acreage, though that was common procedure, so whether he had yet married Lucy Mouse, at that time about nineteen, is uncertain.

It is certain that they were married fourteen months later, when Lucy Mouse senior deeded by gift her gold ring to "Lucy Tondue, my youngest daughter." In the same document she gave to her grandson William Norton the fifty-acre tract on Skidaway where the Mouses had originally settled; to her granddaughter Elizabeth Young, the town, garden, and farm lots which the Trustees had granted her in 1747 due to her destitution; and all other possessions to her son-in-law Isaac Young. Her spelling of the name—*Tondue*—is intriguing as the only instance of that version on this side of the Atlantic; Peter himself spelled it *Tondee*.

During this time Peter's life and Richard Milledge's continued to run parallel. Though as younger brother Richard should have inherited nothing, John had given him, as far back as 1744, "for the love and affection that I do bear unto Richard Milledge, my true and well-beloved Brother," the original town, garden, and farm lots granted to their father. To this Richard added, between 1752 and 1755, five more farm lots in the same area just south of town, to total two hundred seventy acres, paying between £3 10s. and £12 10s. for each parcel. He built a house on this land, and probably died there.

Detail from Archibald Campbell's "Sketch of the Northern Frontiers of Georgia," showing vicinity of Savannah from Bloody Point, S. C., to Shannon's Point on the Ogeechee River, 1780. *(Courtesy, Georgia Historical Society.)*

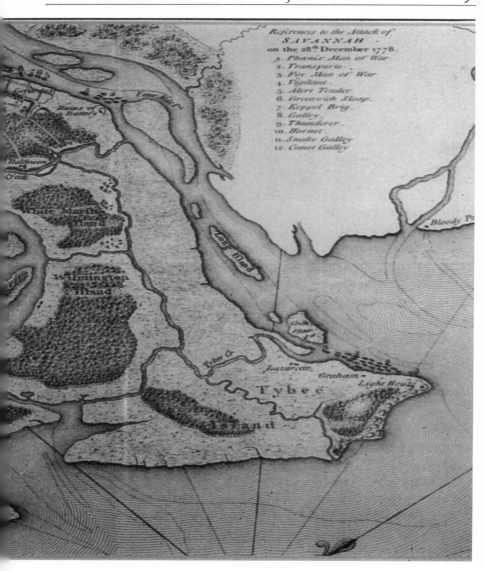

Within a year of Peter's marriage to Lucy Mouse, Richard wed Mary Camuse, daughter and namesake of the volatile antagonist of Paul Amatis. As boys Peter and Richard must have been familiar with the rantings of Mary senior when she clashed with the silk man over the fledgling sericulture, but she had been dead several years when her daughter married, and there is no indication that the younger Mary inherited her mother's temperament.

One other event occurred in 1752 which signalized the acceleration of change in the colony over the next two decades: Great Britain finally abandoned the old Julian calender for the Gregorian, and Savannahians went to bed on the second of September to wake up on the fourteenth.

Royal Omens

IF THE ROYAL ERA IN GEORGIA could be said to have had a royal carpenter, Tondee was he. From the 1760s through the end of the century, much of the business of government—royal, rebel, and municipal—took place in buildings which he had designed and constructed. Aptly enough, though, his first appointment under royal rule came not from the Governor's Council, but from the opposition to the Crown.

The event which prompted this appointment was preternaturally ominous, both ultimately for the fate of royal government in Georgia and quite immediately for the reign of the first governor, Captain John Reynolds. As exuberant as Savannahians were to welcome him, less than three years later they would send him off with even greater glee.

When the forty-one-year-old naval officer stepped off the barge that had brought him upriver from Cockspur Island to Savannah on October 29, 1754, the little town on the bluff was a vision of squalid decay. Christ Church had already sunk to "a ruinous state," the courthouse needed constant repairs, and only from necessity had the log foundation of the Council House been replaced by a stone cellar. Reynolds numbered the private dwellings at "about a hundred and fifty Houses, all wooden ones, very small, and mostly very old." Wood, the most readily available construction material, either rotted in the humid heat or burst ablaze from the merest spark.

But Savannahians drew themselves up for as festive a welcome as they could imagine. Bells jangled, musketfire split the sky and sputtered through the evening, and bonfires glowed like the hopes of the revelers. So transported were the "lower Class of People" that—"being unprovided with materials that they commonly use in testifying their Joy on public Occasions, and unwilling to lose their Share of Rejoicing"—they set fire to the guardhouse and had nearly torched the old Council House before their betters intervened.

Less than a week later, His Excellency met in the Council House with his Council, composed of the previous President and his Assistants, and as they turned their attention to the decrepit and dangerous state of the building, a stack of chimneys at one end gave way and took the wall with it. Reynolds and his Councillors scrambled to safety, and "very providentially escaped being buried in the Ruins."

They reconvened in a shed behind the courthouse, and after concluding that a suitable alternative in which to hold council meetings would be the large vacant building across the street from the silk filature, originally constructed two years earlier as an annex for sorting and storing cocoons, the Governor and Council summoned the most recent successor to the late Mrs. Camuse, Joseph Ottolenghe. He assured them that he would have no further use for the place—it had never been put to the intended use anyway, "being ill-calculated for that purpose"—and the Governor ordered Councillors Noble Jones, James Habersham, and Jonathan Bryan, eventually one of the largest landholders in the province, to have the building fitted out for offices.

Nine days after the old Council House fell, Reynolds and his Council received a petition pleading the interest of William Bradley, an early colonist who had built the Council House as his residence at a reputed cost of £500, and then, after a checkered career in Georgia, had returned to England. Bradley's agent requested that whatever remained of the structure be appraised—before it could be hauled off for salvage—to protect his constituent's investment.

Without entering into a debate over the validity of Bradley's claim, which was doubtful at best since the Trust's servants had actually constructed the house using the Trust's material, the Governor and Council agreed to an appraisal. Accordingly, Bradley's agent appointed Peter Tondee appraiser on his behalf, and the Council chose Richard Milledge on behalf of the Crown.

Papot's apprentices had arrived as masters of their trade, but in no further records would they be paired. More and more Richard Milledge would turn to his landholdings, which at his death were extensive. He registered his brand with the record office—a reverse R joined to an M—and though he designated himself "carpenter" in his will, his brother John, calling in his debts as executor of his estate, termed him "planter."

Ominous Endings

UNDETERRED BY THE COLLAPSE OF HIS seat of government, Reynolds plunged resolutely into the problems that beset the struggling province, and his early efforts show his clear grasp of Georgia's dilemma. They also show clearly the personal qualities that would prevent his dealing successfully with it.

Foremost in his mind was the defense of the frontiers. Though the Spanish threat had diminished, the new alarm of the French and Indian War placed Georgia in jeopardy from Indians to the west and discouraged settlers from moving into the region. With the decline of Frederica, the province had no effective military presence and no defensible fortresses.

As would both his successors, Reynolds appealed again and again to England for troops and munitions, and like them he was continually disappointed. The true fronts against the French were far from the new settlement, and England reserved her strength for those.

But even the modest measures for defense which were in his power to take, Reynolds bungled. From Oglethorpe on, Georgia's leaders had always recognized that neighboring Indians needed constant and attentive courtship. At his first meetings with his Council, Reynolds was urged to initiate diplomacy with them. Letters from Indian traders and reports in person from concerned friendly Indians warned that the Upper Creeks were being wooed with gifts and promises by the French in Mobile, and the Lower Creeks by the Spanish in St. Augustine.

But a full year passed before Reynolds arranged a meeting in Augusta with the chiefs of the Creeks, and when after ten days they had not arrived to receive presents and restore alliances, he returned to Savannah, leaving as proxy his minion William Little. The chiefs, some of whom had come many miles for a talk with the English King's new Governor, were unimpressed. They had not forgotten that fifteen years earlier Oglethorpe had traveled more than twice the distance from Savannah to Augusta to talk with them in their own town, Coweta, and though seriously ill with a fever for much of the ten-day conference, had treated them with respect and solicitude.

Even the Board of Trade and Plantations, reviewing Reynolds's aborted attempt to meet with the Creeks, observed that they were "concerned to find that you did not think it advisable to wait the Delivery of the Presents at Augusta, because your presence at the first Interview might have had great Influence with them at this Conjuncture . . . ." They then added, with pointed tact: ". . . but we do not mention this with a view to condemn your Conduct herein, as there might be sufficient Reasons, tho' you do not mention them, for your return to Savannah."

In his behavior toward his Council—the men who had run the colony before he came—Reynolds showed the same finesse. He failed to seek their advice before issuing orders, he shared with them instructions about their duties and privileges only when occasion required, and in general treated them with bald superciliousness. When the former President, Patrick Graham, did not appear at the fourth meeting of the Council, the one during which the old Council House collapsed, Reynolds devoted the rest of the meeting, after the Council had moved to the courthouse shed, to the secretary's reading aloud the attendance policy for Council members and grounds for suspension or expulsion, despite the fact that the full contingency of eight Councillors had attended each of the three previous daily sessions.

Even when he supported the colonists' efforts, his style was redolent of hauteur. Almost a year prior to his arrival, forty-five settlers in the area of the Ogeechee River had petitioned the President and Assistants that a town be laid out on a peninsula within a great loop of the river then called the Elbow, and now known as Seven Mile Bend. This land had in fact been reserved for public use as a town site from the first year of the colony, and the President and Assistants, in wholehearted agreement that the place would make a fine port, ordered the province's surveyor to draw up a plan for it. Three months later the name George Town, after His Majesty, was proposed.

On touring the southern regions of Georgia in the spring of his first year as Governor, Reynolds was enthralled with the spot, and not only offered to rename it Hardwick after his own relative the Lord High Chancellor of England, but decided to move the capital of the colony there. At the time just one house had been built on the land, but he expressed as much enthusiasm for Hardwick's location as he did contempt for Savannah's.

Consequently, petitions proliferated for town lots in Hardwick. Peter Tondee applied in June of that year, but was rejected, and did not apply again until Reynolds's successor, Henry Ellis, had assumed the governorship two years later. He then requested and was granted lot number 234, on a corner, like his one in Savannah at Broughton and Whitaker.

The lack of public funds, though, prevented construction of any of the buildings necessary for a town—courthouse, church, assembly-house, prison—and despite persistent optimism for the site even to the end of the century, Hardwick never achieved a status above that of trading village. The main result of Reynolds's fixation on the place was his neglect of the public buildings in Savannah.

He galled Georgians most, though, by his virtual dotage on his secretary William Little, a former naval surgeon and for twenty years a shipmate of the Governor. Disregarding the talents and experience of men who had proved their worth to the province and could reasonably expect recognition, Reynolds conferred on Little seven royal appointments, including commissioner of Indian affairs and clerk of both the general court and the House of Assembly. Not content with merely too many jobs, Little charged inflated fees for performing his duties, and his political tactics ranged from questionable to blatantly dishonest. Within a year he had alienated Georgians irrevocably.

Early on, Reynolds too had displayed unbecoming greed. His first letter to London, recounting his jubilant reception, closed with a request for a raise in pay. At the February "land day," after three months in the province, he observed that the Trust's garden east of town had never fulfilled its purpose and asked for those ten acres. The Council complied, and the next day also approved his application for two thousand five hundred acres south of the Ogeechee. By June he had acquired as well, from the three former owners who resigned their rights to the land, all of Hutchinson's Island across the river.

Only at the point of bankruptcy did Reynolds recognized that he had squandered his credibility, and by then letters from important Georgians condemning his performance in office had already reached London. In the summer of 1756, less than two years after he arrived to acclamation, the Board of Trade wrote to recall him to explain his actions.

By the end of October he had learned of the inquiry and foresaw his removal, but he blamed the failures of his administration on the policies of the previous President and Assistants and on bad advice from his Councillors; and he worked assiduously with William Little to subvert the prospects of his successor, Henry Ellis.

Reynolds's career as Governor ended with as fitting a mischance as it had begun. En route to England, his ship was taken by the French, and when he finally made his way to London and presented his defense, the Board of Trade suggested he resign his office and return to sea. Just before the outbreak of the War of Independence, he was promoted to rear admiral, and three years later vice admiral; and though paralyzed on one side by a stroke and mentally impaired, he made admiral at the age of seventy-four, and died the following year.

Perhaps the most important achievement for Georgia during Reynolds's term was the passage by the House of Assembly of an act creating a paper currency. So economically dependent was the colony on South Carolina and England that no gold or silver coin could be kept in Georgia for long, being needed to pay creditors outside its borders. One of the first acts of the royal legislature established a commission to print money and—equally important—to lend it out at six percent interest, thus increasing the available currency in the province and giving colonists the means to generate a cash flow for conducting business.

To Peter Tondee it meant £60 in hand. In July of 1755, he mortgaged for seven years his town lot at Broughton and Whitaker, his farm lot west of town, his one hundred twenty acres near the glebe land, and three slaves named Simon, York, and Flora.

Money's Worth

THAT TONDEE MORTGAGED FOR £60 all of his real estate and three slaves raises the question, How much was all this really worth? and its corollary, How much did things cost then?

In colonial Georgia, cash came in three denominations: twelve pence made a shilling; twenty shillings made a pound. Farthings, at four to the penny, and guineas, at twenty-one shillings, were used, but rarely. Inflation did exist, but the rate was so low compared to the modern perception of the term as to be negligible. Other market factors exercised far greater influence on prices, and the form of payment—whether British pound sterling or colonial currency—mattered considerably: one British pound equaled roughly seven of South Carolina's.

The price of real estate varied, as might be expected, according to the quality and location of the land and the improvements made on it. Tondee sold his swampy garden lot to John Milledge for 2s. per acre; Richard Milledge paid between 1s. 6d. and 5s. 6d. per acre for his farm lots on higher ground south of Savannah; and in 1759 Tondee sold his farm lot for 6s. 8d. per acre to Thomas Burrington, a well-to-do gentleman who owned the adjacent tract. Town lots ran a great deal more: in 1764, Tondee paid Moses Nunez, the son of Doctor Nunez, £40 for the lot next to his on Broughton Street. Houses in town rented for £10 to £30 a year, depending on their size, although the impatient Whitefield paid £20 to rent a large house for only six months.

Slaves comprised a substantial part of many Georgians' wealth. At the time of his death, Whitefield possessed forty-nine, accounting for well over two thirds of his estate; Tondee's seven slaves totalled three fourths of his. The standard price for a healthy adult male slave was £40, but special skills added to his value, just as age, injury, or temperament could subtract. Women and children were appraised by age and condition: an infant might bring £5, a girl £10, a sick woman £25, and an old woman £12.

Household furniture, on the other hand, generally simple and serviceable, did not represent much investment: a large mahogany table might cost £2; a dining table, £1 5s.; a pine bedstead, 10s.; a straw-bottomed chair, 2s. or 3s.; a Windsor chair, 4s. Among other household goods, a dozen white delft plates went for 6s.; a large china bowl for 5s.; and an axe for 4s. 6d.

By contrast, fabric items were particularly expensive, especially feather beds, which with bolster and pillows would run £5, or the value of two large mahogany tables and a few chairs. Even blankets, at 5s. each, were worth the same as roughly one hundred pounds of rice.

Clothes were usually made by the colonists themselves, but there was no shortage of tailors in Savannah, although James Habersham had a low opinion of them on the whole and ordered some garments to be made in London. Of the types of cloth available, osnaburg, a coarse cotton for work clothes, ran 8d. per yard; Irish linen, 2s. 6d. A pair of thread stockings would cost 3s.; white cotton stockings, 6s. Boys' shoes would average 4s.; adults' double channel pumps, 10s. Ribbon went at 1s. a yard; colored handkerchiefs at 1s. 6d. each. A suit belonging to carpenter Thomas Tripp, valued in 1769 at £5 pounds, must have been sumptuous indeed.

At the standard food prices, 5s. would buy about thirty pounds of beef or a little less of pork, twenty-five of veal, or twelve of mutton; five and a half pounds of butter, or fifty of fine white flour; half a barrel of cider, a gallon of rum, or almost two of Madeira; or a pound of tea.

Despite the poverty of the province, Georgia was deemed by most of the colonists and many visitors, even in the early years, an expensive place to live. This disparity explains in part the high cost of labor in Georgia: unskilled labor brought 2s. a day, and skilled laborers like carpenters and bricklayers charged 4s. to 5s. a day.

In offering his real estate and slaves as collateral, Tondee guaranteed his loan with almost everything of value that he owned. The real estate totaled about £80 and the three slaves certainly £50 or £60 more. So why all this property to secure a sum of £60?

To discourage default on these loans, the House of Assembly had stipulated in establishing the General Loan Office that security would have to be posted equivalent to at least twice the amount lent out and that slaves could account for no more than one third of the total. On the same day that Tondee took out his loan, John Milledge mortgaged all of his four-hundred-acre tract on the Little Ogeechee, a town lot, a farm lot, and two male slaves for only £80 pounds. That the mortgagees clearly did not expect to default attests to their faith both in themselves and in the economic future of Georgia under royal rule.

Though disappointed by Reynolds, they would see their hopes resurrected by the achievements of his successor, Henry Ellis.

Rule of Reason

A MORE DRAMATIC CONTRAST TO Captain John Reynolds than Henry Ellis could not have been invented. A gentleman and a scholar, Ellis brought to the office of Governor the personable qualities and social savoir-faire needed to work effectively with disparate groups of people—those traits the Captain so patently lacked. Unlike Reynolds with his benighted self-absorption, Ellis approached the problems facing Georgia with an almost clinical objectivity. He observed; he gathered information; he analyzed, formed a hypothesis, and acted on it, with resounding results. By the end of his three-year administration, the province had more than doubled in population and wealth.

Born into landed gentry, Henry Ellis had seen a good deal of the world before coming to Georgia. He had run away to sea as a boy, visited equatorial Africa and the West Indies, and joined an expedition in 1746 to search for the Northwest Passage, declining the command of one of the two ships for the more interesting role of general scientist: charting waterways, recording temperatures, measuring tides and salinity, and gathering "Metals, Minerals, and all kinds of natural Curiosities." On his return, Ellis published an account of the voyage, for which he was elected a Fellow of the Royal Society.

When he landed at Savannah in February of 1757, "loud Huzza's" greeted him from the bluff. Bonfires crackled in a twofold celebration, burning William Little in effigy and welcoming the new Governor. A Georgian who styled himself "Americanus" offered odes both for Reynolds's departure:

'Tis done at Length, the Tumults past,
The storm that Threat'ned us blown o'er
R . . . :ds's Power has breath'd it's last,
Little's vile Threats are heard no more.

—and for Ellis's arrival—

Welcome! thrice welcome! to our Land,
Georgia break forth in rapt'rous strain;
Great George our Sovereign is our Friend,
Be thankfull and forget thy Pain—

How has this infant Province shook,
Under a lawless Tyrants Sway;
But lo! the iron Rod is broke,
Ellis is come to cheer our Day—

Even before he set foot in Georgia, Ellis had begun educating himself about the problems there. He stopped in Charles Town for two weeks to confer with Governor Lyttleton, whose primary contact from Reynolds had been complaints about the delivery of his mail, and his counsels with Lyttleton established a mode of diplomacy that Ellis was to follow throughout his term in Georgia.

Once in Savannah, the young Governor—despite his accomplishments, at thirty-six he was just two years older than Tondee—adopted the same attentive approach. He listened to all opinions, which colonists were only too eager to share; but he sided with no one. His Northwest Passage expedition had given ample proof that when men train their eyes against each other, they lose sight of the common goal: during the icebound winter, the captains of the two ships had fallen out, and their unwillingness to coordinate subsequent efforts had doomed the project.

First, Ellis identified and put to use the strengths of the men on his Council, consulting with them extensively and delegating responsibilities. Next he adjourned the House of Assembly until Reynolds and Little had left the colony. Both remained in Savannah well into spring, preparing their defenses for the Board of Trade and trying to sabotage Ellis's plans as much as possible.

With deft ingenuity, Ellis avoided directly confronting Reynolds's forces. Faced with a general court on which two of the three seats were held by Reynolds's men—the third had been vacated by Little's departure—he declared that the great importance of the matters before the court required a panel of five judges, giving himself a majority of appointments on the bench without having to remove anyone. Rather than overtly reclaiming the prerogative of controlling the public accounts, a right which Reynolds had yielded to the House in a belated appeal for popularity, Ellis explained that the province's credit had so thoroughly collapsed during the previous administration—a fact no one could dispute—that to restore economic viability he was obliged to call in all debts for immediate payment. The colony achieved instant financial credibility, and the House of Assembly, still adjourned at the time, could only applaud.

Ellis had also the acumen to turn obstacles into advantages. Among his final conciliatory acts as Governor, Reynolds had raised a troop of forty rangers, but without providing for equipment or pay. Instead of disbanding them, Ellis commissioned officers of his own choosing and, at least for a while, paid the troops himself, an act of liberality unthinkable in Reynolds.

By the time he called the House of Assembly back into session, any opposition from the Reynolds's camp had dissolved. United, the colonists could get on with the formidable business of addressing the three main issues that stunted Georgia's growth: the threat of Indian attack, the scarcity of settlers, and the lack of wealth.

To bolster defense, Ellis shifted the focus of the customary civic work days from repairing roads to constructing forts and erecting a palisade around Savannah, and he succeeded in finally getting some regular troops stationed in the colony. Despite protests that the province could not support the hundred men offered, Ellis requested they be sent anyway, and by autumn of his first year in office the Virginia Regiment of Blues had arrived.

To attract settlers, he proposed that Georgia provide protection to debtors from their creditors for a period of seven years, with the exclusion of South Carolinians. Given the colony's inception as an alternative to debtors' prison for London's poor, the idea had a sound precedent and brought rapid results.

To encourage commerce, Ellis reinforced the worth of the paper currency issued by the General Loan Office by accepting it at face value for public debts, even though the Board of Trade had never ratified the original act; and five months after assuming office, he signed a new bill to print more money.

Having set in motion the machinery to promote growth in Georgia, Ellis devoted the remainder of his years as Governor to strengthening alliances with the Indians, and his reception of the chiefs in Savannah in October of his first year showed a panache not seen since Oglethorpe's time.

The chiefs at first were loath to come to Savannah at all, remembering the treatment they got from Reynolds at Augusta. But when news reached Ellis that a large party of Indians had gathered at the Altamaha River and were headed to town, the Governor sent Captain John Milledge and his troop of rangers to Fort Argyle on the Ogeechee to escort them the rest of the way. As the group neared Savannah, Ellis had the "Principal Inhabitants," who were most likely to give an impressive appearance, ride out to meet them in a clearing about a mile south of town, where a tent had been pitched to regale them. The whole assemblage then paraded in order— gentlemen, Indians, and rangers—to the town gate, where cannon saluted them.

Riders parted into two lines, the Indians marched between them, and Noble Jones and his militia ushered the party through the streets, past the Governor's House—where more cannon announced them, and volleys answered from the bluff and from the ships in port—and on to the Council House. There the Virginia Blues fired another salute, then fell into lines flanking the door, and the Indians passed between them and entered the council chamber to be welcomed by Ellis.

Cordial addresses and assurances of mutual friendship were exchanged, and when the Governor read to the chiefs a document of his own composition titled "A Letter from the great King George to his beloved Children of the Creek Nations," the Indians "at every Period declared their Approbation aloud!"

Ellis then presented them the prepared treaty, and before a throng of Principal Inhabitants and Indians, he and the Head Men pledged that "the Present Treaty of Peace and Alliance shall remain firm and inviolable as long as the Sun shall shine and the River run into the Sea."

Establishmentarianism

THAT GEORGIA ADOPTED ANGLICANISM as its official religion as late as 1758 resulted primarily from the zeal and political maneuvering of a converted Italian Jew. Presented and passed as an innocuous recognition of the religious majority, the measure became the legal basis, right up to the Revolution, for Anglican attempts to seize property and fees from both the Presbyterian and the Lutheran congregations.

Its sponsor and main protagonist, Joseph Ottolenghe, had been raised a devout Hebrew in the Piedmont region—the same part of Italy from which Amatis had hailed—but had embraced Anglicanism a couple of years after moving to England. Sent to Georgia by the Society for the Propagation of the Gospel in Foreign Parts with a mission to Christianize slaves, he arrived in the colony during the summer of 1751, when interest in silk production was reviving after a decade of mismanagement and neglect. With overseeing the silk business by day and catechizing the slaves at night, he found ready outlets for his prodigious energy. Though he never met with the success he sought in either enterprise, within four years he was elected to the House of Assembly, and it was from there that he engineered passage of the bill to establish Anglicanism officially.

The establishment act also divided the province into parishes, which functioned as political as well as ecclesiastical districts. Savannah and its environs became Christ Church Parish, the predominantly Lutheran area upriver became St. Matthew Parish, above that was the sparsely settled St. George, and beyond, St. Paul, which included Augusta; down the coast were St. Philip, St. John, St. Andrew, and St. James. Representatives to the Commons House of Assembly were chosen by parish, with the number of representatives from each determined by its proportion of the total population. Thus Christ Church Parish contributed one third of the members.

The act did not prevent non-Anglicans' being elected, however, and they often were. In fact, it had little immediate effect at all on religion or politics in the province, and only several years later, because of the self-righteous intolerance of a few men, like Zouberbuhler's fractious successor Samuel Frink and Ottolenghe himself, did manipulation of the law breed animosity.

Where Peter Tondee attended church is somewhat ambiguous. Brought up a Huguenot in London, he would have found Presbyterianism the closest equivalent in Savannah, but not until 1755 did an organized congregation emerge, and the first minister, the Reverend John J. Zubly, did not assume the pulpit until 1760. His pastorate at the Independent Presbyterian Church lasted until the Revolution, and among Savannah's clergy he was the clear leader of the cause for American rights and one of Georgia's delegates to the Continental Congress. Eventually he balked at breaking with England, though, and his abrupt departure from Philadelphia incurred the wrath and resentment of Georgia's Liberty Boys.

During his orphan years, Tondee undoubtedly attended Christ Church with his guardian, but neither Amatis nor Parker showed any sign of regular worship. Indeed, given the incompetence and contentiousness of most of Georgia's Anglican priests before and after Zouberbuhler, colonists rarely flocked to services. Tondee did pay £10 10s. in 1767 to lease a pew in Christ Church, but pews there were also leased by two of the founders of the Presbyterian church, perhaps for status or to reserve seats for special events. Even the Nunez brothers, Daniel and Moses, occasionally went to services at Christ Church. Tondee's pew, in the back corner of the gallery, was the very last leased.

Of necessity, society in Savannah had been heterogeneous from the first year. Tondee's circle of friends, as did most Georgians', crossed lines of religion and nationality and language. He knew Anglicans and Lutherans, Presbyterians and Congregationalists, Jews and even a Catholic or two, despite the official ban on Papists and the lingering bias against them. His neighbors were Germans and Scotsmen, Portuguese and French, Swiss and Italians and South Carolinians. He spoke English and French and likely some German. The social fabric, in short, was a broad and various weave, and when revolution finally ripped it apart, there were few seams to rend clean.

For Peter Tondee, though, a more important event involving Ottolenghe than passage of the establishment act occurred in 1758. Between four and six on the morning of the fourth of July, in a fire so hot that it threatened the Council House one hundred feet away, the silk filature burned.

The Filature

FOR MANY GEORGIANS, THE SILK business never lost an aura of mystification. From the hatching of the silkworm "seeds" to the unwinding of the single long filament from the cocoon, raising caterpillars as a crop must have struck the colonists as inscrutably alien, and the Trustees' plans for an industry based on insects clearly quixotic. The mystery that veiled it was deliberately maintained, also, by the successive silk managers in Georgia, who jealously guarded the secrets of curing and unreeling the cocoons. Despite repeated assurances from the Trustees, they viewed their exclusive knowledge of these techniques as job security and were reluctant to train anyone else thoroughly enough to replace them. By the 1740s, the experiment in sericulture seemed defunct.

But the French and Indian War of the 1750s and the consequent French embargo on silk sent prices up, and the silk business enjoyed a resurgence in Georgia, driven primarily by the enthusiasm of James Habersham. He saw in silk Georgia's economic redemption, and two of the three structures erected during that decade for conducting silk manufacture were built at his urging and under his supervision.

The first public filature in Savannah—indeed, the first public one in any colony—went up in 1751 on the northeastern Trust lot in the Lower New Ward, later named Reynolds. Formerly the baking, soaking, and unreeling of cocoons had been done in the house of the current silk manager or in a shed added on for that purpose. But making the process public and enlisting numbers of apprentices to learn it seemed certain to promote expansion of the culture.

The first filature had hardly been completed before Habersham concluded that another was necessary and implored the Trustees for more funds, citing the renewed interest among colonists in the silk business that the public filature had generated. In one of their final acts as administrators of the colony, the Trustees voted £300 for a second filature, which was erected on the adjacent southeastern Trust lot.

But the interior of this second building—a larger two-story house—was never completed, and it was this unused shell that became the new Council House after the old one collapsed around Governor Reynolds and his Council.

The fire that consumed the first filature in 1758 began about four in the morning, probably ignited by embers which had fallen between the floor boards and smoldered since the previous day. Constructed of yellow pine, rich with resin, the building had burned so fiercely that the outer wall of the Council House across the street streamed resin itself, threatening to detonate the magazine of gunpowder stored inside. Not until some resolute sailors braved the danger and started removing the powder did Savannahians rouse themselves to help. Lost were over a ton of cocoons, the copper basins for soaking, £40 in cash, and other valuables belonging to Ottolenghe.

In less than three weeks, Governor Ellis and his Council advertised for bids to rebuild the filature, and within another two weeks Peter Tondee and Benjamin Goldwire had been awarded the contract, agreeing under penalty to finish construction by the end of January 1759, six months later. With their bid they submitted a list of the lumber needed, and for their labor were promised £114.

The Governor and Council had originally advertised for proposals to erect two buildings on that lot, one to be a filature of one story, sixty feet by twenty, and the other a warehouse of two stories, forty-eight by twenty-two.

Workers at basins and reels in silk filature, c. 1760s.
(V. & J. Duncan, Antique Maps and Prints.)

There is no evidence that the one-story house was ever built, though. Subsequent references to the filature concern the two-story house facing Reynolds Square, and its dimensions were the same as the Council House, sixty feet by twenty-four.

Preparing the cocoons, unwinding the thread, and reeling it up took place on the first floor, and sorting the cocoons and storing the silk on the second, a large open room with numerous windows and dormers. This spacious chamber would become known as the Long Room in the Filature, and thirty-two years later President Washington would attend a ball there. Over its eight decades, the upper and lower rooms of the filature would serve as city hall, a succession of schools, a theater and concert hall, barracks and a hospital, and two concurrent boarding houses.

Even during the years of silk production, the filature occupied a singular position among Savannah's buildings. It had to be large enough to hold an adequate number of workers and machines to process the colony's harvest of cocoons, but like a stadium, it saw only seasonal use, standing idle for most months.

Tondee and Goldwire apparently completed construction of the filature on time—no records reveal otherwise—but they were not ordered payment until the following July, almost exactly a year after the old filature burned. One month earlier, perhaps in anticipation of the profit from his work, Tondee had applied for and been granted five hundred acres of pine land up the Savannah River "for the conveniency of cutting lumber." Three hundred acres he requested "in Family Right," and the remaining two hundred he proposed to purchase. Four miles above the old Euchee town, renamed Mount Pleasant, his tract bordered land of his partner Goldwire. Several months earlier, Richard Milledge had been granted five hundred acres a few miles below Mount Pleasant, at a placed called Tuckasee Kings, where he planned to build a sawmill.

Tondee's family in the summer of 1759 numbered six, with two slaves, down from the three in 1755. Peter and Lucy, at thirty-six and twenty-six, had by that time a son, also named Peter, and daughters Lucy and Ann; the fourth child may have been Elizabeth, or one who did not reach adulthood. Peter junior would later carry on the business of revolution after his father died, and the young Lucy would uphold the legacy of spunk and independence that both her mother and grandmother bequeathed, marrying in succession a headlong Liberty Boy and a Frenchman whose Anglicized surname was Hero.

Like Tondee, Richard Milledge saw his family increase to six by the end of the Fifties, and as responsible freeholders, both men discharged their share of civic duties. Tondee served as constable of Decker Ward in 1756, an office that required the disposition to act forcefully on occasion. It was a trait he would rely on in future positions as well. Milledge, five months after he and Tondee had been chosen to appraise the Council House, was appointed along with Thomas Tripp and Benjamin Goldwire to survey the repairs "absolutely necessary" to make Christ Church safe for services; and in the summer of 1757 he was nominated by Governor Ellis as one of ten superintendents of the watch.

At the close of Ellis's brief term in Georgia, Richard Milledge and David Cunningham, in their capacity as stewards of the Union Society, presented a parting address to the Governor, thanking him warmly for "that series of happiness enjoyed by us" and the "encouragement given to persons of our Station." Specifically mentioned were the law to prevent the use of slaves as artisans, the act to recover small debts promptly, and Ellis's decisive steps to establish the public credit. Members of the Society experienced daily the "salutary effects" of these measures. More generally, they also lauded his success in diplomacy with the Indians at a time when the province lay "exposed and defenceless." Signed by both Milledge and Cunningham—who was Tondee's brother-in-law, having married Anne Mouse Brooks—the valedictory expressed genuine affection for Ellis and regret at his departure.

It concluded with a wish for the Governor's renewed health, a reference to the reason he gave for his leaving. Though he had traveled to Africa and the West Indies, he believed that Georgians "breathe a hotter air than any other people on the face of the earth." Ever the scientist, during the summer of 1758 he had walked the streets of Savannah with a thermometer suspended at eye level beneath his umbrella, and recorded on three occasions temperatures of 102°.

Accompanying the address was a "small remembrance of our lasting esteem," described in a newspaper footnote as a "handsome piece of plate" with the inscription "Georgia. The Union Society Present this Token of Public Gratitude, To His Excellency Henry Ellis, Esq., Their Governor. 28 October 1760."

Having seen what they considered the worst of governors in Reynolds and the best in Ellis, Georgians awaited with some uncertainty the advent of their next royal governor, James Wright. His accomplishments for the province would be extensive as well, though, especially in the acquisition of land from the Indians, and he would enjoy the unanimous respect and admiration of the people right up to the Stamp Act crisis in 1765, when suddenly everything changed.

Halcyon Days

IT IS A PARADOX THAT ONE of the primary duties of a good parent is to prepare the child for separation. The same holds true for a teacher and student, a master and apprentice, and the success of the relationship may often be judged by the degree of independence achieved. In just this way did the wise guidance of James Wright bring the province to maturity, and ironically instill in the Sons of Liberty the confidence to cast him off.

If, amid the tumult of 1775, Georgians looked back to an age of growth and harmony and blithe hope, it was surely the first five years of Wright's government. As a result of Ellis's diplomacy, Indian affairs had stabilized, and after the Treaty of Paris in 1763 and the consequent withdrawal of France and Spain from all territories east of the Mississippi, Wright was able to gain three and a half million acres from the Indians for Georgia. During these five years of peace and relative security, the population of the province nearly doubled to seventeen thousand. Settlers came from Pennsylvania, Virginia, Maryland, and the Carolinas, as well as England, Scotland, Ireland, and the West Indies.

Early in his tenure, Wright earned the trust of Georgians. Though he had lived most of his life in South Carolina and had served as Attorney General there for over a decade—even at the time of his appointment in Georgia he was acting in London as agent for South Carolina—he rapidly shifted his substantial land holdings to his new home. And when—after the Treaty of Paris had ended Georgia's role as a buffer zone—South Carolina attempted to claim all lands south of the Altamaha River, Wright defended adamantly his new province against his old. Georgians could not mistake his earnest allegiance, and at least for a few years, Governor and governed enjoyed an era of good faith and cooperation.

After the opening of direct trade with London by the firm of Harris and Habersham during the previous decade, Savannah by the early Sixties had come into her own as a port and was no longer a mere annex to Charles

Town. To ensure that Georgia exported only wares of quality, the Assembly established inspectors for beef, pork, and lumber—Tondee would cull and inspect lumber at the end of the decade and the beginning of the Seventies. Harbor pilots were hired to steer ships up the treacherous Savannah River channel, and the lighthouse on Tybee Island at last got regular maintenance. On Cockspur Island, just within the mouth of the river, Fort George was built to protect shipping and regulate trade. And finally, like her sister colonies, Georgia sent to London an agent, William Knox, to facilitate commerce and urge measures for the benefit of the province.

The wharves on the river grew crowded with barrels of rice, beef, and pork; pitch, tar, and turpentine. Into ships whose masts were hardly visible from town, so high was the bluff, were loaded bundles of skins, stacks of staves and shingles, pine and cypress and oak lumber. Out of their holds and into the shops of Savannah came English shoes and Queensware plates, pewter dishes, delft bowls, candles and castile soap; pigtail, cut, and dry tobacco; coffee and tea, muscovado sugar, Jamaican rum, Philadelphia double beer, Vidonia wine and Madeira; flour, cheese, apples, potatoes, split peas and onions; walnuts and almonds, figs, olives, raisins, currants, capers, and spices of all kinds; herring and mackerel and even anchovies.

To treat what ailed them, Savannahians could dose themselves from Lewis Johnson's shop on the Bay with Squire's or Daffy's elixir, Bateman's drops, Godfrey's cordial, oil of anise or juniper or peppermint, Anderson's pills, Epsom salts, or opium. There was ipecac to induce vomiting, Peruvian bark for a touch of the intermittent fever, tincture of valerian for nervous disorders, and tincture of sage for preventing the decays of age. And to help it go down, there was white, brown, and barley sugar-candy. Johnson also sold the best lancets, and instruments for drawing teeth.

At the office of printer James Johnston—who began publishing the colony's first newspaper, the *Georgia Gazette*, in 1763—the more literate could purchase Shakespeare's works in eight volumes, *Robinson Crusoe, Gulliver's Travels, Aesop's Fables, Tobler's Almanac,* and other titles, as well as a four-sheet map of South Carolina and part of Georgia, surveyed and drawn by fellow townsman William Gerard DeBrahm. From Johnson and Wylly's store on Bay Street, with which the Tondees had an account, one could also buy for the parlor wall a Hogarth print, lambasting lawyers or ridiculing some folly of fashion.

The price of real estate in town went up, and new construction, though lacking the opulence of Savannah's homes during the cotton era, surpassed by far the modest cottages of the first decade. Though only a handful of the two hundred houses in Savannah at that time were brick, many stood on brick foundations, and brick was required for chimneys. With the constant danger of fire, any violation of this law incurred bitter resentment from neighbors. Kitchens and privies, as well as stables and cart-houses, were out back, under a separate roof.

Houses were painted in various shades of red and blue, and deep piazzas, or porches—often running the length of the house and sometimes embracing two or more sides—gave relief from the notorious summer heat. There was little protection, though, from windblown sand, and many visitors to Savannah, including Washington, complained of winds whipping up the sand from the bluff and driving it like a blizzard down the unpaved streets.

What the Tondee home at the corner of Broughton and Whitaker looked like in the early Sixties is a matter of some conjecture. It was certainly built of pine, likely cut from the higher ground of Tondee's farm lot or from his first grant of one hundred twenty acres, and it was at least two-story: later references to Tondee's allude to its size—"large house," "Capital Dwelling House." The Long Room, expansive enough to host a convocation of all the Freemasons in the colony or an assemblage of over a hundred delegates to the Provincial Congress, would not be added for several years, after Tondee had taken out a liquor license. Also built of pine, it would stand behind the house, along Whitaker. In 1775 saddler George Dresler, who owned the lot diagonally across Whitaker and the lane, would advertise his new shop "opposite Mr. Tondee's Long Room."

Intimate with sweltering Savannah summers, Tondee doubtless provided his home with a piazza fronting Broughton, the main street in town, and possibly one on Whitaker too. Both would catch the prevailing southeastern breezes and offer a pleasant setting for visits from neighbors. On the back of the lot were the stable and storehouse for lumber, as well as quarters for the slaves.

In 1760 Peter and Lucy's son Charles was born, and two years later another daughter, Mary. The other young Tondees—Lucy and Peter juniors, Ann, and one more, ranging in age from six or seven to toddler-size—found playmates nearby among their family's friends.

Just over a block east on Broughton Street lived Richard Milledge's brood. At the beginning of the decade, his oldest, Jacky, was six; Elizabeth was five; James, three; and Richard junior almost one. Appended to Richard's household and his brother John's were Billy Stephens, grandson and namesake of the old President, and his sisters Elizabeth and Mary, orphans of Frances Milledge and Newdigate Stephens.

John and his wife Ann Skidaway Smith, who was born on Skidaway

Island four months after its settlement, had by 1760 John junior, then three, and daughter Mary; these two would be their only children to reach adulthood. Indeed, so high was infant and child mortality that of Richard Milledge's nine children, only four boys would survive him; of James Habersham's ten, only three—Jemme, Joe, and John—would live to carry on the name; and of Noble Wimberly Jones's fourteen, though several would attain maturity, only George would outlast his octogenarian father.

The small Tondees might have expected welcome, though no playmates, at the home of Benjamin and Hannah Sheftall, across the lane on Duke Street. In 1760 Mordecai Sheftall, Ben's son by his first wife Perla, was twenty-five and well into a lucrative career as a merchant, owning a warehouse and wharf lot; a year later he would marry, and in 1763 become the Tondees' neighbor to the west, across an empty lot. Ben and Hannah's son Levi, then twenty-one, would join his half-brother in business, and both would eventually tender their fortunes and fates to the Revolution. The Tondees and Sheftalls maintained strong ties, personally and politically, well beyond the deaths of their patriarchs.

Since Lucy Tondee was the youngest of the five Mouse sisters, cousins on that side were generally older than the Tondee children. The Brooks twins, John and James, were then twenty-two; Elizabeth Young, daughter of the late Elizabeth Mouse and Isaac Young, was eighteen; and William Norton junior, Aunt Katey's son, was around ten. On the Tondee side, Peter's brother Charles probably lived in the vicinity of Purrysburg, South Carolina, at this time, so his children would have seen Peter's infrequently.

With the increase in construction during the Sixties, Tondee and his partner Benjamin Goldwire likely found steady work, and between jobs there was timber to cut from his five-hundred-acre tract near Mount Pleasant. He used this land in 1762 as collateral, along with a slave named Tom, for another loan of £50 from the General Loan Office.

When Tondee was not building houses or harvesting pine trees, Savannah offered diversions enough for entertainment. Since the early days, cricket in Johnson Square had been a favorite holiday pastime for both players and spectators, and occasionally there were horse races to fire the blood and to swell the purses of the lucky. In August of 1760 a memorable race was run between John Maxwell and John Fitch; Maxwell's horse won, but the real loser in the race was Morgan Sabb, who "had the misfortune of having his leg broke." Sabb may have been simply an onlooker; riders galloping their horses through town were a continual peril, and fines were handed out regularly for the offense.

Savannahians also had a variety of social clubs to engage them. Within a year of the founding of the colony, the Freemasons had organized, and besides quarterly communications, they celebrated the feasts of St. John the Evangelist in December and St. John the Baptist in June. Since 1750 the Union Society had held periodic meetings and anniversary dinners on St. George's Day in April. Over time, both these groups had attracted substantial membership, but it was during the Sixties that clubs rapidly expanded. The St. Andrew's Society gave annual dinners on November 30 to honor the patron saint of Scotland, and the Society of St. Patrick inaugurated the festival of March 17 which two centuries later would become Savannah's official bacchanalia.

Other clubs catered to the whimsical as well as the serious. While the Georgia Library Society promoted culture by lending books, the Amicable Club and the Ugly Club likely aspired to no more than convivial company over good food and drink. All met at one or another of the popular taverns, where fellowship flowed in bumpers and bowls.

Centers of social life, the taverns not only hosted club events but offered a congenial atmosphere for the individual patron. During the Sixties, one tavern especially fostered the refinement of social graces and appreciation of the performing arts. Late in December of 1763, Mrs. Sarah Lyon advertised a ball to be held at her house; tickets, "which admit a Gentleman and a Lady," could be bought from the hostess. Though within two years Mrs. Lyon had died—"greatly and justly regretted," the *Gazette* opined—her husband John upheld the custom in 1766 with a public concert by the new organist of Christ Church, probably on the harpsichord, followed by a ball. Two years later, Lyon's Long Room, with the imprimatur of Governor Wright, presented a popular farce by London actor David Garrick titled *Lethe, or Aesop in the Shades*, featuring personages called "the Fine Gentleman and the Fine Lady, with a Song in Character," and instrumental music as well. The play began promptly at seven o'clock, and tickets cost half a crown each, or two shillings sixpence.

State occasions too provided respite from the daily routine. Georgians observed anniversaries of the King's birthday, accession, and coronation, and Oglethorpe's birthday; and declarations of both war and peace brought demonstrations of rejoicing. One of the most impressive ceremonies—and a singular one in the life of the province—occurred a few months after Wright's arrival, and it epitomized the sense of unity and hope with which the Sixties began.

During her brief career as a colony, Georgia saw only one change on the English throne. In February of 1761, Savannahians celebrated the accession of George III with all the pomp they could muster. The regulars and militia were drawn up before the Council House on Reynolds Square, and after the windows of the Council Chamber had been thrown open, the proclamation announcing the new King was read by the clerk "audibly and distinctly under a Discharge of twenty one Pieces of Cannon." Governor Wright then led the principal inhabitants and the regulars and militia to the city market, at that time on the square in Percival Ward, where the proclamation was read again, to the same discharge of cannon. And finally the procession marched to Fort Halifax, a fortress at the northeast corner of town built only the previous year, where the ceremony was repeated.

Despite the radical shifts in popular sentiment over the succeeding decade, Georgians' devotion to their new monarch would remain curiously constant. Their quarrel was with Parliament, not with the Crown. Even on the threshold of the Revolution, the Sons of Liberty, dining at Tondee's Long Room after erecting a liberty pole, would toast first The King, and then American Liberty.

Number Nine Heathcote

THE LOT NEXT TO THE TONDEES' on Broughton Street—number nine, Heathcote Tything—had always been vacant, and in 1764 Peter bought it. The purchase meant double the frontage on Savannah's main residential street. With a total of one hundred twenty feet, Tondee now owned two fifths of the block. But it would be his last acquisition of land. Though his province and his career were thriving, so was his family, and over the next decade Tondee's finances fluctuated.

One setback arose within months of his purchase of number nine. Though the port of Savannah would endure a brief interruption during the Stamp Act of 1765, more damaging to the colony's economy, and directly antagonistic to Tondee's interests, was the Sugar Act of 1764. A revival of the earlier Molasses Act, which had targeted New England's rum distilleries in an attempt to give British sugar planters a monopoly of the American molasses market, the Sugar Act also introduced regulations on the timber industry. By requiring prohibitive security bonds from shippers of lumber, it threatened to eliminate entirely one of Georgia's chief exports, and seriously jeopardized the value of Tondee's five hundred acres of pine land up the river. Even James Habersham, a King's man to the last, recognized that no sane merchant would risk financial disaster for a shipment of pine that would bring comparatively small profits. He wrote Georgia's agent William Knox in London that if this law were left standing, four fifths of the province's lumber trade would cease.

Unlike the Stamp Act, though, the Sugar Act was not repealed. So some shippers turned to smuggling, as they had under the Molasses Act; and in the ports, customs commissioners found the regulations a steady source of private income. Ultimately, for colonists, the effect of both these acts was the same: Parliament forfeited credibility and encouraged Americans to disobey the law.

When Tondee bought number nine Heathcote late in February, two months before the Sugar Act was passed, he paid £40 5s. shillings for it. Originally granted to Abraham Molina, the lot had been given as payment for a debt to Moses Nunez, who had never built on it, though he claimed to have kept it "in Repair." Both men had come to Savannah among the Jews on the *William and Sarah* during the first summer of the colony, and for Nunez the village on the bluff had marked the final port in an odyssey which began in Lisbon in an elegant mansion on the banks of the Tagus River.

Moses Nunez's father Samuel had been physician to the Grand Inquisitor in Portugal and a man of eminence and wealth, but a rival had denounced him to the ecclesiastical council and the family had been imprisoned for heresy. At the intercession of the Inquisitor, the council agreed to place guards in the Nunez household to prevent lapses, and they were paroled, but not before Moses' sister had been questioned—the ropes left scars like bracelets on each wrist.

While Doctor Nunez arranged for their escape, the family maintained an appearance of acquiescence and normalcy, and according to their custom, entertained other eminent families of Lisbon. On one occasion, a dinner in summer, the guests included the captain of an English brigantine, then at anchor in the river. As the party amused themselves on the lawn, the captain invited the doctor and his family and a few others to his ship for a lunch he had prepared. Accompanied by the spies of the Inquisition, the ensemble went on board the brig, and while they were eating in the cabin below, the mates weighed anchor and sailed out to sea, spies and all.

The doctor had converted into gold as much of his assets as he could and had dispersed it among the men of the family to conceal in leather belts; the ladies had quilted their jewels into their gowns. All else was relinquished, and later seized by the Inquisition.

The Nunez family lived in London for about seven years before emigrating to Georgia, and the voyage of the *William and Sarah* had imposed further tests. Before the ship had cleared the Thames, she suffered serious damage, and the passengers had to disembark during repairs. When finally at sea, she met with storm after storm in her passage and was almost wrecked on the coast of North Carolina, where once again repairs caused a delay of several weeks. By the end of the ordeal, as they rode at anchor below the Savannah bluff, mere yards from their goal, they must have found the cold ambivalence of Oglethorpe's reception utterly apt.

In Georgia, Moses and his older brother Daniel—twenty-eight and twenty-nine at the time of their arrival—rapidly learned the Indian language, became traders, and served as interpreters throughout the colonial period.

As early as 1736, Daniel had assisted in Indian talks at Frederica, and Moses was present at conferences between the Creeks and both Ellis and Wright.

At the height of the Spanish threat in 1740, after Oglethorpe's abortive siege of St. Augustine, all of the Nunez family except Moses had removed to Charles Town. Having fled Catholic Portugal, they did not relish the prospect of invasion by Catholic Spain. From there Doctor Nunez and his daughter continued to New York, but Daniel returned to Georgia, and during the summer of Bloody Marsh, Moses coxswained the scout boat *Skidaway* between Savannah and St. Simons. Stationed at Noble Jones's fort at Wormslow, the *Skidaway*, with six oars and a swivel gun, comprised the other half of the Northern Company of Marines.

When he sold Tondee the lot on Broughton, Moses was living in Yamacraw on the west side of town. Seventy at the onset of the Revolution, he would remain curiously aloof from the upheaval around him, and when he died at eighty-two, would bequeath property to his three mulatto children, along with instructions that they be raised as Christians.

Peter intended to will number nine to his second son Charles. He left it vacant, and at his death it was the only piece of real estate in his possession other than the corner lot, number ten, originally granted to his father by the Trustees in 1733.

1765

WHEN AMERICAN NATURALIST JOHN BARTRAM stopped in Savannah in September of 1765, he recorded in his journal that Governor Wright was "universaly respected by all ye inhabitants." John and his son William, who would return in 1773, were making a tour of the Carolinas, Georgia, and Florida to survey the flora and collect specimens, and it was on this trip that they discovered the *Franklinia alatamaha*, named in honor of their friend Benjamin Franklin and the river Altamaha, the banks of which were the sole habitat of this peculiar and beautiful shrub. Last seen in the wild in 1803, it survives now in gardens and nurseries through the seeds gathered by William on his second visit.

The Bartrams dined with Wright at his invitation, and John found him "A very agreeable humane kind gentleman," observing that Georgians "can hardly say enough in his praise." Within a couple of months, however, the universal respect had dissipated and the mutual trust vanished, for though he had defended Georgia against her sister colony in the land dispute, he sided squarely with the mother country—at the clear expense of his province—in the Stamp Act controversy. That he alone, of all the colonial governors, succeeded in enforcing the Stamp Act galled Georgia's Liberty Boys all the more.

Parliament had passed the act in March of that year—to become effective the first of November—and so long as the conflict had remained merely hypothetical, Wright and his colonists showed reciprocal civility. Though he never revealed his personal opinion, Wright too seemed to think the act unwise. But few at the beginning of that year could have foreseen the rancor that would erupt by the end.

To the Tondees and the Sheftalls the year brought triumphs and trials, often mixed. At two o'clock on a Friday morning early in February, fire broke out in an old house on the lot adjoining Ben Sheftall's and burned it to the ground. Luckily the night was calm and the flames were kept confined, and neither Sheftall's home nor Tondee's across the lane was touched, but to the Tondee brood in the dead of night, it was an unsettlingly close spectacle. To their father the house carpenter, it was the persistent face of a personal nemesis.

His career reached its zenith that year, at about the same time that demonstrations broke out against the Stamp Act. He had continued his partnership with Benjamin Goldwire—they were paid for some work on the Council House in March—but for his magnum opus he teamed up with Joseph Dunlap, who had come to Georgia at the beginning of the Sixties, and, doubtless rather reluctantly, also with Robert Kirkwood and his partner John Hall. The hiring of both these pairs of carpenters for the courthouse project arose from a dispute, and it is unlikely that the match was ever a happy one.

As far back as February of 1764, the General Assembly had voted to build a new courthouse and had appointed commissioners to advertise the construction and take bids. But not until July of 1765 did any notice appear in the *Gazette*. It ran for three weekly issues, calling for bids by the middle of August, and adding that since "a considerable quantity of lumber, bricks, and lime, are wanted for building and finishing the said house," proposals for supplying these materials were also invited. Significantly, the notice stated that bids for building the courthouse were to be "agreeable to a plan in our hands." This plan would become the point of contention between the partnership of Tondee and Dunlap and that of Kirkwood and Hall.

The previous courthouse had been only one story, and since the act passed by the General Assembly had specified that the old courthouse was to be torn down and rebuilt, the plans presented—except for Kirkwood and Hall's—had been for a one-story structure. How Kirkwood and Hall came into possession of the plan drawn by Tondee and Dunlap is not clear, nor is the reason that they were the sole partnership to offer a two-story design. Kirkwood himself had just arrived from South Carolina that summer, possibly as late as August; Hall had been in Georgia three or four years.

What is apparent, however, is that irregularities occurred on the part of Kirkwood and Hall and the commissioners as well. In March of 1766, Tondee and Dunlap presented a petition to the Commons House claiming that Kirkwood and Hall "had found Means in Injury to the Petitioners to possess themselves of the said Plan" and had simply added a second story to it—"it manifestly could be made appear the Scheme and Ichnography [a scale drawing of the ground floor] was the Study and Labor of the Petitioners." Tondee and Dunlap then submitted an estimate of £430 to build the two-story design and asked for redress of their grievances.

Oddly enough, six weeks earlier the commissioners themselves had entered a memorial to the Commons House attempting to explain their choice of the two-story plan and their award of the contract to Kirkwood and Hall. They protested that they had used "every Means in their Power" to procure the best plan, that they had obtained estimates for both the one- and two-story designs, and that the difference in cost between them would be offset by reducing the size of the roof. Left unmentioned were the procedure used to solicit plans and the failure to reopen bidding once the decision had been made to build a larger courthouse.

By that time, though, all this was relatively moot. The commissioners had resolved the issue the previous November by employing both pairs of partners for the project. The date that construction actually began, however, is harder to pinpoint: the bill to fund it did not pass until March of 1766, on the same day that Tondee and Dunlap presented their petition for redress, and work on the two-story brick edifice continued for several years. As late as 1768 court was being held in John Lyon's Long Room; and because of a stalemate between Wright and the Commons House—and the consequent shutdown of the Assembly for two years—Tondee would not be paid the balance of his account until 1773.

When completed, the courthouse fronted Wright Square, with a wide pediment supported by columns shading the entrance. Court was held in the large room upstairs, the smaller being used for the judge's chamber; and of the three rooms downstairs, one was reserved for the chief clerk and the other two for the grand and petit juries.

Though no records of private homes built by Tondee have been found, one likely candidate was that of James Habersham, constructed in the spring of 1765. Peter had not yet begun work on the courthouse, and Habersham seems to have held the former Bethesda boy in some regard. As late as 1772, despite their political differences, which by that time must have been apparent, he would cite Tondee in a letter to Wright, then in London, regarding the price of reels for the silk culture.

Usually owners of large tracts of land, like Habersham and Noble Jones, placed their principal home on their plantation, but with the death of his wife at Silk Hope and the painful memories of that house, Habersham had chosen to live in town: "In short," he wrote his friend William Knox in London, "I am now a perfect Citizen of Savannah, and that has made me lay out 4 or 500 £ in a neat and comfortable Habitation in it." Facing Johnson Square at Bull and Bryan, the house reflected Habersham's preference for simplicity and utility over ostentation.

During the summer of 1765, Noble Jones's plantation Wormslow on the Isle of Hope provided Savannahians the diversion of a botanical marvel. The *Gazette* of July 11 reported that during the previous week parties of people from town had gone there to see an agave plant, with a bloom stalk said to be twenty-seven and a half feet high, containing thirty-three branches and "a vast number of blossoms." Tondee may have been familiar with this plant already, from his years on the Isle of Hope, but to a fourteen-year-old the mound of green spikes would have been an object of avoidance.

Summer's end and autumn brought to a close one of Tondee's oldest friendships. Early in August, Peter witnessed the will of Benjamin Sheftall, then seventy-three and "infirm in bodily health"; two months later, this venerable neighbor died.

Also during the first week of August, Peter's brother Charles petitioned for two hundred fifty acres on the south side of the Altamaha River, in land ceded by the Indians in 1763. With a wife and two children, but no slaves, Charles was living outside Georgia, probably in Purrysburg, the Swiss Huguenot village up the Savannah River on the Carolina side. The petition was initially postponed until Charles could appear before the Governor and Council in person; and when he did, on the following land day, his request was approved, but only on condition that he first bring his family into the province. A month later Charles registered the grant and put his signature beside the entry in the record book, but whether he ever took up that land remains a mystery. After 1765 he drops out of sight.

Chagrin

NOBODY WON THE STAMP ACT conflict in Georgia. The whole miserable affair produced only acute embarrassment for both Wright and the Liberty Boys, and it was this deep personal chagrin, as much as their ideological differences, that stiffened the spines of Tories and Whigs alike and made future clashes inevitable. Forced to choose between obeying a bad law or endorsing bad behavior, reasonable subjects on both sides felt betrayed and insulted.

Few were more keenly torn by the dilemma than John Milledge. As a member of the Commons House of Assembly, he had defended colonial rights against the intrusions of Parliament and had harshly criticized the Stamp Act, which placed a tax on all legal documents, newspapers, licenses, ship's papers, even playing cards. He was clearly in sympathy with the sailors who demonstrated on November 5, the anniversary of the Gunpowder Plot, by parading through the streets with one of their crew carried on a scaffold to represent the stampmaster. At intervals the sailors would stop and cudgel the mock-agent, whose neck was noosed with a rope that also looped securely under his arms, and he would cry out, "No stamps, No riot act, Gentlemen." They had concluded by hanging him before Machenry's Tavern on Ellis Square, to the delight of a crowd of spectators. The *Gazette* pointed out that no property, public or private, had been harmed, and no outrages committed.

Two months later, though, John found himself obliged, as Captain Milledge of the rangers, not only to warn the Governor that the Liberty Boys were gathering in town but also to square off against them—many of whom were his friends and neighbors—to protect the stamps which were stored in the guardhouse. In his long and laudable military career, few orders could have aroused in Milledge more distaste. For the entire month of January, he and his rangers stood watch over the stamps, until the unused bulk of them were finally loaded on a British ship and returned.

Sir James Wright, last royal governor of Georgia.
(Courtesy, Georgia Department of Archives and History.)

For his part, Governor Wright handled the crisis deftly and decisively. When a crowd assembled at his gate to demand whether he had appointed a temporary stampmaster, he walked into the middle of the group with his musket, admonishing them that this was no way to wait upon the Governor of a province and assuring them that in any event he would fulfill his oath to His Majesty. After the crowd dispersed, he personally led a patrol of forty rangers through the streets of Savannah, and for four nights he slept in his clothes.

When the royal stampmaster finally arrived at Tybee, Wright had him escorted secretly to town and then, once the stamps had been issued to collectors, lodged him in the country to avoid the mob. Soon afterward the backwoods Liberty Boys marched on the town, but Wright worked through his channels of influential planters to dissuade them, and those not convinced by argument he confronted with troops.

For their part, Georgia's Liberty Boys were ambivalent and divisive. Though the majority opposed the use of stamps, Savannah's merchants stood to lose heavily—not to mention the owners of rice plantations—if the sixty-odd ships trapped by the closing of the port were not allowed to sail with their cargoes of the previous year's rice crop. Fearing financial disaster, the merchants had first petitioned Wright to allow the ships to sail without stamps, as no stampmaster had yet arrived in the province, and later they struck a deal with the Liberty Boys to use stamps only to clear those vessels. Men like Mordecai Sheftall and planter Jonathan Bryan, both of whom would play prominent roles in the Liberty Party a decade later, found themselves in equivocal circumstances during the Stamp Act turmoil.

But even when their numbers were great—and they were in every confrontation greater than Wright's—the Liberty Boys had no central leadership and quarreled themselves into sullen factions. From a body of six hundred in the back country, they had shrunk to less than half that size by the time they mustered on the town common. There, stymied by Wright's hundred troops, they splintered in dispute, and by evening they were gone.

His success would seem to have been a source of satisfaction for Wright. But he had seen the face of the mob, and its insolence was an affront to decency and decorum. That British subjects had dared offer armed resistance to His Majesty in the person of the royal Governor shook him deeply; that they had opposed a Governor so distinctly devoted to their welfare struck him as gross ingratitude. To his credit, Wright never identified by name any of these "Sons of Licentiousness," some of whom he must have known, but he smarted from their indignities.

The most biting chagrin for Wright, however, came with the news in late spring that Parliament had repealed the Stamp Act. After sacrificing the trust and good will of the common people in the performance of his duty—and succeeding where no other colonial governor had—he now bristled that it had all gone for nothing. The Board of Trade even hinted in a letter that perhaps he had been somewhat too zealous in his response to the colonists' "just & decent Exercise of that Liberty which belongs to the People."

At this time, though, Wright was still early in his tenure as Governor. Another decade would pass before he suffered the final indignity of being arrested by the twenty-five-year-old son of his recently deceased, closest friend in Georgia, James Habersham.

A different kind of embarrassment beleaguered Peter Tondee during this year, the effects of which would bear strongly on events a decade later. On March 6, 1766, the same day that he submitted his petition for redress of grievances and that funds were voted for the courthouse, the Assembly also amended an act which had prohibited tradesmen from selling liquor. Henceforth licenses could be issued to such men if they could demonstrate to five justices of the peace that by their trade alone they could not support their family. Tondee was issued his license in January of 1767, retroactive to the previous October, and for it he paid a fee of £3 sterling, Savannah's rate being the highest in the province.

Friends and Family

THE AMENDMENT TO THE ACT Regulating Taverns listed a variety of reasons why a tradesman might not be able to support his family and should be granted a license to retail liquor. Advanced age, any losses or misfortunes, sickness, and the number of members in a household were all deemed qualifying circumstances. In Tondee's case, the first of these can be ruled out—Peter was forty-three when he applied—and sickness is also unlikely. His work on the courthouse and offices he later held do not reflect a sick man.

But he may have suffered financial losses from the Sugar Act, and it is certain that there were more than a few places at his table. Allowing for the high rate of mortality among children, the fact that at least seven of Peter's reached adulthood suggests that the actual number in his household at this time was probably greater. It is a fair assumption that during the second half of the 1760s, the Tondee home at Broughton and Whitaker echoed with the din of young voices and the stampede of small feet.

This was not yet the age of Tondee's Tavern. Though Peter's license in 1767 entitled him to retail spirits in quantities of less than three gallons, he is not included among those licensed to keep a tavern, which would permit billiard tables, shuffleboard, and ninepins, as well as allowing the proprietor to charge for food and lodging. Not until 1770 does any evidence apear that the Tondees hosted large groups on a regular basis, and since the *Gazette* did not publish the list again until 1781, the year in which Tondee officially commenced operating a tavern remains unclear.

The taverns listed in 1767, though, included Machenry's, Creighton's, and Abigail Minis's, along with five others in Savannah, four down the coast in Sunbury, and two up the river in St. Matthew Parish. Licensed retailers in the province, like Tondee, numbered fifteen, among whom were Lucy Tondee's sister Ann Cunningham and her son James Brooks, and Margaret Pages, a friend of the Tondee family. Georgians could purchase rum, brandy, gin, beer, wines, and cordials—in amounts greater than three gallons—from many of the general stores.

This ready access to spirits implies a deep and persistent thirst among colonists, confirmed by a Savannah customs official's estimate of Georgians' drinking habits in 1770. He calculated that adults consumed an average of half a pint of rum per day, in addition to smaller quantities of gin, wines, and beer. Generally, working folk at home drank their rum straight, while taverns offered it in grog, a mixture of rum and water; in toddy, the same mixture with sugar; and in punch, a warm lime daiquiri served in a bowl, which was passed around the table without the bother of cups or glasses.

For the most part, alcohol taken in moderation was thought salutary, stimulating the blood and bracing men for hard labor. Oglethorpe himself had supplied beer and bread for both breakfast and dinner on civic work days, and in at least Maryland and Virginia it was common practice for some mothers to administer a glass of rum to children in the morning as a tonic.

But public inebriation rarely met with approval. A sketch in the *Gazette* in January of 1768, titled "The Character of a Sot," lampooned the typical drunk: "His eyesight is best when he is stone blind, for till then he can never see his way home. He is a postboy's horn to alarm a quiet neighbor at the unseasonable hour of one in the morning. ... His frugality is very remarkable, for a shirt always lasts him a month without washing. ... He is a key to the doors of workhouses, and keeps alive the charitable practice of burying the poor *gratis* ... and after his death there are no traces of his memory but on the chalked walls of alehouses." Two years after this parody appeared, Peter Tondee would join in demonstrating the second of the traits described, though with a drum instead of a horn.

In May of the year that work on the courthouse probably began in earnest—1766—Tondee's former partner Benjamin Goldwire died on Ossabaw Island, mourned by a wife, three sons, and two daughters. To his oldest son and his son-in-law, he left his carpenter's tools and his books of architecture. His personal possessions, including his two slaves but not his land holdings, amounted to £115, almost exactly one third of the total of Tondee's possessions a decade later.

One of the appraisers of Goldwire's estate, Peter Gandy, would also witness Peter Tondee's will, and in fact the two men's lives intersected at many points. Gandy served as secretary of the Union Society in 1766, and his name is third on the membership roster of Unity Lodge, the second Masonic chapter in the province, founded by Tondee in 1774. By then Gandy had also become Tondee's accountant. Though probably somewhat

Signatures of Peter Tondee, family and friends—Peter's brother signed his name *Chas;*
(across) Peter's son, *Charles.* Note the date *1768* embedded in Sheftall's signature
and the change in signature of John Shick after the Battle of Savannah,
in which he lost an arm.

John Oates

Peter Tondee

John Gandy

Lachlan + McGillivray

Lucy Tondee

Charles Tondee

More signatures of Peter Tondee, family and friends.
Note the bold letters of Lachlan McGillivray.

different in temperament—Gandy's signature was florid with embellishment while Tondee's was simple and regular—the two Peters clearly trusted one another.

A clerk and schoolmaster, Gandy had been teaching in Savannah since 1763, and in May of 1768 advertised his intention to open a school on Monday, June 6, in part of Mrs. Cunningham's house. In the ad he claimed that his method of teaching was well known in Savannah and requested that "those gentlemen and ladies who formerly favoured him with the tuition of their children will still continue them." Gandy promised "sobriety, due care, diligence, and constant attendance." On Wednesday, June 8, he confirmed that he had opened school at Mrs. Cunningham's, but within two weeks he had moved to another house. He offered no reason for the change, though perhaps he found the Cunninghams' business in retail liquor inimical to his promise of sobriety and academic diligence.

Some of the young Tondees likely learned their letters under Gandy's instruction. Peter and Lucy juniors, Ann, Elizabeth, and Charles—ranging in age from fourteen to eight in 1768—might all have sat in his classroom, and five-year-old Mary and toddler Sally would have been ready for lessons by the early Seventies.

As well as scholastic education, Savannah offered instruction in the arts of dancing and self-defense, for both children and adults. In September of 1765, a notice in the *Gazette* announced the opening of a dancing school by a woman with the felicitous name Medley D'Arcy Dawes, so reminiscent of do-si-do. Perhaps for the sake of modesty, though at the sacrifice of appropriate partners, Miss Dawes proposed to teach young gentlemen on Monday, Wednesday, and Friday evenings; and young ladies and children on Thursday and Saturday afternoons. For the truly modest, she would give private instruction at the lodgings of the student, between ten and noon.

Gentlemen desiring to hone their martial arts skills could apply to John Revear, who published in July of 1768 his intention to teach "THE NOBLE SCIENCE OF DEFENSE, in the most comprehensive and easiest method which is taught in all Academies in Europe at this present time." Revear's schedule of classes—from six to nine in the morning and five to seven in the evening—seems designed to allow both him and his students to work full-time during the day.

For the Tondees, 1767 ended with brighter financial prospects than it had begun. Besides the added income from retail spirits, Peter's wages for work on the courthouse were augmented by his fees as culler and inspector of lumber for the port of Savannah. Both he and Joseph Dunlap were among six inspectors appointed in March, and three years later they would be the only two reappointed.

But 1767 brought setbacks as well. In May, Tondee had entered a caveat against the Crown's allowing Lucy Mouse's gift of the original fifty-acre lot on Skidaway Island to pass to her grandson William Norton. "Others" joined him in this suit, likely the Cunninghams, but Norton won the judgment, which was fortunate since he had previously sold the property to John Milledge.

And another event which occurred in 1767 or early 1768 must have disconcerted the Tondees considerably. One of the family's slaves was executed.

Slavery

TONDEE'S SLAVE WAS ALMOST CERTAINLY hanged—the great majority of condemned slaves were—and since the goal of deterrence dictated a public execution, the site was most likely the common south of town. After the prisoner had mounted a ladder at the scaffold, the noose was fitted around his neck and he was pushed off the ladder. The experience, some were told, was no worse than an apoplectic fit. To heighten the deterrent effect, especially in the case of murder, the head of the executed slave might be severed and fixed on a post near the place of his crime. In at least four instances, for acts judged particularly heinous, slaves were burned at the stake.

Georgians went to such lengths not just to prevent future crimes, but to preclude future punishments. No one gained from the execution of slaves. They were valuable assets, the backbone of many estates. Masters objected to their wanton destruction, and the provincial government, obliged to compensate owners for slaves executed, wished to get the most deterrence for the pound. Despite the increasing severity of Georgia's slave laws, no more than about twenty-five slaves were put to death during the royal era, and more than one third of those were executed in a single year, the same that Tondee's was.

In estimating government expenses, the Commons House routinely budgeted compensation for one slave per year; any reimbursements to specific colonists were then incorporated into the next tax act. In some years there were no executions, and according to surviving records, slaves executed before 1767 may have numbered no more than three. So the fact that in the tax act of April 1768 six other colonists besides Tondee were compensated for a total of nine slaves invites speculation, for insurrection was one of the offenses listed as capital.

But the *Georgia Gazette*, never shy of publishing news of slave troubles both abroad and at home, mentions no uprising during the period covered by the tax act of 1768. That two of the seven colonists were compensated for two slaves each implies some degree of complicity, but several of them lived in the southern parishes, where plantations were far apart and any concerted effort between slaves of different owners would be difficult.

In the case of one of the slaves executed that year, the crime can be determined from a petition to Governor Wright. In July of 1767, William MacKenzie requested a reprieve for a slave condemned for robbery. At that time MacKenzie was living on Skidaway Island and owned about thirty-five slaves, one of whom had run away the previous summer. Although none of the other six masters that year, including Tondee, appealed for clemency, such petitions were not uncommon. As in MacKenzie's case, however, they were seldom granted.

Other developments in Georgia in 1766 and 1767 besides possible insurrection, though, could account for the sudden proliferation of slave executions. With the colony's rapid growth and prosperity during the Sixties had come an abrupt increase in the slave population, many of whom were new slaves imported for the expanding rice culture. So brisk was the slave business that in late October of 1766, two Savannah firms sold in one day a total of two hundred sixty recently captured slaves. Though many of the owners of large plantations had lately relocated from South Carolina and thus brought with them some experience with slavery, the province as a whole was yet green at handling it. Between new slaves and new masters, a consistent code was hard to establish, not least because laws affecting both were openly flouted.

To regulate slave behavior, the Assembly had adopted in 1755 a slave act similar to South Carolina's, imposing conditions and restrictions on what slaves could do. To leave town or his plantation, a slave needed a permission ticket, and no more than seven male slaves could travel together without a white person with them. To carry a weapon required a ticket or the company of a white over sixteen, and only with permission could slaves purchase liquor, or buy, sell, or barter anything. Prohibited outright were assemblies of slaves, especially on Saturday nights, Sundays, and holidays; and slaves were forbidden to play drums, horns, or other loud instruments "which may call together or give Sign or Notice to one another of their wicked Designs . . . ." Through this last injunction and the proscription against teaching a slave to read and write—punishable by a fine of £15— Georgians hoped to prevent any methods at all of widespread communication between slaves.

Slave laws addressed the behavior of masters as well. They must provide "Sufficient Cloathing Covering [and] Food," and they could not work slaves more than sixteen hours a day, or at all on Sunday. Acceptable forms of punishment included whipping or beating with a horsewhip, cowskin, switch, or small stick; or putting in irons or in prison. Masters were admonished, however, not to kill a slave, or cut out his tongue, or put out his eye, or castrate, scald, maim, or burn him.

But reality differed substantially from the law. Depending on their master, some slaves without tickets traveled freely, carried weapons, bought and sold goods, and worked and lived apart from their owners. Interpretations of sufficient clothing, shelter, and food varied widely, and the clause against working slaves on Sunday, which allowed exceptions for "absolute necessity" and domestic service, was generally ignored. Far from discouraging slave musicians, colonists frequently hired them for entertainment at dancing assemblies and banquets.

Even the colony's leaders showed a public disregard to the ban against teaching slaves to read and write. As early as 1751, within a year after the Trustees had approved slavery in Georgia, the Society for the Propagation of the Gospel in Foreign Parts had sent Joseph Ottolenghe to Savannah to teach religion to Negroes. Ottolenghe had applied himself diligently, managing the silk business by day and holding classes at night for anywhere from ten to fifty slaves. He taught reading and writing and expounded the principles of Christianity, sustaining his efforts until the end of the decade, long after the first slave act had declared educating slaves illegal.

Likewise, in the middle Sixties, the Reverend Bartholomew Zouberbuhler provided funds in his will for a catechist to live on his plantation Beth Abram and instruct the fifty-two slaves there. And as late as 1775, James Habersham, who had personally taught several of his house slaves "to read a little," set up a school on one of his plantations with a Moravian teacher and about thirty young students.

In each case the goal of educating slaves was to win their souls to Christianity, not to liberate their minds, and assuredly not to abolish slavery itself. Most masters, though, resented the efforts of Ottolenghe and his successors and suspected that enlightenment for slaves could lead only to discontent and rebellion. Many refused to let their slaves attend classes, and even Ottolenghe eventually concluded that "Slavery is certainly a great Depresser of the Mind."

Meanwhile, the steady flow of slaves into the province strained the ability of society to assimilate them and heightened pressure on the government to maintain control. By 1765 numbers of fugitive slaves had assembled in the swamp on the Carolina side of the Savannah River and regularly raided plantations in Georgia. In an effort to quash them, the Commons

House had offered £5 reward for every renegade male slave over sixteen delivered to the workhouse and £2 for every head. But a year later the Grand Jury in Savannah complained that "the negro act is not put in force" and that slaves were attending "funerals in large bodies in the night, rioting, and frequenting tippling-houses . . . without tickets from their masters, and in a most notorious manner breaking the Lord's Day."

The Grand Jury of June 1768 elevated the same complaint into a "very great grievance," and targeted specifically masters who allowed their slaves "to live so much at large." But by 1770 a body of two to three hundred blacks were living below the Trustees Garden bluff, and fears of an uprising moved the Commons to include in that year's slave act a requirement that white males attending church carry arms and ammunition.

So the sudden rise in slave executions in 1767 seems not the result of any particular event, but a reaction to the general decline of order. Tondee himself would demonstrate two years later his own apprehension at the growing threat, and it prompted his entry into the political arena.

The memoirs of a black sailor who came to Savannah several times during the middle Sixties confirm graphically the level of white anxiety toward the end of the decade. On a trip in 1765, Olaudah Equiano—or Gustavus Vassa—had been beaten almost to death by a drunken doctor who resented the stranger's presence in the yard among his own slaves. On another trip in 1766, after having bought his freedom, Vassa escaped flogging only through the efforts of his captain, who had hidden him at the house where he lodged in Yamacraw until their vessel sailed. On his last visit, the year Tondee's slave was executed, Vassa had spent a night in the guardhouse for burning a light at a friend's home after nine, again was almost flogged, and before he left had narrowly eluded being kidnapped by two white men on the outskirts of town.

Doubtless the Tondee family's other slaves witnessed the execution of their compatriot, at least the males Tom and Joe, the latter of whom was African and bore "his country marks upon his cheeks." Tondee may also have owned by this time another slave named Will, who would later be valued at £80 because of his carpentry skills. These men, whether they viewed the hanging as justice or homicide, were perhaps in the best position to judge.

What they thought of Tondee as a master is a point of conjecture. There is no record that he freed any of his slaves, nor is there evidence that any ran away from him, though even that would have proved primarily that the slave objected to slavery, not necessarily to Tondee. Two of his former slaves did run away from masters who bought them during the British occupation of Savannah, when the possessions of Liberty Boys were seized and sold at auction, but they rejoined the Tondee household after the British withdrew.

One change in Tondee's attitude toward slaves is apparent in his ownership of Will. Whether he trained Will personally or acquired him with skills, Tondee clearly had abandoned his earlier conviction that slaves should not be used as artisans. The change was likely motivated, as was the conviction, by economics.

At least one other Savannahian, however, considered Tondee an acceptable master. In December of 1768, less than two years after his slave had been executed, Peter was bequeathed by Margaret Pages a female named Cumba, who over time became a well-known face in the tavern.

Estates

ANTHONY AND MARGARET PAGES HAD come to Savannah on the *Charming Martha* in mid autumn of 1750, with three other French families sent by the Trustees to help with the silk culture. The men were given contiguous fifty-acre lots four miles west of town, not far from Tondee's first grant of one hundred twenty acres, on which to plant mulberry trees for silkworms. Within a year, though, Anthony, a baker by trade, was supplying provisions to the colonial government, and in January of 1764 he was included among the retailers of spirits in Savannah in the first list published by the *Gazette*.

The following year's list, however, named his wife Margaret, not Anthony. He had given notice, in the same issue that carried the first list of retailers, that he intended to leave the province and wished to settle his accounts. In March of 1764 he sailed for London on the *Epreuve*, along with the wife of Governor Wright and two of his daughters. But the ship never made port. In October of that year, James Habersham wrote a friend that he feared the Governor's wife and daughters were lost at sea, and in March of 1765 the *Gazette* ran an elegy titled "The Mourning," lamenting the loss and alluding to the ship's name, French for a trial, proof, or ordeal. Two months before the poem appeared, Anthony Pages's estate had been appraised and valued at £119.

The Widow Pages continued to retail spirits until her death in 1768. In her will, as well as leaving the wench Cumba to Tondee, she directed that her mulatto slave boy named Peter, the son of Maria, be educated, and at twenty-one manumitted. Her solicitude was not unique. Other colonists freed slaves in their wills, usually for faithful service rather than from any objection to slavery itself, and some masters during their lifetime accorded freedom by deed of gift, as did Daniel and Moses Nunez for several of their slaves.

During the second half of the Sixties, Peter Tondee was called on more and more to appraise estates of deceased Georgians, and their names, as well as those of the men who bonded themselves with him to conduct the estate inventories, indicate his network of friends and the types of colonists with whom he associated. Not surprisingly, many were mechanicks like himself, a few were relatives, and a substantial portion were German.

Tradesmen whose estates he helped to appraise or administrate included Matthias Kugle, a brickmaker killed by a fall from a horse in 1765; carpenters Thomas Tripp in 1769 and Thomas Lee, Senior, in 1772; and saddler Frederick Holzendorf in 1768. Tondee's relations with the Holzendorf family were extensive, and may have dated from the early years of the colony.

During the summer of 1733, Frederick's father, John Frederick Holzendorf, had brought to Governor Johnson of South Carolina a letter of recommendation from the Duke of Newcastle in London, affirming that he came from "good family in Brandenburg" and requesting the Governor's assistance on his behalf. Holzendorf was granted land near Purrysburg, but by the 1740s he lived on St. Simons Island, practicing medicine as Surgeon's Mate to the Regiment. Though he owned a lot in the town of Frederica, he made his residence on a plantation nearby, purportedly living in the country "out of cheapness, rather than in town, where he must be liable to company."

At his death, this property passed to his son Frederick, who exchanged it for acreage on the mainland near Midway. There he sold leather goods until 1765, when he moved to Savannah and set up shop across the street from Abigail Minis's tavern, advertising that he had just imported on the last vessel from London a wide assortment of saddle trees, brass and iron harness buckles, worsted chair reins of different colors, best snaffle and palm bits, chair and car whip thongs, fringe, blue and white lace, and harness complete for two English-made chairs—"in short all kinds of saddlery, and supposed to be the most complete assortment ever yet brought into Georgia." He promised as well "Chairs lined with livery lace on the shortest notice" and "Fire buckets on the shortest warning." Holzendorf's terms were cash, rice, deerskins, indigo, or short credit.

In April of 1767 Peter Tondee and Adrian Loyer, a silversmith who maintained the public arms and kept the town clock ticking, signed a bond for Frederick Holzendorf's guardianship of his brother William, then nineteen. But by December Holzendorf was dead, and in April of 1768 Tondee, Mordecai Sheftall, and John Shick appraised his estate at less than £10. Three years later, Frederick's younger brother John apprenticed himself to a Savannah cabinetmaker, pledging in the contract not to commit fornication nor haunt alehouses, taverns, or playhouses. Brother William, however, would come to know Tondee's Tavern well: in 1777, his signature was one of three on the four-dollar denomination of Continental currency in Georgia, and during the British occupation of Savannah, he was branded "a rebel Counsellor."

Perhaps the best illustration of the interwoven fabric of Tondee's friends and family, though, begins in July of 1768 with the estate of Adam Croddy, a Savannahian who owned six slaves, a piragua—a long, flat-bottomed barge for transporting loads of up to thirty-five tons—and several small canoes, as well as furniture, household goods, and clothes, all of which Tondee, his partner Joseph Dunlap, and two others assessed at £350.

Croddy's will was to be executed by carpenter John Street, but the following spring Street announced that he intended to leave the province for some time to recover his health. By autumn he too was dead, having appointed Tondee his executor. The two were related by marriage: Street's wife, also deceased, had been Tondee's niece, the daughter of Ann Cunningham. Their son John Street, Jr., apparently lived for several months with his Grandmother Cunningham, for soon after her death, he became the ward of Jacob Oates, who had recently married Tondee's daughter Lucy.

Four years later, Tondee bonded himself along with Jacob's father John Oates to appraise the estate of Jacob's sister Jane. Joining them was John Shick, whose son Frederick would marry Tondee's daughter Sally ten years afterward. Meanwhile, the estate of Adam Croddy, having passed from John Street to Peter Tondee, still showed up as late as 1788 in the accounts of Tondee's estate, which was then being administered by another son-in-law.

Finally, that Tondee felt an affinity with Germans is manifest in the names of those bonded with him. The Holzendorfs from Brandenburg, the Sheftalls from Frankfurt-on-Oder, the Shicks from Salzburg—all would have spoken German as fluently as English. Indeed, Shick put his signature on a petition to the Society for the Propagation of the Gospel asking for a German-speaking preacher for the Savannah area. On the same petition were the names of bricklayer John Eppinger and tavernkeeper Mathias Ash, both of whom signed bonds with Tondee and were also members of Unity Lodge, the Masonic chapter headed by Tondee in 1774.

The purpose of listing and appraising possessions in a colonist's estate was to ensure the proper disposal of his assets according to his will, but inventories incidentally provide extensive details about the daily lives of individuals. In Peter Tondee's own estate inventory, for instance, the tools identified suggest a great deal about his career as a carpenter, most emphatically that his forte was finishing work. With the long planes and jointers listed, he could even the long edges of doors or windows; with the workhorse jack planes he could rough out a surface, and put a sheen on it with smoothing planes. His strike block planes could trim the end grain of boards, as on a paneled door; and his chisels, augers, and drawbore pin could mortice the frame surrounding the panels and draw the joint up tight. He could lift a tongue with a raising plane and cut a groove to receive it with a rabbet; shape window sashes with a fillister; form with a "Cornish" plane the cornice board that fitted into the angle between ceiling and wall; carve a concave surface with a round plane or a convex with a hollow, or both at once with an ogee plane to produce an S-curve.

By far, the major portion of Tondee's tools, however, consisted of planes designed to create decorative molding. At his death Tondee owned one hundred forty-three molding planes, comprising almost two thirds of his total investment in the implements of his trade. Though he referred to himself throughout his career as a "house carpenter" and practiced all the skills of construction from drawing plans to boxing window frames, his heart was with the finer trim work, and he must have put the final details on some of the most impressive homes in Savannah. In the estate inventory of no other carpenter is there such a wealth of finishing tools.

One carpenter's inventory which has not been preserved is that of Richard Milledge. Ill as early as 1766, Milledge had died "near town" in November of 1768 at the age of forty-four, survived by his wife Mary and four sons, ranging in age from nine to one and a half, the youngest twins. On the day of his death, unable to write his signature, he had signed his will with an unsteady cross.

For much of their time in Georgia, the lives of Tondee and Milledge had run parallel. Roughly the same age, they had lost their fathers ten days apart in that first, sick summer; had been seized from their homes by Whitefield in his frenzy for orphans; lived together as apprentices and learned from the same master; founded a tradesmen's association, and married not long after—the Frenchman an English girl, the Englishman a French. Only with Richard's shift to the country and the divergence of their careers do the records cease to pair them.

Six months after Richard died, his brother John advertised that all his estate would be sold at auction, including the six hundred acres he had accumulated just south of town, with "a good dwelling house"; fourteen slaves, some of whom were sawyers, squarers, and carters; a stock of cattle, horses, hogs, and sheep; farming and carpentry tools; and household furniture. Proceeds from the sale, to be held at Richard's plantation, would go toward discharging his debts.

With Milledge's death, Tondee became the only surviving founder of the Union Society, which was soon to line up solidly on the side of

American rights. That his two co-founders would have endorsed this trend of their brotherhood is almost certain, given their previous attitudes and allegiances. But what they might have thought of Tondee's behavior during the early hours of December 28, 1769, is anyone's guess.

The Guardhouse Incident

ACCORDING TO THE DEPOSITIONS, the incident at the guard-house occurred between three and four on the morning of Thursday, the 28th of December, 1769. In a public display of pique, Tondee and William Graeme, Attorney General for the province and member of the Commons House, woke up the town. In fact, Graeme gave the order to sound the alarm at that hour—the political motivation and the flair for the dramatic were both distinctly his—but he was roundly seconded and stoutly defended by Tondee. The two had been celebrating the Feast of St. John the Evangelist with their brother Masons on the preceding day, and no doubt were still warm with the solidarity of fellowship.

The general point at issue was the need for a reliable town watch. The Assembly had addressed the problem as far back as 1757, early in Ellis's tenure, by creating a night watch of townsmen. Savannah males from six-teen to sixty were required to stand guard, five to ten men each night, under the direction of ten superintendents, two of whom were Noble Wimberly Jones and Richard Milledge. During guard duty—which began at eight in winter, nine in summer, and lasted until dawn—patrols were to make at least three rounds through the streets and lanes, with particular care to enforce the ten o'clock curfew for slaves.

But two years later this arrangement was judged "deficient and ineffectual," and despite repeated attempts over the next decade, neither the Assembly nor the militia succeeded in establishing a viable system of patrol. Volunteers objected to the number of exemptions from duty, military commanders were negligent, and hired guards balked at the low pay. By 1767, the year that Tondee's slave was executed, the lapse of the town watch in Savannah had aroused enough concern to draw criticism from the Grand Jury.

So when in December of 1769 the Assembly considered another bill for reinstating the town watch, most Savannahians were enthusiastic, even though the guard would be supported primarily by a tax on townsfolk. Undoubtedly one of the most enthusiastic was William Graeme, a recent Georgian and member of the Commons House assigned to work on the bill.

Graeme's career in Georgia politics had been truly meteoric. He had moved to the colony little more than two years earlier, and in fact had been obliged to decline a seat in the Commons in November of 1768 for not yet meeting residency requirements. In October of 1769 he was elected again, but most notable is that even before the first election—when he had lived in Georgia for less than a year—Governor Wright had already appointed him Attorney General.

Though the Governor's patronage might seem hasty, it was based on a long acquaintance with Graeme's family in Charles Town. When Wright had been made London agent for South Carolina in 1757, William's brother David had assumed his duties as Attorney General and officially replaced him after Wright became Governor of Georgia three years later. And when Wright's brothers Jermyn and Charles had filed suit in the South Carolina Court of Chancery in the summer of 1764—two years before both moved their families and slaves, one hundred fifty in all, to Georgia—William himself, fresh from a five-year clerkship in the office of his brother the Attorney General, had represented them.

But Wright's opinion of Graeme was shared by other Georgians as well, who were impressed with the lawyer's patent erudition. It was hard to miss. In his dress, in the decor of his rooms, in his library and his wine cellar, the man scintillated class.

On the street he might be seen in a "full Trimmed sky blew Coat and Waistcoat," or a "blue Coat & laced Scarlet Waistcoat," or a red coatee—close-fitting with short tails—with a black cloth waistcoat. Over these, on the rare bitter days in winter, he might wear his scarlet surtout or brown greatcoat. For formal occasions, he had two black coats and waistcoats, one "full Trimmed"; for court business, a barrister's gown and wig; and for military functions, a suit of scarlet regimentals, laced.

His accessories included stone knee buckles and silver shoe buckles, a silver watch, a gold-headed cane, and an officer's sash for the regimentals. He owned a silver-hilted sword, one pair of silver-mounted pistols and another pair of steel, and a silver-mounted couteau, a large knife worn as a weapon. But more expensive than any other article in his wardrobe—worth even more than all his arms combined—were his "Yards of rich broad gold lace." If his name were not enough to announce his Scottish heritage, his penchant for lace removed any doubt.

His dining table and bureau were mahogany; his guests sat in green

Windsor chairs, chairs "with Green Bottoms," or more expensive "hair Bottomed Chairs." Graeme could look at his face in a pair of mirrors, or his entire person in a pier glass, all framed in mahogany. His red bay bookcase held over seventy volumes, roughly two thirds of which were law books, but among the rest were Shakespeare, the letters of Locke, and a Latin dictionary. From his walls, prints of the King and Queen, William Pitt, the classical philosophers, and Amorous Beauty gazed on his labors and leisure; and at day's end he slept in a feather bed, nightcapped, beneath a flowered quilt.

Though with two china punch bowls, pewter and whitestone dishes, and eighteen whitestone plates, Graeme was well equipped to entertain, the mere two decanters and four wine glasses he owned belie the magnitude of his cellar. To slake the thirst of his guests, Graeme could draw on a keg of brandy, two casks of rum, a barrel of northward beer and about two dozen of weaker brew, and seven and a half dozen bottles of porter.

The depositions against Graeme, which were published in the *Gazette* at the insistence of the court, relate three separate incidents. For two, all depositions taken were printed. But in the matter of the guardhouse incident, they were "too numerous to be inserted," so the account of that night relies on the four which were chosen for publication.

The episode apparently took its impetus from an event the previous evening reported by Robert Kirkwood, the carpenter whom Tondee and Dunlap had charged with plagiarism and with whom they were teamed to build the courthouse. Between eight and nine, Kirkwood had assisted a Mr. Blyth in binding a mulatto named Billy, who had "snapped a gun at a white man," and afterward the two had taken him to the guardhouse. Finding no one there, though all the doors were open, Kirkwood and Blyth had then proceeded to the workhouse, where runaways and unruly slaves were held, and delivered Billy to the warden.

A few hours later, Tondee and Graeme found the guardhouse again empty, despite a large fire in the grate. They waited several hours more, and when no guard appeared, Graeme ordered a Negro drummer to go outside and beat to arms. Then, after a while of that, he told the drummer to beat a point of war.

Thus three of the four versions of the incident begin with the deponent's waking to the drumbeat between three and four in the morning. In the exception, Kirkwood was wakened by his wife telling him for God's sake to get up and see what was the matter, she feared there was a fire. Kirkwood, for his part, suspected that the sailors had risen and overthrown the guard.

Minis Minis, the son of Abigail and Abraham, also presumed the drumbeat to be a fire alarm, but when he opened his bedroom window, he could see no sign of fire. So he put on clothes, took his sword, and headed for the guardhouse on Wright Square. On his way down Broughton, he met John Lyon, the blacksmith and tavernkeeper, carrying his gun and powderhorn, and the two continued together.

Lyon had been baffled by the call to arms as well, and had opened his door to hear it more clearly. Then he told his slaves to look for a fire anyway, and waked his family before dressing and rushing out. By the time he and Minis reached Wright Square, though, the tattoo had changed to a point of war, and on approaching the guardhouse Lyon went directly to the Negro, struck the head of the drum with the butt of his gun, and said, "You rascal, what do you beat for?"

The drummer pleaded that it was not his fault, but Mr. Graeme's orders, at which Graeme seized Lyon by the collar, avowed that it was by his order that the drum was beat, and that it should go on beating, as there was no guard.

This ostensible stalemate was settled smartly by a proposal of Levi Sheftall, who had also joined them, that if the Negro beat any more, he would cut the head of the drum.

Sometime earlier Joseph Clay, the nephew of James Habersham and a partner in business with his oldest son Jemme, had arrived at the guardhouse to much the same reception, adding in his deposition only that Peter Tondee supported Graeme and thought he was right in what he did. So supportive was Tondee that, according to Minis and Lyon, he nearly came to blows with a Mr. Parker, probably James, possibly Joseph, but certainly one of Henry's sons. Under cross-examination, both Lyon and Minis conceded that, to Graeme's credit, he had interposed in the quarrel between Tondee and Parker, which the latter had concluded by stating that Tondee might say what he would, he should take no notice of it.

When Robert Kirkwood finally reached the guardhouse, the drum had ceased. He found Graeme, Tondee, and a Mr. Jenkins sitting by the fire and talking very peaceably and quietly. To his inquiry what was the matter, Graeme answered that himself and Mr. Tondee had been there several hours, found no guard but a large fire in the fireplace, and thought it proper to beat to arms, on purpose to have a guard, and now they had enough, and wanted no more, and said they would keep guard all night. To this Tondee appended that if he guarded Kirkwood's property tonight, Kirkwood ought to guard his tomorrow night.

In the other two incidents for which depositions were sworn against Graeme, his behavior inspires less admiration. The first occurred two weeks after the guardhouse affair, and in this instance the object of his spleen was a carpenter from England, George Eastmead, who had just brought his wife and two children to Savannah. Graeme had shown up at two in the morning at the house where they were staying, pounding on the door and threatening in the King's name to break it open. After the landlady admitted him, he called for some grog, and noticing the family lying side by side on the floor in the next room, accused Eastmead of being a sailor belonging to some ship.

Graeme then seized him by the collar and sent a slave to fetch his sword, and after waving it around for a while, searched the carpenter's pockets. On finding a watch, Graeme declared that it was stolen, he knew who the owner was, and handed it back to Eastmead. With the collar still in his grip and the slave taking the other collar, Graeme led the carpenter to his own house.

There, after the doors were locked, he announced to Eastmead that he was the Attorney General of the province and would send him to jail. At this point, Eastmead, observing him to be in liquor, tried to humor him by complying with his whims. Graeme ordered his shoes and stockings taken off, and his coat and waistcoat, and finally, with his sword drawn, told the carpenter to take the candle on the table and go upstairs with him. When Eastmead declined, Graeme protested that he was not sleeping downstairs and kicked him out of the house, after first making a pass with the sword that nicked the carpenter, though he stepped back, in the pit of the stomach.

This fondness of Graeme's for waving his sword found expression in the third incident as well. Two months after the Eastmead confrontation, he challenged another carpenter named Skinner with being an interloper and a scrub, and for his impertinence had him confined overnight in the black hole. An hour before dawn, Graeme returned and hit the carpenter on his shoulder and arm with a cane, and at daylight he drew up the guard in front of the guardhouse and ordered Skinner to ask their pardon, which he did. His hesitation, however, incurred a blow from the flat of Graeme's sword and the command to repeat the apology, after which Graeme hit him again, knocking his hat off.

In this last incident, Graeme acted in his capacity as captain of the guard, not as Attorney General. He had resigned that office—"thought proper to resign," Wright laconically phrased it—not long after the Eastmead affair, which was the only one for which he expressed any remorse. In fact, he had conceded that if the Grand Jury brought in a bill against him for that offense, he would confess it.

But the Grand Jury threw out all three bills against him, and that is what prompted the court to order the publication of the depositions. Such an obvious miscarriage of justice could not pass without notice, and the three judges who heard the evidence wanted Savannahians to know the entire story.

Subsequent issues of the *Gazette* carried letters from jurors adamantly defending themselves, and others from readers vehemently attacking them. One juror characterized Graeme as the embodiment of "probity, discernment, and justice"; a letter refuting this description pointed out that the juror himself had attempted to horsewhip Graeme on one occasion and to dash out his brains on another. Graeme's drinking was alluded to; events from jurors' personal lives were detailed to prove their bias toward him; his partisans even brought up his Scottish heritage to suggest that he was a victim of English prejudice. What outraged his camp most, though, was that in publishing the depositions, the court did not appear "tender of a gentleman's memory."

For when the accounts of his escapades were printed in the *Gazette* in June of 1770, just a couple of weeks after the Grand Jury's deliberations, Graeme was dead. He had fallen ill several days earlier, and died as the paper was going to press. A supplement to the same issue that ran the depositions included his obituary, which affirmed that "his ability, integrity, and faithfulness, in discharge of the duties reposed in him, were so conspicuous as to merit universal respect and esteem." He was attended to the grave by the Grand Master and the Lodge of Masons; the Light Infantry Company, which paid him all military honors; and "many gentlemen of distinction in this place, who all seemed deeply affected at the loss of so sincere a friend and useful member of the community."

As for the issue of the town watch, the bill was passed in May, but by the following October the guard were refusing to perform further duty without a raise in pay. Three years later Governor Wright wrote to London that he was hopeful a night watch would be established in the next Assembly, and though the Commons did approve it, the Upper House rejected the bill in form as a circumvention of their rights. It never came up again.

As for Tondee's part in the guardhouse incident, Savannahians seem not to have held a grudge. In an April election which was itself a minor revolution, they voted him a seat on the Workhouse Commission.

Part Three

The Tavern

Politics and Religion

TONDEE'S ELECTION TO THE Workhouse Commission was not simply an endorsement of his stand on law and order, so clamorously publicized at the guardhouse. It also coincided with a radical shift in the attitude of voters. Before the balloting on Easter Monday of 1770, the Workhouse Commission had consisted primarily of principal inhabitants, men whose names were suffixed with *Esquire*. After that election, no member of the upper class would win a seat on the commission again. With the Seventies had dawned a belief in the common man, and by the middle of the decade Wright would lament that government had fallen into the hands of "a Parcel of the Lowest People Chiefly Carpenters, Shoemakers, Blacksmiths, &c."

It was admittedly a modest victory. The power of the Workhouse Commission extended only to hiring and overseeing the warden. But that included his use of the slaves held there, which at times could amount to a significant labor force. For the gentlemen on the commission to be turned out by artisans, who had to compete most directly with slave craftsmen, suggests that voters were no longer willing to concede control of their welfare as a matter of social deference. If those in power did not attend to their interests, they would put power in the hands of men who would. That they trusted Tondee in this capacity is conspicuous; he was one of only two members re-elected each year until the Revolution.

The same spirit of self-determination had moved the Union Society, just before the elections in 1770, to pass unanimously a resolution praising the efforts of Jonathan Bryan to promote a boycott of British goods. One of the largest landholders in Georgia and a member of the Governor's Council, Bryan had chaired a public meeting in Savannah the previous September to discuss nonimportation as a response to the Townshend Acts, the latest attempt by Parliament to tax the American colonies. For his role in this meeting he had been suspended from the Council late in February. By mid March the Union Society had reacted, voting to present Bryan "a handsome PIECE OF PLATE . . . as a Token of the Sense we entertain of his *upright*

Conduct, as a worthy Member of this SOCIETY, a real Friend to his Country in general, and the Province of *Georgia* in particular." The resolution ran as a notice in the *Gazette* for three successive issues.

The ensuing twentieth anniversary meeting of the Union Society on April 23, St. George's Day, is the first record of any assembly at Tondee's, and it betokened the kind of patrons the tavern would attract. Having honored one of their own, a man whom the *Gazette* described as "a Gentleman of Revolution principles," members could congratulate themselves on being at the vanguard of the movement for American rights. There was some business to conduct—annual officers were elected at this meeting—but the event was celebrated as a holiday, with guests swelling the party. The *Gazette* reported that "A general entertainment"—meaning victuals and drink—"was provided for the occasion, at which a number of gentlemen invited by the members were present, and the day was spent in their usual sociable manner."

As gratifying as it was to Tondee to win a seat on the Workhouse Commission and to host the Union Society, he doubtless found the greatest pleasure that April in the marriage of his daughter Lucy to Jacob Oates, a son-in-law nonpariel for a nascent revolutionary.

The Oateses were a diverse and colorful crowd, one of many families that the Revolution would divide. The patriarch, John, had brought his wife Elizabeth and five children to the colony in the autumn of 1760, but his connections with Georgia preceded the move. The previous June he had been designated by Lachlan McGillivray, Esquire—an Indian trader and wealthy landowner who had immigrated from Scotland—to oversee fifty slaves leased to Charles Wright, the Governor's brother, at his plantation on the Carolina side of the Savannah River.

In late 1764 McGillivray made Oates overseer on his own plantation Vale Royal, just upriver from town. Within six months, however, Oates's wife Elizabeth, whom he had married in North Carolina twenty-two years earlier, moved to Savannah without him, and John placed an ad in the *Gazette* to warn creditors:

> Whereas Elizabeth my wife hath taken upon herself to come and reside in Savannah, and hire a house, and run herself into other unnecessary expences, (with which I have been charged) contrary to my express order, and notwithstanding she had every necessary provision made for her; This is therefore to caution all persons not to credit my said wife on any account, as those who are imprudent enough so to do may not expect any recompence from
>
> John Oates

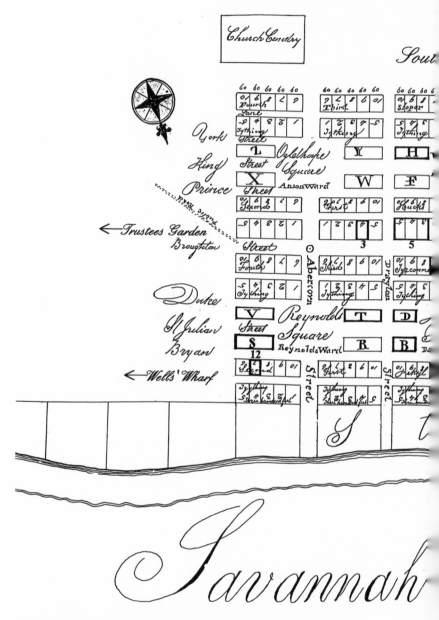

Savannah in the Time of Tondee's Tavern. Based on a map of Savannah by Thomas Shruder dated 5 February 1770; prepared by Glenn Rivers.

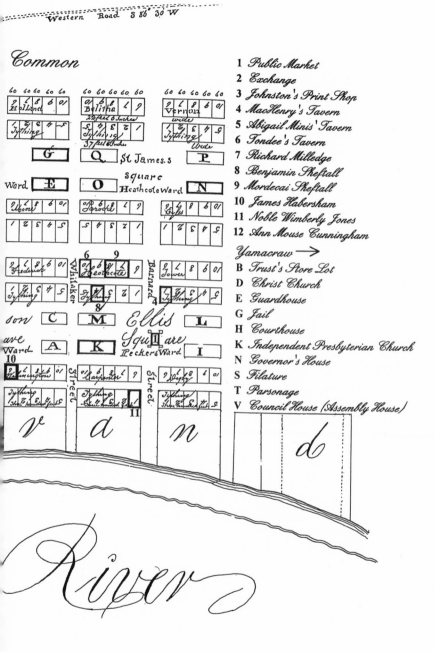

Common

1 Public Market
2 Exchange
3 Johnston's Print Shop
4 MacHenry's Tavern
5 Abigail Minis' Tavern
6 Tondee's Tavern
7 Richard Milledge
8 Benjamin Sheftall
9 Mordecai Sheftall
10 James Habersham
11 Noble Wimberly Jones
12 Ann Mouse Cunningham

Yamacraw →

B Trust's Store Lot
D Christ Church
E Guardhouse
G Jail
H Courthouse
K Independent Presbyterian Church
N Governor's House
S Filature
T Parsonage
V Council House (Assembly House)

Oates stayed on at Vale Royal into the Seventies, forming a lasting friendship with his employer; and certainly his daughter Tamer made a strong impression on McGillivray. In 1767, when she was twenty, he gave her two Negro girls, "for and in Consideration of the Good will and Affection which I have and bear unto Miss Tamer Oates," and both she and her father were remembered in McGillivray's will.

Jacob Oates worked as a merchant's clerk for Edward Telfair, but as his family grew over the next few years, he would augment his income by acting as a real estate broker in Savannah. In his politics he emulated his father-in-law, not his father, who would remain a staunch Loyalist, but the grandson he provided both was named, tactfully, John Peter.

The wedding ceremony of Lucy and Jacob, on a Tuesday evening in April of 1770, was almost certainly performed by the Reverend John J. Zubly in the Independent Presbyterian Church. Their son would marry in the same church twenty-seven years later, and considering the rancorous state to which religious affairs had sunk in Savannah in 1770, the alternative to Zubly—the Anglican clergyman Samuel Frink—is unimaginable.

With the death of Bartholomew Zouberbuhler, twenty years of religious stability and good faith had ended. The thirty-two-year-old Frink came to Savannah with a Harvard education, a barbed pen, and the unscrupulousness of the convert. On his arrival in 1767, Zubly had treated him with civility, but after Frink declined to conduct the funeral of Zubly's child, or even to walk beside him in funeral processions, relations turned frosty.

It was finally a matter regarding funerals that brought into the open their mutual antagonism, as well as the exasperation with Frink of many Georgians, including faithful members of his own congregation. Because Anglicanism had been established as the official religion of the province, Frink claimed that the Anglican sexton should be paid for the tolling of the funeral bell, even when it had been the Presbyterian bell rung by the Presbyterian sexton. To force the issue, he brought suit for the sexton's fees against Joseph Gibbons, a Presbyterian who had paid for the burial of a poor man.

The judge in the case was Ottolenghe, author of the establishment bill and an equally intolerant convert. After manipulating a judgment against Gibbons, he gratuitously fanned the blaze by declaring that Dissenters had no right to the use of a bell at all and that Frink was to blame for not having had it pulled down.

As the Commons entered the fray, Frink brought another suit against a recent widow for the same fees. Clearly the money was never the issue; the fees were negligible. Frink's real purpose—reflected in Ottolenghe's judgment—was to set a legal precedent enforcing the supremacy of Anglicanism by officially oppressing non-Anglicans. But his insistence on pursuing a legal technicality, to the obvious detriment of his own ministry and the religious harmony of the province, betrayed a myopic bent for contention.

Frink's contempt for other clergymen had early embraced the Reverend Whitefield, whose broad beam he liked to ridicule. And not surprisingly, in the two most elaborate religious events of 1770, both occasioned by Whitefield, Frink was notably absent.

The first, an affair of grand pomp and ceremony, had commemorated the thirtieth anniversary of the founding of Bethesda. Whitefield invited the Governor and his Council, the Commons House, the Chief Justice—in effect, the government of Georgia—and various other gentlemen, who rode out to the Great House in carriages and on horseback. They were conducted to the library on arrival, and offered cold tongue, ham, and tea to refresh themselves after the ten-mile journey. One guest reckoned the number of carriages at twenty, aside from horsemen.

They were then led in procession to the chapel by orphans and staff in black academic gowns, singing as they walked, and addressed by Whitefield on a verse from Zechariah, "For who hath despised the day of small things?" Particularly affecting had been his account of the obloquy he had suffered and the hardships he had endured in maintaining for so long a time such a numerous orphan family in such a desert, but he also recalled the providential support that had assisted him in raising the orphanage to its present height. Before his sermon, prayers were read by the Reverend Mr. Ellington, the former priest at Augusta but now the president of Bethesda; and afterward, to another hymn from the orphans, the company proceeded back as they had come. The day was consummated with an elegant dinner, of many different dishes, some plain, some well-dressed, and the domestics waited at table, serving round plenty of wine and punch.

The second occasion, which rivaled the first in spectacle, was Whitefield's memorial service nine months later. He had died in Newburyport, Massachusetts, on a preaching tour, and had been buried there. When word of his death reached Savannah, a paroxysm of mourning swept the town. In Christ Church the pulpit, desks, candelabra, organ loft, and pews for the Governor and Council were draped in black, and at the service both Ellington and Zubly delivered funeral sermons. Frink, though the priest of Christ Church, did not take the pulpit.

For a while the controversy over the sexton's fees continued to breed resentment. Bills regarding it were bandied like a shuttlecock between the Upper House and the Commons, but finally both lost interest. There were, after all, more pressing issues to consider. With Frink's death, a year after Whitefield's, the matter was effectively put to rest.

In the spring of 1771, Georgia embarked on a period of governmental stalemate that would last for a year and a half, preventing new legislation and virtually shutting down the operations of the General Assembly, including the passage of any tax bills. For Tondee this was especially unfortunate, as the province still owed him and his partners over one fourth of the cost of building the courthouse.

Limbo

AT THE END OF 1770, PETER TONDEE, Joseph Dunlap, and Robert Kirkwood submitted a petition to the Commons House claiming that the cost of work completed on the courthouse, calculated according to the lowest rates, exceeded their original estimate by £145. They found themselves "great losers thereby," suffering "a Loss much more than the Petitioners are able to bear," and asked that one of them be allowed to explain their accounts to the House. They concluded by pointing out that a considerable balance was still due them on the first estimate, "the Want of which, Causes the Petitioners to labour under great Hardships and Distress." But the petition was tabled, along with their accounts, and like the rest of the legislative agenda, lay untouched for almost two years.

The Governor and the Commons had locked horns over their respective rights, and with each new point of dispute the object became more the assertion of prerogative than any specific matter at hand. At first the House, recognizing that the four southern parishes created in 1763 were not represented in the Assembly, refused to pass a tax bill until elections were held in them, citing "no taxation without representation." Wright had in fact recently obtained permission from London to hold elections in those parishes and showed the letter to the Speaker of the Commons, Noble Wimberly Jones, but when on the following day the House persisted in declaiming on its rights rather than voting on a tax bill, the Governor dissolved the Assembly and ordered new elections.

When the next Assembly convened two months later, it was Wright's turn. Exercising a prerogative never before used by a royal governor in Georgia, he rejected their unanimous choice of Jones as speaker. The Commons subsequently elected Archibald Bulloch, but resolved that Wright's action was a "high Breach of the Privilege of the House." When they refused to revoke the resolution, he dissolved that Assembly as well, just after the

by John Sartain. Phil.

after

James Habersham. *(V. & J. Duncan, Antique Maps and Prints.)*

House had agreed to settle their outstanding accounts, but—inconveniently for Tondee—before they could pass a new tax bill.

Three months later, in July of 1771, Wright sailed for London on a visit that would keep him out of the province for over a year and a half. To act as governor in his stead, he appointed James Habersham, the President of his Council and a good friend—though a reluctant head of state—and left him instructions to reject on principle the first speaker chosen by the next Assembly.

Habersham delayed calling new elections for almost a year. In fact he had been advised by Wright to await further word from London on the speaker issue before reconvening the House, but for Habersham the year imposed other ordeals that exhausted his energy and damaged his health, and he simply could not bring himself any sooner to face the inevitable confrontation with the Commons.

To begin with, as well as executive duties that proceeded regardless of the Assembly, like holding land day on the first Tuesday of each month, he was heavily burdened with business affairs, not only of his own three plantations—Silk Hope, Dean Forrest, and Beverly—but also of the eleven plantations owned by Governor Wright, which had been left in his care. The spring floods that year were the worst in memory, and the damage to the rice crops compounded his worries.

Habersham also blamed the erratic weather for breeding fevers among colonists. In mid autumn his business partner and old friend Francis Harris succumbed, and by year's end Habersham's own attacks of gout had become agonizing. The turbulence peaked in December with a winter storm, which Habersham described in a letter to Wright: "It began with a cold rain, which soon turned into a frozen sleet, afterwards snow, and which froze so intensely, that for 2 or 3 days, the Boys were sliding upon the sandy Streets and Squares of this Town."

In addition to all this, Habersham was deeply shaken in February by the death of a mulatto boy belonging to his youngest son John. Bitten on the cheek by a rabid dog two weeks before Christmas, the boy had shown "more than pretty Behavior in taking leave of all around him" when the disease struck two months later. But eventually his shrieks became so dreadful that his mother begged he be put to death. Even the doctor attending him, after his second visit, took to his own bed from distress. Habersham immediately summoned his Council, and with their approval announced a reward of 2s. 6d. for any dog at large killed in or around Savannah for one month to come. The same bounty was offered to owners of confined dogs, with no mention of sickness.

During this afflicted season, one of the few pleasures in Savannah for Habersham was watching the dancing assemblies held at the courthouse. Though unable to rise from a chair without help, he found these occasions "brilliant," and "conducted with Harmony and Decency." When the Chief Justice complained that dancing in the courtroom was improper, Habersham made sure that the organizers hired the courthouse keeper to clean the room and close up afterward.

By the time the new Assembly met in April of 1772, Habersham claimed to be in somewhat better health, though he also wrote to Wright, "I wish you was here to take the Government from me." He obeyed his instructions faithfully, however, disapproving the Commons' predictable choice as speaker, Noble Wimberly Jones.

When the House elected Jones a second time, Habersham rejected him again, explaining that he had no personal objection to the gentleman—although his letters reveal he was rapidly developing one—but that he had an express command from his Majesty to disapprove him. When the House elected him a third time, Jones himself declined, thanking the members for their trust but pleading the pressing demands of his private business. So the House chose Archibald Bulloch, like Jones a member of the opposition but at least an acceptable resolution to the impasse, and Habersham approved him.

Only after delivering a speech to the Commons declaring his faith in their cooperation and urging harmony did Habersham learn of the third election of Jones and his refusal. With indignation he demanded the Commons remove that entry from their journal, and when they instead protested they had meant no disrespect to the Crown, he dissolved the Assembly.

When he finally called them back into session in December, the Commons were ready to get to work. After the obligatory election of Noble Wimberly Jones as speaker and his politic refusal for the sake of private business, they chose William Young, an attorney and current Grand Secretary of the Masons. Next they resolved that Peter Tondee be Messenger of the Commons House, to replace the late Thomas Lee, Senior. The position carried an annual salary of £25, a welcome supplement to his income, but early on Tondee discovered that the messenger often put in long hours, and sometimes found himself in awkward situations.

Custody

AT THE END OF TONDEE'S first year as messenger, the Commons voted to pay him £10 beyond his salary "for Extra Services from the great length of the present Sessions." Usually the Assembly convened in October and sat through April or May, with a break of several weeks for Christmas. But the late start in December of 1772 and the backlog of business, plus a three-month adjournment for spring planting, kept members at work well into the following autumn.

The ten days of meetings before the Christmas holidays were devoted to setting up the operations of the Commons: taking the oaths of office, selecting a speaker, hearing an address from Habersham on matters important to the province, and returning one pledging dedication to duty. Sessions were held in the Assembly House, adjacent to the filature on Reynolds Square, with the Upper House on the second floor and the Lower House or Commons on the first.

Within a week after reconvening on January 18, the Commons issued a call for all outstanding accounts, and Tondee again submitted his request for reimbursement for the cost of building the courthouse, closing with the observation that this same petition had been presented almost two years earlier but had not been acted on before the House had been dissolved. With characteristic inertia, the Commons would examine and reexamine the accounts until late in the summer.

Governor Wright returned in mid February, to a reception that warmed quickly after news spread of the accomplishments of his trip. In anticipation of his arrival, the Commons had discussed appointing a committee to inspect his house for needed repairs, but the motion had failed. Another motion two days later to send a delegation to welcome him at the bluff passed by a margin of two to one, however, and by early March the House had voted unanimously to congratulate Wright on his efforts in behalf of the province.

Wright had in fact achieved impressive results in London, both for Georgia and for himself. By arranging a cancellation of trading debts owed by the Cherokees and Creeks in exchange for a land cession, he had acquired for the colony an additional two million acres, to the northwest beyond Augusta and on the frontier west from Savannah, increasing Georgia's size by more than half. Also, in recognition of his performance as governor, the King had honored him with the title of baronet. For a while, at least, Sir James and the Commons enjoyed a period of "Confidence and Harmony."

With so much to get done, there was compelling need for harmony, and as Messenger of the Commons, Tondee soon found his main duty to be summoning absent members so that the House could conduct its affairs. Often this amounted to no more than posting letters, but sometimes he was instructed to deliver the message immediately, for which he was paid 6d. per mile one way, and 10s. each day for keeping a person in custody. It was this last matter of custody that bred predicaments.

Among the members he was ordered to bring in were Isaac Young of St. Matthew Parish, who had married Lucy's sister Elizabeth Mouse and, after her death, had continued to manage affairs for his mother-in-law; Sir Patrick Houstoun, for whom he had to travel to Darien; and Edward Barnard of Augusta, who had donated the first organ to Christ Church in 1765. In most cases, the truant member offered an excuse, which was usually accepted, and he was allowed to take his seat after paying Tondee his fees.

Ironically, it was Jonathan Bryan—the man honored by the Union Society three years earlier—who incurred the strongest censure given by the Commons to one of its own members. Late in July, Tondee was issued a warrant to take him into custody for unexplained absences, but that same morning Bryan had left the province "in a Contemptuous Manner . . . without asking leave or even making his Intentions known." He was promptly expelled from the House, but what the members did not realize, nor could have condoned, was that he had gone into Creek territory to arrange a ninety-nine-year lease of four to five million acres in present northern Florida. Having been removed from the Governor's Council for his support of the embargo of British goods, Bryan had wisely concluded that he would be granted no more land in Georgia, and sought to create a private empire elsewhere. Only the upheaval of revolution finally halted his project.

The Commons also censured other colonists besides its own members, and the task that probably proved thorniest for Tondee was bringing in his son-in-law's father John Oates. With the tongue of a sailor and the temper of a fyce, Oates had insulted on the street one of the members of the Commons, John Adam Treutlen, who represented the Ebenezer district of St.

Matthew Parish and who four years later would govern the infant state of Georgia. Not confined merely to Treutlen, Oates's remarks had reflected on the honor of the entire House, and after being summoned, he was questioned, instructed to apologize—which he did, acknowledging his fault—and was reprimanded by Speaker William Young.

Without doubt, though, the House vented its indignation most vehemently during this session on cabinetmaker James Muter, who submitted a memorial to the Commons concerning two roads through his plantation south of Savannah. One he had built and kept in repair at his own expense to transport lumber to town; the other had been built by the government for the convenience of a member of the House, Thomas Netherclift, who owned an adjacent rice plantation. But by a bill under consideration, both roads were to become private for the use of Netherclift. Understandably vexed, Muter had pleaded the British constitutional protection of freehold, and argued that this seizure was "not for the Good of the publick in General but to serve the purpose or Caprice of a Single Individual who your Memorialist is Informed has given out that he will spend a Thousand pounds rather than not have the said Road established."

Livid at the insinuation of abuse of power, the Commons voted without demur to burn the memorial in the square before the Assembly House and ordered Tondee to take Muter into custody immediately. This was on a Friday. On Tuesday Muter sent a petition to the House explaining that he was "in Custody of the Messenger of your Honorable House for some Expressions which he may have made use of in a Memorial lately presented" and that he was "Sorry any Act or Expression of his shou'd have given offence to the House as it is a thing he never had in Intention." Like Oates, he was called before the bar of the Commons and professed to be "extreamly Sorry" to have given the least offense. The members accepted his apology, and after paying Tondee his fees, which amounted to at least £2, Muter was discharged.

Though Tondee and Muter doubtless knew each other already, through their work if not socially, the four days gave them ample time to talk shop. A year later, Muter bought from Peter and Lucy for £250 the five hundred acres of pine land in St. Matthew Parish.

Lightning Rods

THE TAVERN WAS FLOURISHING, but with Peter's attention divided among the sessions of the Commons, the Workhouse Commission, the inspection of lumber for the port, and his trade of carpentry, tavernkeeping fell primarily to Lucy. Indeed, as Tondee's Tavern acquired over the next few years the sobriquet of the cradle of liberty, Peter might fairly be called the husband of the hand that rocked it.

Late in December of 1772, not long after the Commons appointed Tondee messenger, the Masons held their Grand Anniversary and General Communication on the Feast of St. John the Evangelist in "the Lodge Room at Brother Tondee's." The brethren in the province were advised to meet at nine in the morning, and from Tondee's they proceeded to Christ Church to hear a sermon suitable to the day preached by the Reverend Brother Lowten, Frink's successor. As tickets were required for admission, the celebration doubtless included dinner.

The following March, the Society of St. Patrick held its anniversary festival at Tondee's. Though not the first observance of St. Patrick's Day in Savannah, the event attests to the growing community of Irish in the province. Since the late 1760s, Wright and the Assembly had encouraged immigration to Georgia in order to populate the Indian cessions in the back country, and ships of Irish Protestants, responding to the offer of large land grants to groups of settlers, had begun arriving in 1768 and had continued almost yearly. The town of Queensborough was established for them on a branch of the Ogeechee River one hundred twenty miles from the sea, but many made their home in Savannah.

Tondee's Tavern also furnished provisions for a committee of both Houses to inspect the lighthouse on Tybee Island. Late in January, three members of the Upper House and nine of the Commons went downriver to view the repairs recently completed under the direction of John Mullryne, a former member of the Commons for the Sea Islands—Skidaway, Green

Island, Wilmington, and Tybee. Over £2 per member was spent on victuals and liquor for the outing, and the committee returned with glowing reports of the work and with praise for Mullryne.

The catering was shared by Abigail Minis, who had provided a dinner in the courthouse for upwards of seventy for the King's birthday the previous June. After that occasion, Habersham had written to Wright that her prices were higher than in past years and that he had heard complaints about both food and drink. He delayed paying the bill for several weeks, but lest "the old Woman . . . make a Murmuring about docking her Account," he had eventually discharged the full amount. Seventy-one when Habersham wrote the letter, the old woman would live for almost twenty years after his death.

Tondee and Minis were not reimbursed for the lighthouse committee's picnic until the tax bill was signed at the close of the session in late September, at which time the courthouse account was also paid, as well as Tondee's salary of £25 as Messenger of the Commons and the £10 more "for Extra Services." In addition, the tax act included payment of £16 15s. to the partnership of Tondee and Dunlap for boxing window frames at the courthouse.

The very next item in the tax act was a sum of £3 10s. due to blacksmith John Lyon "for making and putting up an Electrical road to the Court House." Lightning had in fact struck the building three years earlier in June of 1770, within a week after the grand jury failed to return bills against William Graeme for his misadventures. During a short but severe thunderstorm, the top of the north chimney was struck and thrown down, one of the windows in the courtroom was shattered, and the casing of one window in each of the jury rooms below sustained serious damage. On the same day lightning toppled the chimney of another house in Savannah, and the following Sunday the roof of Noble Jones's house in town was struck. The bolt had "communicated to five rooms, broke many panes of glass in the windows, and tore the casings, &c. of them to pieces in a very surprizing manner. Although Mr. Jones and some of the family were in three of the rooms, providentially none of them received any hurt."

Though the tax act does not indicate when the Commons hired Lyon during the three preceding years, he probably erected the lightning rod on the courthouse soon after the events of that June. The efficacy of Dr. Franklin's invention was subsequently put in doubt, though, by another disaster attributed to lightning in late spring of 1773. Around dusk on the evening of the last Sunday in May, despite a lightning rod which had been recently mended, the Great House of Bethesda was struck and burned to the ground.

The fire first appeared on the roof near the cupola. Only a few of the Family were there at the time, most being in Savannah, and a Negro man sent up to extinguish the flames at the outset was overcome by smoke and heat and fell off. He survived the fall, and seemed likely to recover after he had been bled and his neck set right.

Unchecked, the flames spread swiftly throughout the wooden orphanhouse and the chapel. The library was entirely lost, the full-length portrait of Whitefield, his wax effigy, and a bust were consumed, and most of the household and chapel furniture destroyed. A brass candelabrum in the chapel melted, and a witness to the blaze described firespouts whirling from all parts of the orphanage, one comparable in size to the Tybee Lighthouse.

The conductor of the lightning rod had run from the prong atop the cupola, along the roof ridge, and down to the ground at a corner of the building adjacent to the chapel. Curiously, the only lightning that day had occurred in the morning, along with some light clouds and a thunderclap or two. Those present claimed that after one flash, the house had been filled with smoke and the smell of sulfur, but no fire then broke out. They maintained, also, that they had made no fire in any of the chimneys for two days past.

This paradox inspired one reader of the *Gazette* to offer his observations on the phenomenon of electrical fires. While conceding that new inventions were rarely flawless and that certainly Dr. Franklin's would be improved with experience, he hypothesized that the proximity or strength of a bolt produced the sudden destructiveness of it; and inversely, that a distant or weaker bolt could account for a slow, smoldering effect and a delayed outbreak of flames. In support of his theory he recounted examples of similar fires in Hessia and France. But he did not pretend to fathom fully the natural dynamics at work, and closed rhetorically, "May we not hence conclude that the effects of lightening, as they are not always equally destructive, are also not at all times equally sudden; or does lightening ever kindle without at the same time causing an apparent flame?"

Probably more deeply grieved than anyone else at the loss, Habersham had decided two weeks before the letter was published that the fire had been caused by latent sparks in one of the chimneys, which were poorly designed and difficult to clean. But the theory of the distant thunderbolt and the slow burn to a sudden flashpoint would find application by the end of the year in the political sciences. On December 16, a party of fifty Bostonians dressed as Indians dumped three hundred forty-three chests of tea into the harbor, and the rumble echoed down the coast.

Unity

WHAT IS MOST TELLING ABOUT Unity Lodge—the second Masonic chapter in Georgia, founded in 1774 and headed by Tondee—is that virtually all of its twenty-five brothers came from the working class. Not one would have been considered a principal inhabitant; none were designated Esquire. It was as though, through Unity Lodge, the Union Society, founded by and for artisans but long since embracing men of the upper class, had been created anew.

Among the members of Unity were several with whom Tondee had personal ties or professional connections. His son-in-law Jacob Oates, Jacob's father John, and brother-in-law Sinclair Waters—Tamer's husband—appear on the roster, as well as Tondee's accountant Peter Gandy; David Tubear, who had been elected to the Workhouse Commission with Tondee and had served as warden; and the current warden Thomas Corn. Second on the list, just under Tondee's name, is that of John Eppinger, a well-known bricklayer in Savannah; and other trades plied by brothers included those of butcher, tailor, cooper, clerk, planter, gunsmith, and sailmaker. Two members besides Tondee had kept taverns, and after the Revolution and the demise of Tondee's, Eppinger's widow would open her own.

Surely the central question about Unity Lodge, given the year of its founding, is the political stance of its brothers. At the beginning, at least, the chapter was not a faction of Liberty Boys, numbering about seven who would side with the King in the coming conflict. Also, it is probable that Unity was constituted early in 1774, since events during that summer tended to polarize Georgians, and three of the members would sign a dissent to resolutions adopted at Tondee's Tavern in August. But it must be allowed that many Georgians vacillated regarding revolution up to the point of war, and beyond. Another of the signers of the August dissent became a charter member six months later of Grenadier Lodge, the third Masonic chapter and a more predominantly rebel group, and by January of 1776 had risen to secretary of the Provincial Congress. Conversely, even among the sixteen brothers of Grenadier Lodge—which included Joe and John Habersham, Samuel Elbert, Oliver Bowen, and Francis Henry Harris, all major figures on the rebel side—one fourth of the chapter eventually emerged as Tories.

Besides Tondee, Unity members initially most active in the rebellion were Jacob Oates and Joseph Rice, both of whom took part in clashes as early as the spring and summer of 1775; Aaron Pickren, who as second lieutenant in October of that year led a company of volunteers in St. George Parish; and Thomas Hamilton, who in March of 1776 helped set fire to several ships loaded with rice to keep them out of the hands of the British.

Of the Unity members who remained loyal to the Crown, one of the most steadfast was John Oates. He was joined by his son-in-law Sinclair Waters and about five others, but there were also a few members whose allegiance, from ambivalence or necessity, seemed to accommodate which-ever side held sway at the moment. Mathias Ash and Robert Gray appar-ently worked with both governments, and even Lucy Tondee, during the occupation of Savannah, rented the Long Room to the British "for Public Uses" and provided a dinner for Wright to celebrate the King's birthday in June of 1782. At that time she had five mouths to feed and no other source of income.

For whatever reasons, none of the Loyalist members of Unity Lodge were prosecuted after the Revolution. But Georgia patriots were not always so inclined to forgive. One of the Liberty Boys of Unity, Doctor Frederick Rehm, took part in a case that exemplified their bitterness toward some who had willfully collaborated with the British. The closest to gentry of any brother, Rehm had treated sick prisoners during the war, dispensing his own medicines, and he had represented Chatham County in the fugitive rebel assembly of 1782. In the summer of 1783, he signed with Mordecai Sheftall and several others an affidavit accusing Donald McLeod, a doctor in the British service, of mixing pulverized glass in medicines to be given American prisoners on board prison ships.

At the time of the incidents, Dr. Rehm himself had been a prisoner on the ship *Whitby*, and suspecting the medicine which McLeod had delivered, he and two other American doctors had "made experiment of the medicine by extraction" and removed fine glass from it, which they wrapped in paper to show McLeod when he returned. The alleged response of the British doctor on seeing the glass was a shrug of the shoulders and the remark that it was only so many rebels dead.

Other affidavits were also presented, though, attesting to the doctor's innocence, from such patriots as Colonels Samuel Elbert, George Walton, and John and William McIntosh, as well as a host of private citizens treated by McLeod. All swore to his kindness and humanity, his solicitous attention to the sick and wounded, and his personal generosity. He was credited with securing a hospital ship so that the sick prisoners could be separated from the well, and at his own expense clothing several wounded Americans.

The committee on petitions, after reviewing the affidavits for and against McLeod, recommended that the House of Assembly accept him as a citizen of Georgia. The evidence against him was insufficient, they concluded, and the charges based on a "keen and jealous sensibility of the sufferings of the said deponents." After all, they noted, had McLeod's heart been truly wicked enough to wish the destruction of the unhappy prisoners, he might have made use of many other means more effectual and less subject to detection.

The House of Assembly, however, voted eighteen to sixteen against McLeod. That opinions in his case were so evenly divided, and rancor so deeply rooted, reflects the continual dilemma which Georgians, both Liberty Boys and Tories, faced during the war and for years afterward. Neighbors became scapegoats; injuries, imagined or real, demanded retribution. Among the objects of enmity, no man would feel the backlash of resentment more keenly than the Reverend Zubly, who sailed to the Continental Congress in July of 1775 in high esteem and returned in December an anathema, unable to endorse separation from England. He was arrested the following summer and banished from rebel Georgia, and half his considerable estate was confiscated, which included a one-hundred-twenty-acre tract near the glebe land that he had purchased from Peter Tondee.

A decade after its founding, the former members of Unity Lodge might have looked back on the name of their chapter as a fine piece of irony. In 1774, though, ardent idealism was the spirit of the age, and as turmoil gathered on the horizon, a state of unity with one's brothers was a consummation devoutly to be wished.

Resolution and Dissent

AS TONDEE'S TAVERN GREW IN popularity, it swelled also with accounts receivable. In February of 1774, Peter announced in the *Gazette*: "The subscriber gives this notice to all persons anywise indebted to him, that they do forthwith pay their respective accounts to Peter Gandy, who is authorized to receive the same and give due charges.—Peter Tondee." These debts were almost certainly owed by customers of the tavern rather than clients of Tondee's carpentry—his partner Joseph Dunlap is not mentioned—and they reflect the difficulties inherent in the tavernkeeping business.

The genial ambiance of a tavern and the boost of a bowl of warm punch sometimes inspired patrons to exceed their funds, and since payment was often rendered in goods or services rather than in cash, those in the throes of a good time found it easy to squint at the bottom line. In extending substantial credit, Tondee was typical of tavernkeepers, who frequently fell into arrears themselves because of overdue tavern bills. But his sense of charity had been exhausted, along with the patience of his accountant, when a year later, one week before the Provincial Congress first convened, the *Gazette* ran this threat:

> As little or no regard has been paid to the former advertisement for a settlement with sundry persons indebted to Mr. Peter Tondee, it is therefore requested, for the last time, that they do forthwith pay or settle their several accounts with the subscriber on or before the 30th day of this instant January. Those accounts that remain unsettled will be then put into an Attorney's hands, to be sued for without distinction.—Peter Gandy.

Bad debts notwithstanding, the tavern thrived, and over the next two years the Long Room became center stage for the drama between Governor Wright and the Liberty Boys. In April of 1774, Tondee's Tavern hosted the

Miniature of Peter Tondee, artist unknown.
(Photograph courtesy of Walter Wright; enhancement by David A. Hammond.)

twenty-fourth anniversary of the Union Society, at which Dr. Henry Bourquin—whose deathbed will Tondee would witness the following December—was chosen Senior Steward, and David Zubly, Jr., nephew of the Reverend Zubly, Junior Steward. The *Gazette* reported that "an elegant entertainment was provided, at which his Excellency the Governor was present."

Though Wright would not have attended the business part of the meeting, which began at eight that morning, but only the "elegant entertainment" at midday, what moved the members to invite him at all tempts speculation. His closest ally in the Society—Grey Elliott, who sat on his Council—was then in London in the anomalous capacity of alternate agent for Georgia should Benjamin Franklin leave England. True, Wright enjoyed renewed esteem after the huge Indian land cession the previous year, and battle lines between Whigs and Tories were yet indistinct. But he must have felt like Daniel among these men who four years earlier had resolved unanimously to honor another member of his Council, whom he had expelled, a "Gentleman of Revolution principles."

To Mistress Tondee must go credit for the elegance of the entertainment, a reference to the variety and taste of the food. Many different dishes comprising several courses were commonly presented at banquets, and diners took small portions to permit the widest spectrum of flavors. Though her menu remains a mystery, it probably featured local seafood—shrimp, oysters, fish, and blue crabs—and nearby game like venison and turkey. Savannahians were especially fond of oyster bisque and oyster pie, okra gumbo with chicken and oysters, jambalaya with shrimp, Ogeechee shad with roe, bass or flounder stuffed with crabmeat, crab stew, and deviled crab. There might have been a turtle soup, there likely was a beef roast or a ham, perhaps some veal, possibly a sweet potato soufflé, some cornbread, and always there was rice, plain with butter or gravy or boiled with peas to make Hoppin' John, or red rice with shrimp and bacon. Wine accompanied each course, and the meal would have ended with raisins, nuts, and fresh or dried fruit. It is doubtful that at this time Lucy offered tea; Georgians preferred coffee anyway.

Guests at Tondee's dined at two large mahogany tables, on white Queensware plates, and were served from large Queensware and pewter dishes. With the two slaves Cumba and Jenny and her own bevy of daughters, Lucy could draw on an ample kitchen and waiting staff. When next she provided an entertainment for Wright, however, just before the British evacuated Savannah eight years later, her resources would be severely reduced.

The rift between Wright and most of the men at this dinner widened suddenly in mid summer, spurred as usual by the Sons of Liberty in South Carolina. Early in July they had held a general meeting in Charles Town to oppose taxation without representation, deportation to England for criminal trials, and the Boston Port Act, and to elect delegates to the Continental Congress in Philadelphia in September. The results of their meeting were published in the *Georgia Gazette* on Wednesday, July 13.

The following day Savannah's Liberty Boys scrambled to catch up, and their haste and lack of organization not only confounded many Georgians at the time, but gave rise to contradictory accounts among historians in later years. First, a committee headed by Noble Wimberly Jones submitted a notice to the *Gazette* calling attention to the critical state of affairs in the colonies and announcing a meeting of all inhabitants of the province to be held in Savannah on Wednesday, July 27. No time or place was specified, and the notice was unsigned.

Meanwhile, since the next issue of the *Gazette* would not appear for a week, the committee also had handbills printed with the same announcement, as well as letters copied by hand, and sent them to sympathizers in the more distant parishes. At some point four names were added below the notice—Noble Wimberly Jones, Archibald Bulloch, John Houstoun, and George Walton—and colonists were further advised to "attend at the Liberty Pole at Tondee's Tavern."

The meeting, however, was held at the Exchange on Bay Street, not at Tondee's Tavern, and though St. John and Christ Church Parish were amply represented, the parishes up the Savannah River and others down the coast were not. So those attending established a committee of thirty-one to draw up resolutions similar to South Carolina's, and postponed further action until Wednesday, August 10, when another meeting would be held.

The following *Gazette* published a report of the July 27 meeting, submitted by committee chairman John Glen, along with an invitation to all parishes to send delegates to the August 10 meeting. Significantly, the number of delegates from each parish was to equal its representatives in the Commons House. Again, no time or place for the meeting was given.

Two days later Wright issued a proclamation condemning the meeting of July 27 and outlawing that proposed for August 10, warning colonists that such assemblies were "unconstitutional, illegal, and punishable, by Law." The ban was also carried by the *Gazette* on the day of this second meeting, at which every parish was represented.

Wright's edict did seem to have an effect, however. The Liberty Boys shifted the site of the meeting to Tondee's Tavern, where more control over the makeup of its members could be exerted, and Peter himself stood at the door with a roster of delegates and screened all who presented themselves, turning away some whose names were not listed. Several of the later petitions criticized his refusal to admit these men, but as host of an officially proscribed assembly, Tondee had reason to be wary.

The meeting accomplished most of what the Liberty Boys wanted, with the exception of electing delegates to the Continental Congress. Eight resolutions were adopted covering the familiar complaints of the blockade of Boston harbor, taxation without representation, and deportation for trials, and the members declared themselves a general committee to correspond with other colonies.

With his proclamation flagrantly ignored, Wright chose not to prosecute the delegates but to discredit them. Over the following weeks he had petitions circulated throughout the province objecting to the manner in which the meeting was conducted, the inequity of representation, the change of location—the move to a tavern had been particularly offensive—and the exclusion of some who desired admittance. Several of the interior parishes also expressed concern that if alienated, the King might be disinclined to send troops to Georgia to protect settlers from the Creeks, many of whom were incensed by the recent land cession. This very real danger proved persuasive for Wright in the back country.

In response, the Committee offered extensive rebuttals in the *Gazette*, protesting among other things that one third of those who signed the petitions of dissent were appointees on the royal payroll, some others were "long since dead," and that "as soon as it was known . . . that any person had been refused admittance, positive directions were given to admit all persons whatever." For a while matters rested thus. The General Assembly was to meet in mid November, and the Liberty Boys were content to await news from Philadelphia.

Four days before the General Assembly was to reconvene, however, Governor Wright issued another proclamation delaying its commencement until January 17, allowing only that he "thought it expedient that the meeting . . . be postponed for some time." His announcement, published in the *Gazette* of November 16, was followed in the next edition by an invitation from the Liberty Boys to all parishes to send delegates to another meeting in Savannah on January 18. As before, no specific place or time was indicated.

Accordingly, on Thursday, December 8, voters in Christ Church Parish elected fifteen delegates to the first Provincial Congress in Georgia, among whom were Joseph Clay, Joseph Habersham, William Young, Archibald Bulloch, Noble Wimberly Jones, and Peter Tondee.

Departing from his usual code of editorial neutrality, printer James Johnston concluded his report of this "fair and regular poll" with the assertion:

> It cannot surely at this time admit of a doubt but every parish and district throughout the province will, as soon as possible, follow so laudable an example. Every thinking man must be convinced how much the honour, welfare, and happiness of us and our posterity depend upon a vigorous exertion and claim of our just and natural rights, which the arbitrary system of politicks adopted by Administration is undeniably calculated to deprive us of. This hath been so fully and satisfactorily proved by the ablest men, as well in England as America, that every one who will candidly and seriously peruse their writings cannot hesitate to join heartily in opinion and measures with our Sister Colonies.

Ironically, within two years Johnston would side with the King, though with little relish, and leave the country. But after the war—and after his confiscated property had been restored—he would return to Savannah and resume publication under the masthead *Gazette of the State of Georgia*.

Sons of Liberty

BY THE END OF 1775, the Provincial Congress had replaced the Assembly as the voice of the people, and Tondee's Tavern had supplanted the Assembly House as the seat of government. Even within the first week of that year, though, a spat between the Liberty Boys and a Number of Gentlemen over a proposed meeting at Tondee's revealed that those shifts were already under way.

The first gathering at Tondee's in 1775 was not ostensibly political, although among those present were at least a dozen delegates to the upcoming Provincial Congress. On Monday, January 2, the Union Society met at Tondee's "on particular business," probably to award scholarships to poor children, their primary civic project. The same issue of the *Gazette* announcing the meeting also solicited applications for four vacancies for "Poor Children to be schooled upon the Bounty of the Union Society."

Two days later the *Gazette* carried an invitation to another meeting, pointedly political, to be held at Tondee's on January 12: "A NUMBER of Gentlemen desirous to petition his Majesty on the present State of Affairs, who look upon Acts taxing without Representation as a great Grievance, would be glad of a Meeting of all such Persons as may approve such a Meeting on Thursday the 12th Day of January, at Ten o'Clock, at Mr. Tondee's Long Room, when a Petition will be proposed to their Consideration." None of the number of gentlemen extending the invitation had signed it.

The next issue of the paper contained both an endorsement of it in a letter by "Philaleutheros," a "lover of freedom," and a disavowal of it by Samuel Farley, secretary of the delegates to the Provincial Congress. Farley protested "that the anonymous paragraph in the last week's Gazette, desiring a meeting on Thursday next at *Tondee's* Long Room, has been inserted intirely without our knowledge or approbation; and that we think it highly improper in anywise to interfere, or to adopt any measure, until the meeting of the said Congress. By Order of the Delegates." Apparently, the meeting never took place.

Though anonymous, the invitation clearly resembles an effort by the Upper House to enlist the Commons in a petition to the King at the opening of the Assembly two weeks later. For the Liberty Boys, though, the time to petition had long since passed, and they viewed the proposed meeting as only a ploy to stall action by the Provincial Congress. Whether the gentlemen had consulted Tondee about holding this event at his tavern is doubtful. The notice was unsigned, and as one of the delegates to the Provincial Congress, Tondee officially subscribed to its prompt repudiation. But the incident suggests a tacit recognition that power was changing not only hands but headquarters as well.

The simultaneous sessions of the Commons and the Congress could have posed a conflict for seven members who were also delegates, including Tondee as messenger, but neither the time nor the place that the Congress met was specified. If at the tavern, then the meetings almost certainly began after the Commons had adjourned, since on the third day of the Congress, a land auction of roughly twelve thousand acres took place at nine a.m. in the Long Room.

Governor Wright's opening address to both houses of the General Assembly expressed the anxieties of a distressed parent. He shuddered at the dreadful calamities that must befall the rebellious northward colonies, professed "a real and affectionate regard for the people," and assured them, "You may be advocates for liberty, so am I; but in a constitutional and legal way." There is no reason to doubt Wright's sincerity; his loyalty to Georgia was superseded only by his loyalty to the Crown. But the issue of legality went to the heart of the conflict: the Liberty Boys contended that the recent acts of Parliament had in fact violated their rights under the English constitution. And whereas the Governor advised working within the system to rectify injustices, the Liberty Boys, from bitter experience, judged the system itself incorrigible.

For Wright, this was not an easy time. Late in December arsonists had destroyed two ricks of rice on one of his Ogeechee River plantations, and only providence had spared eleven other ricks, three hundred barrels of rice, and a barn containing a threshing machine. Also, during the following weeks, as his opponents tried to wrest control, the Governor found himself vexed by his Upper House and deprived of any real support from two of his most stalwart Councillors.

Although the answer of the Upper House to Wright's opening address had been couched in terms of deference and optimism, the Councillors cautioned that Americans were entitled to all the rights and privileges of British subjects, "and to that end it now appears highly necessary that the constitutional rights of his American subjects may be clearly defined and firmly established." Doubtless this concern formed the substance of the petition which they wished the Commons to submit with them, but for the Governor it was hardly to the point.

While the Whigs plotted and his Council dithered, Wright had also to manage without the help of two of his oldest allies. In the past he had wielded power less by fiat than by personal influence, preferring to work quietly through principal inhabitants rather than to issue proclamations. But now as he squared off with the Liberty Boys, he could no longer rely on James Habersham, whose gout kept him in constant pain and almost immobile, or Noble Jones, who was seventy-three and, although he would attend Council meetings well into the summer, had largely retired from public duties.

Ironically, sons of these two Loyalists led the assault on the old order. At fifty-one, the same age as Tondee, Noble Wimberly Jones was already an elder statesman to the Boys; at twenty-three, Joseph Habersham was an eager apprentice. During his several years at the College of New Jersey and three more in London, young Joe had developed political views distinct from his prudent father's. Merely an insolent seventeen-year-old when he arrived in England—he was expelled from Woolwich Academy for addressing the maid and landlady as though they were Georgia slaves—he returned in late 1771 a well-behaved clerk and partner of his brother's firm, James Habersham Jr. and Company. Less than three years later he had embraced the liberty movement, serving on the committee which conducted the meeting at Tondee's in August of 1774 and representing Savannah in both sessions of the Provincial Congress in 1775.

Like their counterparts in the Commons, delegates to the Congress were given a kind of opening address on the first day of the session. Though directed to the ladies of the province, a letter from "Margaret Homespun" in Augusta in the January 18 *Gazette* exhorted Georgians to rise to the present crisis. With a keen feminist edge, the author claimed for women the true dispute with England: "After some time and thought I came clearly to one conclusion, 'That the principal bone of contention (to wit the article of tea) lies altogether between the Parliament of Great Britain and the Women of America.' I cannot see what right our husbands have to interfere in it . . . ." Indeed, her opinion of the "tyrant-sex" is little better than of the British—against both she would defend the "undoubted sovereignty of the Tea-Table."

"Let us then rouse, my Sisters," she urges, ". . . we women have a thousand ways of signifying our disapprobation; some chuse to carry every point by storm, others find it more convenient or effectual to employ a *pouting fit."* As the plan adopted by the Continental Congress has amounted to pouting, she concludes, then "with a toss of the head," let us resolve to buy no taxed tea or any other English goods: "From such a conduct we shall convince the men (who bye the bye have not yet given up their wine) that we surpass them as much in public as in private virtue."

Ms. Homespun closes with a charge to the ladies to spurn the expenses of vanity: ". . . where is the difference to us whether we go to church in a *silk* or a *cotton* gown, whether, instead of brocades or sattin sacks and negligees, decorated with flounces and furbelows, we appear in good homespun *embroidered* with a variegated piece of the same kind of cloth . . . . Away with ridiculous fopperies, and appropriate the three hours of each day which you now waste at the toillette to the spinning wheel." Her final injunction broadens to include all "unnecessary diversions and entertainments," and she vows that whatever the outcome, "let it never be said our sex were accessory to the death of AMERICAN LIBERTY."

Assured of their wives' support, delegates to the Congress drafted twelve resolutions. They agreed not to import goods from Britain after March 15, except those essential to the Indian trade, and they would purchase no tea from anywhere. For their part, the men would not buy wine from Madeira. Exports to Britain would stop December 1, except rice to Europe, and merchants who violated the ban or practiced price gouging would be boycotted.

The resolutions encouraged frugality, economy, and industry, and discountenanced "every species of extravagance and dissipation, especially horse-racing, and all kinds of gaming, cock-fighting, exhibition of shows, plays, and other expensive diversions and entertainments." No longer could homespun skeptics have any doubt of the delegates' seriousness; in the one prohibition against horse racing there was sacrifice enough. More than a few at that Congress would have recalled with gusto the race in November of 1766, run for a purse of £50 between delegate Jonathan Cochran's horse and one called York owned by Thomas Heartley of Stono, South Carolina. Or the race in March of 1770 over a course at the east end of town, in which Liberty beat six others to earn £60 for Mr. Randal of Augusta; or the one a year later over the same course, won in three heats by John Bellinger's Brutus.

Forty-five of the delegates signed the resolutions on January 23—Tondee was fifth—and having elected Noble Wimberly Jones, Archibald Bulloch, and John Houstoun to represent Georgia at the Continental Congress in May, the Provincial Congress broke up. In truth, there was nothing else in their power to do. The resolutions depended on the cooperation of the colonists, and since only five of twelve parishes had sent delegates, the Congress had little hope of widespread compliance. Jones, Bulloch, and Houstoun wrote Philadelphia abjectly that because they could not justifiably claim to represent the people of Georgia, they would have to decline attending. St. John Parish, holding in disgust the apathy of the other parishes and having refused to participate in the Provincial Congress, did send fifty-year-old Dr. Lyman Hall on their own. Taking with him two hundred barrels of rice and £50 in cash, Hall was warmly welcomed by the other twelve colonies, but as the delegate of only one parish, he too abstained from casting Georgia's single vote.

Aware of their tenuous position, the delegates to the Provincial Congress had adjourned with the intention of introducing similar measures in the Commons, still in session, and thus gaining legitimacy for their resolutions. A declaration listing American rights and grievances was prepared for vote, lacking only the names of the deputies to represent Georgia at the Continental Congress. But informed of their plans, Wright prorogued the Assembly before the Commons could take any official action.

With proper channels blocked, the Liberty Boys resorted to means less scrupulous. Within a week they had acted, in blackened faces at midnight, and the encounter produced the first casualty.

First Blood

IF THE INITIAL PLAN HAD WORKED, no one would have got hurt, but it must be added that the initial plan was patently half-baked. The Liberty Boys' objective was simply to steal eight hogsheads of molasses and six of French sugar which had been seized by the royal customs collector for unpaid import duties. The molasses and sugar would then be sent down the coast to Sunbury to the patriots in St. John Parish, who had vowed not to trade with the other parishes in Georgia until they adopted the Continental Association, but who now foresaw some shortfalls.

Acting on a tip, the collector had found the barrels on the wharf and in the storeroom of Andrew Elton Wells, an ardent rebel and brother-in-law of Samuel Adams. But as it was evening and he lacked any ready means of transporting them, he had marked each with the sign of the King's broad arrow to show confiscation and assigned customs inspector James Edgar to guard them until morning. To help Edgar, two sailors were sent ashore from His Majesty's armed schooner *St. John*, then lying at anchor opposite the wharf, about a quarter mile east of town below the Trustees Garden.

The two sailors, John Downs and Daniel Martin, were eating some bread and cheese when Joseph Rice—a sailmaker and one of the brothers of Unity Lodge—appeared on the wharf with a bottle of cherry brandy. A rather thin man of average height, Rice was dressed in a white coat, black breeches, and white stockings, and wore his hair tied behind. He joined their supper, but they declined his repeated offers of brandy. After a while, Rice confessed to them that the hogsheads of molasses and sugar were his and that he would be ruined forever if they were taken from him. He promised the men a half joe each to let him take the barrels away (a Johannes was a gold coin worth about 36s.). Soon he would get the inspector James Edgar drunk, he assured them, and then could quickly clear the wharf. But the sailors still refused, and when Rice returned at midnight he brought with him twenty friends.

Brandishing cutlasses and pistols, the men rushed Edgar, tripped him up, and fell on him, and though they were disguised in seamen's clothes, with their faces blackened, he recognized several from town, of the better sort, before he was blindfolded and dragged up the bluff.

Both Downs and Martin were thrown into the river, but one of the crowd objected and pulled Downs out by his coat, saying the two were sailors off the *St. John* and only following the captain's orders. Martin, however—even though he cried out "Murder!" and begged for mercy—was not let out, and Downs ran up the bluff and hailed the *St. John* for help. Martin was being murdered, he yelled, and then hid himself under a tree.

On the *St. John* the officer of the watch called to the master that the two on shore were in danger of their lives, and the master rapidly manned the yawl and attempted to land at Wells's wharf. But the mob, which had now swelled to thirty or forty, warned him that if he landed, there was nothing but instant death for him and his men.

So the master swung about to return to the *St. John* for reinforcements, and heard behind him on the wharf a watchword passed around, sounding like *Flip* or *Tip*, and soon after, the splash of several casks falling into the river. He brought an additional boat and hands back with him, but instructed them to stay on board when they reached the wharf.

He was met halfway up the bluff by eight or ten men, and addressed them, "Pray, gentlemen, what is that man a talking about. He seems to be a black man."

"No," said one of them, in a white Bath overcoat, "he is not black. For we are all of a color."

From the white streaks between the black smudges, the master concluded they were all white men. What was the reason, he asked, that they had treated his people so ill?

When they answered that they had not treated any of his people ill, he returned to his boat, rowed up the river a short distance, and picked up John Downs from shore. Daniel Martin was not seen again.

Meanwhile, on the bluff several of the men had surrounded Edgar and were beating him with their cutlasses, until one who seemed in command stepped in, waving his sword, and stopped them. Then six or seven took him to the Common, along with some tar and feathers from Wells's yard, and among the cedar trees there, they stripped, tarred, and feathered him.

Governor Wright issued a proclamation condemning the riot and offering £50 reward for information, even promising His Majesty's pardon to any accomplices who would give King's evidence, except of course those who had actually forced Martin into the river or tarred and feathered Edgar.

Privately Wright wrote the Earl of Dartmouth that this incident showed the weakness of the executive government in Georgia. Had there been "even one Hundred of the Kings Troops here, Such an Insult Would not have been Attempted."

Having bared their swords with impunity, the Liberty Boys now needed only a rallying call to rouse their timid province. It came in May, with the news that British soldiers had fired on American minutemen on the village green at Lexington.

Opposition Party

REPORT OF THE SHOTS FIRED IN Massachusetts reached Savannah on the evening of Wednesday, May 10. On the following night a number of Liberty Boys met at the home of Noble Wimberly Jones, and afterward Jones and his party broke open the public powder magazine, a brick structure on the northeast edge of town, and removed five to six hundred pounds of gunpowder, roughly half its contents. Lending a hand were Joseph Habersham and his cousin Joseph Clay, William Gibbons, Edward Telfair, eighteen-year-old John Milledge Jr., and unnamed others, principally future members of the Council of Safety, which would include Tondee, the Sheftalls, and Jacob Oates. A portion they sent to Beaufort, to the South Carolina Liberty Boys—legend has it that some of this found its way to the Battle of Bunker Hill—and the rest was hidden in garrets and cellars in Savannah.

The day after the theft, Governor Wright issued another proclamation, offering an extraordinary reward of £150 for information. At the same time, however, he wrote London that he did not "expect or Suppose it will have any Effect towards it." Four days later Joseph Clay, in a letter to the firm of Bright and Pechin in Philadelphia, with whom he did considerable business, alluded with seemly modesty to the night raid: ". . . a Report which arrived here a few Days ago relative to a Skirmish between the Kings Troops & the New Englanders have alarm'd the People very much—a few Night ago our Magazine was Broke open & the Powder taken out by Persons unknown—"

The next three weeks passed without incident, but as the King's birthday approached on June 4, the Liberty Boys mobilized to thwart the Governor's customary celebration. On the first of the month, Wright had ordered cannon assembled at the battery at the east end of town, to be fired in salute on the fourth. Since that fell on a Sunday, he had deferred the subsequent banquet at the courthouse to Monday, the fifth.

But on Friday night, despite the recent return of His Majesty's armed schooner St. John, persons unknown spiked all twenty-one of the cannon and threw them to the bottom of the bluff. Some loyal subjects, with the help of several commanders in port and their crews, hauled them back up on Sunday morning, and after a few of the guns had been drilled out, Wright and those members of his Council who were in town, joined by various others, gathered at the flagstaff at one o'clock to drink His Majesty's health. The British colors were hoisted, and the cannon fired as usual.

On Monday the Governor gave a genteel dinner for his Council, officers of the militia, members of the Commons who could still be counted among the faithful, and sympathetic gentlemen. But through the courthouse windows they could see the Liberty Boys raising a liberty pole and running a flag up it, and their conversation was fragmented by the boom of cannonfire which punctuated each toast at Tondee's Long Room, where the crowd had gone to dine.

The *Gazette* reported of this rival celebration, "They spent the day with the utmost harmony, and concluded the evening with great decorum. Amongst many others the following toasts were drank at dinner, accompanied with a discharge of cannon placed under the Liberty Flag, viz,

"The KING. American Liberty. The General Continental Congress. Unanimity and Firmness to America. No Taxation without Representation. A Speedy Reconciliation between Great Britain and America upon constitutional principles. The Earl of Chatham. The Protesting Lords. Mr. Burke, Governor Johnstone, and the rest of the worthy Members of the House of Commons who distinguish themselves in favour of America. The Lord Mayor and Citizens of London. Mr. Hancock. Dr. Franklin. Mr. Dickenson. The Sons of Freedom in every part of the globe."

These represent about half the toasts given, according to an estimate by one of the Governor's guests of the number of times the cannon fired. Aside from the King, whose birthday it was, the men honored were all supporters of American rights, on both sides of the Atlantic. In addition to Hancock and Franklin, John Dickinson would have been familiar to Savannahians for his efforts to get the Sugar and Stamp Acts repealed, and as chairman of the Philadelphia Committee of Correspondence, he was in touch early on with Georgia Whigs.

The *Gazette* had kept Georgians well informed of their allies in England as well, and several of those toasted had been mentioned in recent issues. The Lord Mayor, Aldermen, and merchants of London had repeatedly petitioned the King to disapprove bills restricting American rights. Edmund Burke, a member of the House of Commons, planned to introduce a motion "intended to restore harmony to this Empire, by removing all cause of jealousy between Great Britian and her colonies." George Johnstone, formerly the first governor of Florida, had also championed the cause of the colonies in a speech before the House of Commons, reprinted in full less than a week before the King's birthday celebrations.

Among members of the Houses of Lords who protested the treatment of colonists were some for whom parishes would be renamed as counties in the new state. Foremost was William Pitt, First Earl of Chatham, the "Great Commoner," a fiery orator who had opposed the Stamp Act and whose address to the Peers in January had attracted a crowd so great that the doors of the chamber had been ordered shut. He had declaimed for an hour and fifteen minutes, concluding with a motion that British troops be withdrawn from Boston. Supporting him were the Duke of Richmond and the Earls of Effingham and Camden. Christ Church Parish later became Chatham County;

Noble Wimberly Jones. *(V. & J. Duncan, Antique Maps and Prints.)*

St. Paul, which included Augusta, Richmond County; St. Matthew, Effingham; and St. Thomas and St. Mary, Camden.

In the House of Commons, as well as Burke, after whom St. George Parish would be christened, John Glynn would find homage in the combined St. David and St. Patrick; and John Wilkes, who had spent time in the Tower for his attacks on the Crown, would have a namesake carved from the Indian cession of 1773.

After the Liberty Boys had finished drinking toasts—between four and five in the afternoon on June 5—Joseph Habersham led a group of them on a few errands around town, the kind soon conducted by the Council of Safety. With him were Oliver Bowen, John Houstoun, and a number of others, armed with guns and clubs, and they went first to the house of a Mrs. McFarlin. There they asked to see William Tongue, a New York merchant who had taken lodgings with her, but he was not in, so Habersham went inside and wrote him a note, suggesting that he leave the province within a week or abide by the consequences. Tongue, whose arrival in the *Charlestown and Savannah Packet* in late May had been noted in the *Gazette*, had expressed himself a friend to government and had attended the Governor's celebration at the courthouse that day. The sealed note was delivered to him at seven in the evening.

By the time they appeared at the house of Mrs. Cuyler looking for Captain Andrew Law, whom they also found not at home, the crowd had swelled and had acquired couteaus and small swords. Twenty-five-year-old attorney William Gibbons and Archibald Bulloch had joined the entourage, and with Habersham they went up to the room of Oliver Bowen, who lodged there as well, to write Law a note. He received it an hour later at the courthouse, forwarded by Mrs. Cuyler's daughter Jane via one of his slave boys.

The Sons of Liberty did find Thomas Gunnersall at home. A Quaker and New York merchant, he had come to Georgia on the brig *Elizabeth*, captained by Matthew White, at about the same time that the powder had been stolen from the public magazine. Sick with the fever and ague when he disembarked and indisposed since, Gunnersall was sleeping on a couch when a Negro boy woke him to say that some men wanted to speak with him. On arising he was accosted by Habersham and given the same ultimatum as Tongue and Law.

Gunnersall protested, "Gentlemen, I don't understand what you mean by this kind of treatment," and explained that owing to his illness he had not been in much company since in Georgia, except for dining with the Grenadiers last Saturday, where he never discussed political matters, only that there was a toast given—Success to American Arms—which caused him some uneasiness as there were gentlemen present of opposite sentiments. But he was told that it did not matter, he must leave regardless, they were determined to keep out people who were obnoxious to American unity, with whom they expected Georgia soon to swarm.

Captain Matthew White they found in a room at Mr. Patton's Tavern. To Habersham's proposal that there were some gentlemen at the door who would be glad to speak to him, White answered that if they wanted to speak to him they might come into the room and speak to him there. Habersham asserted that they only wanted to ask him a civil question, whereupon White went out of the house and was immediately surrounded by armed men.

"As you are looked upon to be an enemy to the friends of America," Habersham announced, "you are desired to depart this province within seven days, otherwise to abide by the consequences." When White replied that he did not understand him, Habersham retorted, "Don't you, sir? Then by God we'll make you understand us."

Among the crowd now were also Edward Telfair, Noble Wimberly Jones, and Joseph Rice, as well as several other additions, who White believed had come from the house of one Mr. Tondee, where they had dined. He further believed that one reason for their ordering him out of the province was his having declared he thought the opposition made by the Americans to the Mother Country was unjust, and another reason was his having assisted on Sunday morning to get up the bluff several guns which had been thrown down and spiked on Friday night, and having helped to hoist the British flag for the drinking of His Majesty's health.

By six the Liberty Boys had done with delivering their warnings. In the evening the Governor provided "illuminations as usual" to light the town, and in this festive atmosphere about forty of the Sons, headed by Joseph Habersham and carrying arms "with firelocks & fixed Bayonets," paraded through the streets.

Two days later William Tongue confronted Habersham at the house of Mrs. Cuyler, objecting to the note as "an arbitrary & unprecedented proceeding." He supposed Habersham meant to intimidate him, but if that was the design, he would fail in his views. Tongue also told him that he had already planned, prior to the delivery of the message, to depart for England.

To Habersham's comment that he had been informed Tongue intended to prosecute him for writing the note, he replied that he had not said any such thing, nor yet determined on the matter. Later in the day depositions were taken from all four—Tongue, Law, Gunnersall, and White—and three days afterward Tongue alone decided to press charges. After the warrant had been drawn up, however, he concluded, "Upon serious Consideration of this Matter & the Consequences that might attend the prosecution of the Parties herein Complained of, notwithstanding the matters relative to me are fact, . . . Yet I Chuse of my own Accord to wave the prosecution and request it may be Laid aside."

Perhaps with the advice of the King's Chief Justice, he had recognized that prosecution would be pointless, if not self-defeating. There were no means in the province to enforce royal rule, or even to protect the King's loyal subjects.

Late in May, Wright had finally received word that the one hundred troops for which he had been appealing would soon be sent up from the garrison at St. Augustine. In mid June, however, he wrote London ruefully that although a year ago such a number could have effectively kept Georgia under the King's control, now so few would only inflame the province and endanger the lives of the troops. He therefore asked that they not be sent, and repeated his humble request for leave to return to England.

Shining Moment

WHEN REBELLION COMES OF AGE there is a moment of stark elation, a surge of euphoria after action long suppressed, like an arrow at last released. It is a condition that thrives on company and scorns sleep, and it was epidemic among the Sons of Liberty in the summer of 1775. For them and for Tondee's Tavern, this was the best of times.

They met incessantly, concluding each meeting with a call for another. A week after the King's birthday celebrations, on Tuesday, June 13, a group chaired by Noble Wimberly Jones gathered at Tondee's to discuss means for an orderly shift of authority. Mindful of the "anarchy and confusion which attend the dissolution of the powers of government," they pledged to unite, "under all the ties of religion, honour, and love to our country," to implement the recommendations of the Continental and the Provincial Congress. To this end they strongly encouraged all parishes to join their association, called for another Provincial Congress in Savannah on July 4—with elections for delegates on June 22—and vowed to expel anyone "who from their conduct shall be considered as inimical to the common cause of America."

This last proscription—applying directly to Tongue, Law, Gunnersall, and White—they set out to enforce that same night, as the week had elapsed for those men to leave the province. Sometime that day the Liberty Boys had erected a "Liberty Tree & a Flagg," and in the evening, between three and four hundred assembled and marched about town.

William Tongue had already sailed for Cowes on the brig *Neddy and Nelly*, whose captain had got word that he too was not welcome in Georgia. Captain Matthew White, entered outward at the custom-house on June 12, steered the brig *Elizabeth* for Jamaica on the seventeenth. Of Law and Gunnersall, Governor Wright reported that they "fell on some method of making their Peace with them."

The true object of the Liberty Boys' muster on the evening of June 13, though, seems to have been simply to salute the day's measures with a

Joseph Habersham. *(V. & J. Duncan, Antique Maps and Prints.)*

parade. A demonstration both to themselves and to the King's men of their strength and solidarity, it effected more of a shift in power than perhaps any other event of the summer, infusing the Sons with confidence and determination and appalling Wright with his impotence and vulnerability. After that night, Liberty Boys would usurp authority in broad daylight, with studied sangfroid, and Wright would acquire a tone of desperation in his pleas to London for help.

The day before the June 22 election, a reminder appeared in the *Gazette*, with the added details that balloting for the town and district of Savannah would take place "at the Pole near Tondee's . . . at ten o'clock in the forenoon." As well as twenty-five delegates to the Provincial Congress,

Savannahians would choose a "Committee for enforcing the Association," later called the Council of Safety. The notice was signed, "By Order of the Meeting, N.W. JONES, ARCHd. BULLOCH, JOHN HOUSTOUN, GEO. WALTON."

The next issue after the election reported another meeting—of "sundry Gentlemen"—at Savannah on Monday, June 26, chaired by Lachlan McGillivray, Esquire, John Oates's former employer. Though McGillivray would ultimately support the King and return to Scotland with the outbreak of war, roughly two thirds of the twenty-one men attending were leaders of the liberty movement, among them Noble Wimberly Jones and at least three others who had broken into the powder magazine. But the meeting produced only the most general agreements, citing as grievances the acts of Parliament which taxed Americans and vowing to work within the law for redress. Another meeting was planned for Friday, June 30, at nine in the morning at the house of Mrs. Cuyler.

Though a lodging house, not a tavern, Mrs. Cuyler's enjoyed the patronage of much of the same clientele as Tondee's. In April, the celebration of the twenty-fifth anniversary of the Union Society, despite being originally scheduled at Tondee's, had taken place at Mrs. Cuyler's. Of the five officers elected—which included Noble Wimberly Jones as President—only one would side with the King. The rest were chosen delegates for Savannah to the Provincial Congress in the vote of June 22.

The proprietress, Jane Cuyler, had come to Georgia from New York in the late Sixties with her husband Telamon, a ship's captain, and after his death in the autumn of 1772 she had opened a boarding house, at first on Broughton Street, later on Bay. It was there that Oliver Bowen lived, Captain Law had lodged, and the Union Society had met in April. Her twenty-one-year-old son Henry would take part in a major heist of British gunpowder by the Liberty Boys in July, which netted more than ten times the haul from the public magazine in May, and in 1778 he would be commissioned Captain of Light Infantry. In early 1781 Mrs. Cuyler herself would be the subject of an arrest warrant issued by Governor Wright during the British occupation.

So it is not surprising that the Liberty Boys were well represented at the meeting at her house on June 26. But at the meeting called for Friday, June 30, the attendance differed radically. Jones returned, along with a few others, but by far the majority of the thirty-four present were already King's men, four of them currently sitting on the Governor's Council. The document that came out of this meeting promised cooperation in maintaining order, in protecting personal rights and private property, and in seeking redress of grievances; but stressed that the welfare of the province was inseparable from that of the Mother Country and recommended "that a humble, dutiful, and decent Petition be addressed to His Majesty . . . ."

As before, the Liberty Boys had no interest in a petition. When the resolutions were submitted to the Provincial Congress on the second day of its session, the two gentlemen who delivered them were admitted and were asked to read them aloud, but the paper was left "to lie upon the table for the perusal of the members." Two days later the members noted that it ought not to have been "dressed in the form of Resolves, but rather as recommendations, or in the nature of a Petition of Address to this Congress." As it was well-intended, though, they agreed to take it into consideration.

By the time the one hundred and two delegates met at Tondee's Long Room on July 4, the operations of the new government—at least the executive branch—were well under way. After the unanimous choice of Archibald Bulloch as President and George Walton as Secretary, members adjourned to Reverend Zubly's meeting-house, the Independent Presbyterian Church, to hear a sermon titled "The Law of Liberty." Nearly nine thousand words long and abstrusely rhetorical, it was meant to urge divine law as the prerequisite for liberty and to counsel moderation in the current crisis. At one point Zubly stated unequivocally, "Never let us lose out of sight that our interest lies in a perpetual connection with our Mother Country," and soon afterward, "In these times of confusion I would press on my hearers a most conscientious regard to the common laws of the land." But these passages came near the end, and by then some members on this July morning may have been nodding. What they came away with seems to have been a vague notion that God, and Zubly, endorsed liberty.

Several members were hardly out of church before engaging straightway to disregard the common laws of the land. Having returned to Tondee's, the Congress concluded the business of the day by appointing a committee to thank the Reverend Zubly for his sermon "on the alarming state of American affairs." But by eleven that morning, President Bulloch and six of the delegates, assisted by Joseph Rice and other Liberty Boys, were busily loading a cart with the guns, carriages, and other military supplies from the storehouse in the yard of the filature.

Alerted by two of his clerks, the Secretary of the Province had notified the Commissary General, who in turn had reported to the Governor, at that moment in conference with his Council in the Assembly House adjacent to the filature. Discussing a previous outrage of the Liberty Boys, they had only just concurred that "the Powers of Government seem to be totally unhing'd," when the Commissary appeared with his news.

Wright directed him to inform the persons involved "That the Guns and other Articles were the Kings Property, and to forbid Them at their peril to remove any part of them; And if They Persisted in so doing to take a list of the Names of such Persons amongst them as he knew."

The Commissary relayed the Governor's message, but the men continued to load the cart with guns from the storehouse, telling him that they would take care of them and would return them, and also that they would furnish him with a list of their names and what they had taken away.

Before they were through, the cart, drawn by three horses, had made several trips to the bluff, where the guns and carriages were unloaded and put on board the schooner *Elizabeth*. Thus outfitted and renamed *Liberty*, the ship saw action within the week.

The Liberty

AT TONDEE'S LONG ROOM THE next morning the first order of business was a motion to ask the Governor to appoint a day of Fasting and Prayer throughout the province "that a happy reconciliation may soon take place between America and the Parent State." It passed unanimously, and Wright—fully aware that the Congress would appoint a day themselves if he did not—replied that although he could not consider them a constitutional body, yet he would certainly grant their request, as it was "expressed in such dutiful and loyal terms, and the ends proposed being such as every good man must most ardently wish for . . . ."

Meanwhile work went ahead on the arming of the schooner *Elizabeth*. Built within the past six months at Bloody Point on Daufuskie Island, just across the wide sound of the Savannah River, the ship was framed entirely of oak, with a fifty-foot keel, a twenty-two-foot beam, and a nine-foot hold with a capacity of three hundred barrels of rice. She was painted light blue, but was so new that the cabin windows had not been sashed nor the interior finished. On each side of her main deck would be mounted five carriage guns, and under the quarterdeck several planks would be cut out for small arms in close quarters.

She was volunteered for service by part owner Samuel Price; the other owner, Richard Wright, did not approve of the idea. A short, slender, "rather well made" man of about thirty-five, Price himself would pilot her maiden mission three days later, the first naval operation of the embryonic state of Georgia.

The goal was a shipment of gunpowder from London to Savannah for use in the Indian trade. Having done without for some time—Wright had stopped the flow of goods until the murderers of several backcounty settlers had been punished—the Creeks were growing restive, and Whigs and Tories alike feared an outbreak of Indian warfare. But the Liberty Boys needed powder to wage revolution, and if any at all were to reach Indian hands, they wanted it to come from them.

The South Carolinians were behind the scheme from the beginning. They had known early on about the shipment; knew the ship's name and her captain, Richard Maitland, having already clashed with him the previous summer over three chests of East India tea brought from London on the same ship, then called the *Magna Charta*. In that affair Maitland had broken his word twice, finally taking refuge on another ship in Charlestown harbor for two weeks before sailing his vessel back to England.

So the South Carolina Liberty Boys relished the prospect of another meeting, and in mid June about fifty had come in several boats to Cockspur Island and the north end of Tybee, at the mouth of the Savannah River, where they camped to wait for him. Governor Wright learned of their presence soon after they appeared, and in a letter to Admiral Graves in late June warned of their plan and repeatedly requested "immediate assistance" in the form of "a sloop of war of some force." But the South Carolina Secret Committee intercepted the letter in Charlestown, along with another of similar urgency to General Gage, and replaced them with forgeries asserting that he had "not any occasion for any vessel of war" and dismissing the powder plot as "some little alarm about two or three canoes from South Carolina."

On July 7, the Provincial Congress chose Noble Wimberly Jones, Archibald Bulloch, John Houstoun, Lyman Hall, and the Reverend Zubly as delegates to the Continental Congress in Philadelphia. Zubly expressed surprise, considering himself "for many reasons, a very improper person," but the members insisted and he acquiesced, contingent on his congregation's consent. On the same day the ship *Philippa*, captained by Richard Maitland, came to anchor about nine miles off Tybee point to wait for a river pilot.

Her cargo of six and a half tons of gunpowder and seven hundred pounds of bullets, as well as bar and sheet lead and Indian trading arms, had been loaded in the Thames in March and April, and the ship had sailed before word of the bloodshed at Lexington and Concord had reached either London or Georgia. So far as Maitland knew, he had arrived in a province still lukewarm about independence and trade embargoes.

Early the next morning the armed schooner *Liberty*, commanded by Oliver Bowen and flying a naval banner and pennant, sailed out the Savannah River as far as the *Philippa* and beyond, but did not approach closer than three or four miles, merely "hovering" around the ship. At ten the river pilot boarded her, and when the wind finally rose between one and two, the *Philippa* got under way.

She first stood out to eastward to line up the channel entrance, but about twelve miles from the bar, the *Liberty* steered directly across her course, at which point Maitland saw the carriage guns and armed men. The schooner fired two musket shots to bring the *Philippa* to, but Maitland veered up sharply and sailed on. The *Liberty* followed and hailed her, and after confirming the ship's name and destination, Bowen announced that he would pilot the *Philippa* into the river.

Maitland replied that he had a pilot on board and asked who commanded the schooner and where she was from, and when Bowen had identified himself and the port of his vessel, his men hauled down their pennant and hoisted to the top of the mast a white flag with a red border and large red letters proclaiming "American Liberty."

Bowen and others on board continued to give directions to the pilot on what course to steer, but around seven in the evening, still four or five miles from Tybee point, a calm and an ebb tide forced the *Philippa* to anchor again. The *Liberty* anchored too, so near that throughout the night her sentinels could be heard passing the "All's well."

Just before dawn the *Philippa* got under way once more, followed close by the schooner, and when they had run within Tybee point, Maitland was ordered to take his ship to Cockspur Island and anchor there. The sailors on the *Philippa* could see encampments on Cockspur and Tybee, numbering about three hundred men, and immediately after she dropped anchor, a majority of them came out in boats and surrounded her. Bowen and several others boarded the ship, examined the bills of lading, and informed Maitland that they would take all the gunpowder, shot, lead, and Indian trading arms.

At that point Joseph Habersham came aboard and showed the captain an order from the Provincial Congress to take all the ammunition and arms out of the ship. Maitland responded that the order from the Congress was nothing to him and that he would not deliver the goods until he had seen his proprietors and got their instructions, but to Bowen's rejoinder that he might see whom he pleased, the captain had no reply, "not being in a Condition to dispute matters with them." He did earnestly implore Bowen to spare the powder that was consigned to a merchant in St. Augustine, but was told, "If it was the King's they would take it." When the Liberty Boys—among whom were Jacob Oates, Joseph Rice, and Henry Cuyler—began hauling up the kegs, Maitland set out for Savannah to inform the Governor.

On that same day, Sunday, July 9, the brig *Neptune* from London put in at Cockspur Island, and after reporting their arrival to the commander at Fort George, the captain and a passenger named Smith, who owned part of the cargo, called on the *Philippa* on the way back to their ship. On board her

they found a body of armed men from South Carolina and Savannah hand-
ing up the kegs of gunpowder from the hold to the deck and loading them
onto a piragua alongside, to be conveyed to the *Liberty* nearby. To Smith's
query what they were doing, Oliver Bowen observed, "We are taking out the
powder."

On shore the captain and merchant had been informed of the changed
situation in Georgia, particularly the recent adoption of an embargo against
British goods. Four days earlier the Provincial Congress had passed the
same resolutions approved at its first meeting in January—including the ban
on horse racing—all to take effect immediately. So the two men left the
Neptune at Cockspur and went up to Savannah to appeal to the Congress for
permission to land and sell their goods.

They appeared first before the entire Congress at Tondee's, but after a
short hearing and some debate, their case was turned over to a committee of
five for determination. That afternoon they were summoned to Mrs. Cuyler's,
where the committee examined their invoices and bills of lading, and Smith
explained that he had not intended to ship to Georgia until a reconciliation
had taken place, but hearing that matters were quiet in the province and that
other merchants had shipped goods here, he decided to do the like. He
would have arrived before any resolutions had been passed, he pointed out,
had not the ship lost a week through running aground and damaging her
rudder.

The committee decided that the cargo on the *Neptune* could be unloaded and stored until the Continental Congress issued an opinion, or that
Smith and the captain could reship or depart with it. They initially denied
Smith's request to dispose of some perishable porter and cheese, but later
told him to go ahead. On returning to the *Neptune*, the captain found that
the Liberty Boys had also disposed of eighteen hundred pounds of gunpowder and sixteen hundred of leaden shot.

Two days after his encounter with the *Liberty*, Captain Maitland had a
conversation with Joseph Habersham and others in Savannah, during which
he heard someone ask Habersham if he would suffer himself to be named in
a protest against the recent episode. Habersham replied that he wished he
could see the man that dared do it, and in fact Maitland did not submit his
deposition until just before leaving Georgia in September, long after
Habersham, in company with the delegates to the Continental Congress,
had followed his father to Philadelphia.

James Habersham had sailed north for the recovery of his health, attended by his youngest son John, who had assumed the care of him. They
left Savannah on the schooner *Industrious Peggy* on July 10, the day after the

Liberty had captured the long-awaited prize and the day before Maitland's conversation with Joseph in town. There was little time then, between shuttling downriver to Cockspur and meeting at the Long Room, for this middle son to bid his infirm father a proper farewell, but he would catch up with him soon enough.

Boys of Summer

WHEN HENRY ELLIS CLAIMED THAT Georgians breathe a hotter air than any other people on the face of the earth, he was sitting in the shade of a piazza along the northeast side of his house, at three in the afternoon in the middle of July. There was a light southeasterly breeze, and the mercury stood at 102°. During his walks around town he had recorded 105°, but Ellis did concede that the weatherwise of the province reckoned this summer an extraordinarily hot one. He blamed the intensity of the heat in Savannah on the tall surrounding woods, which blocked the prevailing winds and let the humid air hang. Of his state at the time, Ellis wrote that "one can scarce call it living, merely to breathe, and trail about a vigourless body; yet such is generally our condition, from the middle of June to the middle of September."

Unlike the former governor, the delegates to the Provincial Congress in July were predominantly well-seasoned Southerners, but even to those natives of Georgia among them, the Long Room by noon could not have been a comfortable place. It was undoubtedly spacious—the long room at the filature measured twenty-four by sixty feet—with high ceilings and tall windows. But the hundred men who met there to create a new government, and who had dressed appropriately for such an occasion, must have felt as though they were forging their destiny with bellows and tongs. Also, since Tondee owned fewer than twenty-five chairs, many representatives likely heard the proceedings from benches, and thus were apt to urge brevity and dispatch.

From the published account of their transactions, unanimity carried most measures, and when the Congress broke up on July 17, after meeting daily in the Long Room for nearly two weeks, they had framed their own administration. To fund state operations, they had voted £10,000, and agreed to issue certificates based on a property tax to raise the revenue. They had assigned committees to correspond with other colonies, to oversee the militia, and to regulate future elections. Before adjourning, they had empowered the Council of Safety and the Parochial Committee to act in their stead during recess, and in a quite specific resolution among five passed at the end of the session, they had censured the Reverend Haddon Smith, rector of Christ Church, for twice refusing to declare July 20 a day of fasting and prayer as they requested.

For Lucy Tondee, who had braved the heat of the kitchen for two weeks, no better respite could have come than a period of fasting. The break also promised relief for her girls—nineteen-year-old Ann, thirteen-year-old Mary, Elizabeth, and young Sally—and for Cumba and Jenny as well. For Peter junior and Charles, roughly twenty and fifteen, there would be time at last to sit by the fire and listen to the adventures of their brother-in-law Jacob Oates. The Council of Safety and the Parochial Committee would continue to meet in the Long Room during the summer, but at least for a couple of days, there would be peace.

The Reverend Smith had in fact declared Wednesday, July 19, a day of fasting and prayer, in compliance with the original request of the Congress and with Governor Wright's proclamation. But the Liberty Boys had learned afterward that the day following had been designated by the Continental Congress for all colonies, so they proposed to observe both in Georgia. At this, however, Smith had balked.

Consequently, on Saturday, July 29, at about nine in the morning, a group of delegates appeared on the porch of the parsonage on Reynolds Square, and when Smith came downstairs to the door, he was read this statement: "Sir from Your late Conduct in disobeying the Orders of the Congress, You are deemed an Enemy to America, & by Order of the Committee we are to inform you that you are to be Suffered no longer to Officiate in this Town." Then, abruptly, they left.

On the next morning, Sunday, also at about nine, the sexton of Christ Church was summoned to Tondee's and told by the committee there that he should not ring the bell for church without their order. On his way to tell the Reverend Smith of this matter, he was recalled to the Long Room and instructed not to deliver the key to the church door to any person whatsoever without their order. Some time later—at their order—he opened the church so that one of the delegates could lock the rector out.

The next evening, in the most celebrated tarring and feathering of the Revolution in Savannah, the Liberty Boys avenged themselves on a mariner who had drunk "Damnation to America." At around nine, as John Hopkins sat with his family at supper, a crowd came to his house and opened the door, and three men entered, one of whom was Captain George Bunner,

Tarring and feathering. *(V. & J. Duncan, Antique Maps and Prints.)*

who would convey the delegates to Philadelphia a week later in his brig *Georgia Packet*. Without speaking, the three seized Hopkins, and the rest rushed in and hurried him out of the house. He was led to the edge of town, where the crowd resolved to tar and feather him; but the majority favored a more public place, so he was taken to the middle of Johnson Square, near the sundial, and stripped of his jacket and shirt. After being smeared with tar and fledged, he was hoisted into a cart and pulled up and down the streets and around the squares. When the procession passed Governor Wright's house on St. James's Square, Hopkins was standing in the center of the cart, holding a candle, and the scene glowed with candles carried by the crowd.

At the Liberty Tree they swore they would hang him, and Captain Bunner vowed that although he was rather fat, he would climb up the tree and hang Hopkins himself unless he drank "Damnation to all Tories & Success to American Liberty," a proposition the mariner was obliged to accept. For three hours they paraded him through town, finally putting him out at the vendue house on Bay Street, with orders to beg "all America Pardon." The very next day Hopkins deposed his testimony on the incident, but after words with Joseph Habersham, he withdrew his request for a warrant against Bunner, "on Account of the Dangerous Consequences that may Ensue."

During his ordeal, Hopkins had heard the Liberty Boys say that if they could lay hold of Mr. Smith, they would put the parson alongside him in the cart. Several had in fact looked into the parsonage earlier, but the Reverend luckily was visiting out of town. On returning and hearing of their intentions, he packed hastily and slipped down to Tybee, and a month later sailed with his family for Liverpool in the brig *Joe*. His pulpit was readily filled by Edward Langworthy, a former teacher at Bethesda who in 1778 would represent Georgia at the Continental Congress. By the time the Reverend Smith's sister arrived from London in mid September, the parsonage was being advertised for rent, and in early November what remained of his personal estate—three slaves, a few horses, and some household furniture—was sold at auction from the parsonage steps.

On the first of August, Archibald Bulloch, the Reverend Zubly, and John Houstoun left for Philadelphia. With them went several Liberty Boys, but not on board were delegates Lyman Hall and Noble Wimberly Jones. Hall had gone up in the spring, and Jones, preoccupied like Habersham with a rapidly declining father, had stayed in Savannah to care for him in his final days. In a curious parallel, these two principal Sons of Liberty would comfort to the grave defenders of the Empire—fathers loved and respected—before turning once again to the business of throwing off the parent state.

Last Days

ALL THIS ANARCHY IN THE STREETS placed a particular burden on the men whose job it was—whichever the party in power—to maintain order and protect the citizenry. Liberty was well and good, but the line must be drawn at lawlessness. As both keeper of the jail and warden of the workhouse, Unity member Thomas Corn was the single town turnkey, and though a supporter of American liberty, he found himself in early August performing his duty with difficulty.

The source of his trouble was a sergeant from South Carolina named Ebenezer McCarty. Sometime after midnight on the first of the month, the day the delegates left for Philadelphia, McCarty had boarded the sloop *Friendship* at the riverside, carrying a cutlass and looking for her captain, Amos Weeks. When a mate told him that the captain was not aboard, McCarty had blustered, "God Dam his blood if he was here I would Cut his head off for taking away two Men that I enlisted here & Carried to Charlestown."

Being ashore that night was one of the few strokes of good luck Weeks had met with since putting into port. He arrived from Guadelupe soon after the King's birthday in June, and nine days later lightning had split the mast of his ship from top to bottom. During this high-voltage summer, another sloop lying in the harbor just two weeks afterward also had her mast "much shattered by lightning, which communicated through the deck into the hold and forced its way out at both sides of the vessel."

The two seamen that McCarty sought on the *Friendship* had accompanied him to Charlestown on the schooner *Liberty* after the recent gunpowder seizure, and while one had in fact enlisted in the South Carolina service since then, the other had returned to Weeks's sloop. Not finding the captain on board, McCarty demanded a light to search the *Friendship*, and when that was refused, he took the cabin boy with him and explored below in the dark.

He emerged unconvinced, claiming that Weeks had hidden the two somewhere on the ship, but the mate assured him that the captain had no business with such sort of people anyway, for they would not answer his purpose, and eventually McCarty gave up and went to look for the men in town.

The next day both Weeks and the mate gave depositions about the incident, and the Chief Justice ordered McCarty brought before him and committed to the common jail. At a hearing the following day, the sergeant was ruled unbailable and returned to jail to await further determination, but hardly had Corn locked him up before a crowd descended on the jailkeeper's home and demanded the keys from his wife Sarah. Corn himself had gone to the other jail, and after his wife convinced the men that he had all the keys on one bunch, they struck off for the common jail to spring McCarty.

There they broke the locks off the door and took out the sergeant, but they posted three sentries to guard the remaining prisoners, one of whom was in for murder, until two new locks could be put into place. The keys to these they then delivered to Corn. Two days later McCarty marched through town with a drummer—passing close by the houses of both the Chief Justice and the Governor—beating up for recruits again, which he promptly took with him back to Charlestown.

Of this last episode, Wright had written to London, ". . . unparalleled Insolence my Lord! and this is the Situation his Majesty's Government is reduced to in the Province of Georgia." During the month of August a petition circulated among His Majesty's subjects in Christ Church Parish, condemning the actions of the "several unconstitutional bodies . . . who have in a great measure subverted our civil and Religious Liberties." Especially mortifying to them was that the chairman and at least one member of the Parochial Committee—which had replaced the Reverend Smith with Mr. Langworthy—were "Persons professing the Jewish Religion." In addition to the expected signatures of the Governor's Council, the Chief Justice, and other royal officials, the one hundred twelve subscribers included three brothers of Grenadier Lodge, one of Unity, the Secretary of the Union Society, and a delegate to the Provincial Congress who had declined taking his seat.

The chairman of the Parochial Committee to whom they objected was Mordecai Sheftall. When in mid August the captain of the ship Clarissa had been called before the Committee and told he could not land ten hogsheads of molasses from Jamaica, Sheftall had conducted the hearing, and with him had sat Abigail Minis's son Philip, blacksmith John Lyon, and Peter Tondee. One month later, Sheftall had led a group down to Cockspur for another seizure of gunpowder sent for the Indians. By that time the Liberty Boys

Mordecai Sheftall. *(Courtesy, Marion L. Mendel.)*

were storing their powder in the public magazine, and this haul of two hundred fifty barrels was "brought up to town in Great Triumph."

The vessel used to capture it was not the *Liberty*, however. Renamed the *Earl of Chatham*, the *Liberty* had been confiscated before then from Samuel Price, along with a Negro fellow belonging to him and a lot in Yamacraw, and afterward sold for cash by the provost marshal to Patrick Mackay of Sapelo Island. Mackay retained possession of the ship, though, for little more than a month.

Around eleven on the night of October 31, as the *Earl of Chatham* lay at anchor at the north end of Sapelo, Price, another mariner named Samuel Wells, and seven other men, all armed, boarded the schooner, cut her cables, and sailed out to sea, taking with them a Negro fellow named Jack. Mackay advertised the theft in the next *Gazette*, offering a reward of fifty dollars for the apprehension of Price and Wells, fifty dollars for the return of Jack, and reasonable salvage for recovery of the ship. The subsequent issue carried a proclamation by Wright enjoining all good citizens to assist in bringing the offenders to justice, and noting the generous reward. But the same issue also reported a sighting of the fugitive schooner by the captain of the brig *Live Oak*—to the southward of Tybee bar, standing to the eastward—and that was the last seen of her.

As autumn advanced, the Parochial Committee in Savannah tightened control of the port, turning away vessels from England and quashing any interference by customs in trade between the colonies. When in early October the sloop *Charlotte*, bringing onions and apples from Rhode Island, had been seized by royal collectors for declaring only ballast, her captain had ignored the order and continued to hawk his wares from the ship. Three weeks later a group of Committee men—including Mordecai Sheftall, his brother Levi, and Jacob Oates—went to the customs house and demanded the sloop's register, and when that was refused, broke open the locked desks, and after two hours of rummaging, found and took it.

The Sheftalls and Oates had been elected to the Parochial Committee in mid September, the same weekend that Mordecai led his band to Cockspur for gunpowder. Among the thirty-one others chosen with them for the parish of Christ Church were Philip Minis, John Lyon, Tondee's partner Joseph Dunlap, and John Shick, whose son Frederick would marry Sally Tondee nine years later. The results of the balloting were announced in the November 15 *Gazette* by Secretary Jacob Oates, who advised "That the above Gentlemen attend, at the house of Mrs. Tondee, on Friday the 17th instant, at 10 o'clock in the forenoon."

Notices

"*S A V A N N A H*, October 25.

"The Honourable JAMES HABERSHAM, Esq. President of his Majesty's Council for this province, who lately went to the Northward for the recovery of his health, died at Brunswick, in the Jerseys, the 28th August. As he was possessed of many valuable and amiable qualities, both in publick and private life, his death is much and sincerely lamented. In the first, where he filled some of the highest stations in this province, he conducted himself with abilities, honour, and integrity, which gained him the general love and esteem of his fellow citizens; nor was he less distinguished in private life by a conscientious discharge of the social duties, as a tender and affectionate parent, a sincere and warm friend, and a kind and indulgent master. To sum up all, he was a pious Christian and a truly honest man.

"A wit's a feather, and a chief's a rod,
An honest man's the noblest work of God.   Pope.

"DIED.] In Savannah, Mr. Peter Tondee, House Carpenter, and Messenger to the Honourable the Commons House of Assembly."

In the odd design of fate, the lives of these two men, concluded here in tandem, had been linked from the time Habersham came to Georgia. Tondee had been one of the first students in his classroom and the fifth orphan at Bethesda, and without doubt had worked on the Great House, probably throughout his career. Habersham had been present at land day when each of Tondee's grants had been approved and when the bid for the filature had been awarded to him and Goldwire; and he had not been, significantly, among the Courthouse Commissioners who had bungled the bidding process and provoked Tondee's petition for redress. From the disparate vantages of principal inhabitant and house carpenter, both had seen the colony struggle and flourish, and despite their diverging politics, had managed to remain on friendly terms. In one last, fortuitous juxtaposition, their wills, proportionate in length to each man's obituary, would be entered in the record book consecutively the following summer.

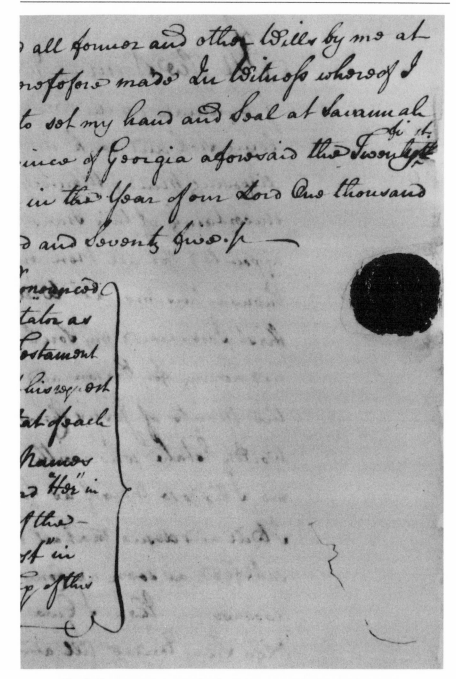

Tondee's attempt to sign his will. Clerks recording the will replicated faithfully his scrawl. *(Courtesy, Georgia Department of Archives and History.)*

Joseph Habersham sent his father's remains from New York to Savannah on the sloop *Hope*, which he hired for that purpose. The vessel arrived on November 5, and the corpse was interred in the family vault the next evening, four days after Noble Wimberly Jones had laid his father to rest at Wormslow.

Two weeks earlier, on Saturday, October 21, Peter Tondee had notified William Young to draw up his will, leaving everything to his wife Lucy and naming her executrix. Tondee was then very sick and weak in bed, and urgent to sign the will and have it witnessed; if he died intestate, Lucy's legal share of his estate would be no more than one of the children's.

On that day he made an attempt to sign it, with Jacob Oates, William Young, Peter Gandy, and tailor William Pickren present in the bedroom. Pickren had helped him to sit up in bed, and with the quill in his hand he had scratched obliquely in the bottom right margin a faint downstroke and a short line to two humps like a camel's back, followed by a squiggle and a curve dropping to the edge of the paper.

Young then decided to postpone the signatures of the witnesses in hopes that Tondee would soon be able to sign his name in his usual manner. But he grew worse over the next day, lingering until the evening, when he died. By the time Lucy submitted the will to Archibald Bulloch for probate ten months later, only two of the witnesses were still alive to swear its validity.

William Young had died on January 18, the same day that Joseph Habersham walked into the house of Governor Wright and placed him under arrest. Young's eulogy in the subsequent issue of the *Gazette* shows the high regard in which he was held by Whigs and Tories alike: "Last Thursday evening died, in the 33d year of his age, the Hon. WILLIAM YOUNG, Esq. a native of this province, Speaker of the Honourable Commons House of Assembly, one of the Representatives for this Town, and an Attorney of his Majesty's General Courts. His warm and natural love to his country was crowned with honour, and his last moments concluded with his earnest wishes for its future prosperity. As Husband, Father, Friend, and Master, few will outshine him; social duties were his particular study and care; in him society has lost a valuable member; nor can his death be more generally than deservedly lamented."

Joseph Habersham had arrested Wright on orders from the Council of Safety. Four British men-of-war had arrived at Cockspur Island in mid January, headed to Savannah for provisions refused them at Charlestown, and after a series of special meetings at Mrs. Tondee's, the Council of Safety had decided to secure the Governor, his Council, and other crown officers.

In conference with his Councillors at the time, Wright had found himself suddenly alone when the young man touched his shoulder and declared, "Sir James, you are my prisoner." The gentlemen were later taken up, but allowed to return to their homes, and put on their honor not to leave town or to communicate with the King's ships. On the night of February 11, however, after two hundred British troops in transports joined the men-of-war at Cockspur, Wright and several others escaped downriver and took refuge on the *Scarborough*.

Early in March, having been denied provisions repeatedly by the Georgia Council of Safety, the British commodore determined to seize the cargoes of rice from twenty boats moored across the river near Hutchinson's Island. He brought several vessels up within three miles of town, where for a few days they paraded under sporadic gunfire from shore. As a precaution, the Council sent Captain Joseph Rice and some volunteers to remove the rigging from the riceboats, but during the night, troops from the transports had landed on the back of Hutchinson's and were already hidden aboard. Rice was surprised and taken prisoner, and two more men sent unarmed to demand his release were taken as well. In response, Liberty Boys confined the Chief Justice, two Council members, and a few principal Tories, until an exchange could be negotiated.

Meanwhile, rather than let the British have the cargoes, the Council instructed Colonel Lachlan McIntosh, commander of the Continental Battalion in Georgia, to burn the riceboats. (In their zeal they had likewise resolved, on the preceding day, to torch the town rather than surrender it, and had ordered appraisals of the property of loyal Whigs for compensation of any losses.) McIntosh directed his men to set afire and cut loose the Tory-owned ship *Inverness*, loaded with rice and deerskins and valued at £20,000, but she grounded before reaching the riceboats. The sloop that was fired next did destroy a couple of them, but the British made off with ten others and about sixteen hundred barrels of rice.

Both sides wrote accounts of victory to their compatriots, but prisoners were not exchanged for several weeks. After sailing from Georgia, Wright expressed the fear that more hostages might have been taken of friends of government following another skirmish which had occurred on May 12. A small armed boat had gone from Savannah down to Cockspur on some errand and had tried to capture a British pilot, who had fired on them and killed one Jacob Oates. Hearing the shots, two of the men-of-war had sent armed boats, and after they killed another rebel, the rest had surrendered.

Lieutenant Oates left a widow and four children, one of whom bore the name Lucy for the fourth successive generation. A spinster, she would be the last.

Discord and Debacle

ONE OF THE STORIES TOLD OF Tondee's Tavern is that Archibald Bulloch read the Declaration of Independence to Georgians from its steps. The scene has appeal and the place would have been appropriate—and the President and the Council of Safety were likely meeting at Mrs. Tondee's when they first read the document together—but the Liberty Pole named in contemporary accounts was almost certainly that erected in early January in Johnson Square, not one before Tondee's.

The Declaration reached Savannah by special messenger from John Hancock on Thursday, the eighth of August, and in a ceremony on Saturday, President Bulloch read it to crowds of citizens and soldiers at three sites around town. They started at eleven in front of the Assembly House on Reynolds Square, and after the reading, the grenadier and light infantry companies fired a general volley. Then they proceeded to the Liberty Pole, where they met the Georgia Battalion, who ended the second reading with volleys by platoon. Last, they backtracked to the battery on the bluff at the Trustees Gardens, where the third reading was consummated with cannonfire.

Afterward, the President and his Council, Colonel McIntosh, various gentlemen, and the militia dined under the cedar trees and drank to the United, Free, and Independent States of America. That night the town was lit up, and a solemn funeral procession conducted, by muffled drums and fifes, to a grave before the courthouse. A crowd judged the largest ever assembled in the province witnessed the mock burial of George III and heard a parody of the funeral service, committing "his political existence to the ground . . . in sure and certain hope that he will never obtain a resurrection to rule again over the United States of America."

Less than two weeks later Lucy Tondee submitted Peter's will to Bulloch for probate, and Peter Gandy and William Pickren gave their depositions swearing its authenticity. Copies were made and entered in the record book, with clerks faithfully replicating the scrawl at the end of the will. At some time during the intervening months Tondee's legal seal had been applied above the signature. In the center of the wax impression a cherub in profile holding a palm branch hovers over a pair of doves on the ground; the motto that rings the upper two thirds of the seal reads "RIEN DE SI DOUX"— "Nothing So Sweet."

In mid September, Peter Tondee's estate was appraised by four Liberty Boys, all fellow mechanicks: his former partner Joseph Dunlap; carpenters John McCluer and Thomas Lee, both of whom had assisted in tarring and feathering mariner John Hopkins; and blacksmith John Lyon. They listed his possessions by area, with a subtotal for each, attending in detail to the carpentry tools; and the sum of all came to £346 6s.

First were the names of his slaves, who accounted for seventy-five

Tondee's legal seal at the end of his will. The French motto
"RIEN DE SI DOUX" means "Nothing So Sweet."

percent of his wealth. Valued at £80, the carpenter Will represented almost one quarter of Tondee's total estate, and Joe, at £60, over one sixth. Jenny was estimated at £20; and Cumba and her children altogether at an even £100—she and Lucy, likely a baby, were listed at £60; Scippio, the oldest, at £23; and five-year-old Bob at £17.

Furniture in the main part of the house included a round tea table, one round and one square dining table, two old desks, a painted "beaufet," eighteen straw-bottomed chairs, five Windsor, one pine bedstead worth 10s., three others worth 4s. each, and a pair of andirons with tongs, shovel, and bellows. Fabric items consisted of two feather beds with bolsters and pillows worth £10 altogether, three others worth £12, sixteen blankets totaling £4, and five pairs of sheets and fifteen pairs of pillow cases at £2 15s. Significantly, the cloth goods were appraised at twice the value of the furniture—one of the two large mahogany tables in the Long Room equaled no more than eight blankets.

The outbuildings held a cart, a cow and a calf, three hundred feet of cypress, fifteen hundred of pine, ten lightwood posts, lots of old planes and sashes, and about three thousand stock bricks; also a gross of bottles, four empty cases with bottles, and two iron-bound quarter-casks.

Of all the entries in the inventory, however, the most intriguing is undoubtedly "1 Sign . . . . 1.0.0." That the sign of Tondee's Tavern was assessed at one full pound—twice the value of his bed—implies a notable piece of workmanship.

About the time that Tondee's estate was appraised, Georgia launched the first of three yearly invasions into British East Florida. All were illconceived, poorly planned, costly fiascoes, promoted by civilians oblivious to the lessons learned painfully by Oglethorpe in the first decade of the colony. Rarely of one mind even under oppression, Georgians found in liberty ample room for dissension; and the fever of democracy, heightened by a phobia of a powerful executive, removed any chance of resolving conflicts. From the first expedition, through the humiliating capture of Savannah, to the disastrous siege by the French and Americans, the failure to cooperate, sometimes merely to communicate, proved the hallmark of martial ventures by the new state. Civil leaders vied for control with military officers; radical Whigs down the coast and in the back country connived against conservatives in Savannah; personal animosities and vainglory overrode expedience.

All these antipathies collided headlong in a meadow southeast of town in May of 1777 in the persons of President Button Gwinnett and Lachlan McIntosh, Brigadier General of the Georgia Continentals. The General had called Gwinnett "a Scoundrell & lying Rascal," the President had sent his second with a challenge that evening, and they met before sunrise the next morning. Their grievances, by that point certainly personal and bitter enough, had been fed from the outset by factional jealousy.

Button Gwinnett had come to Georgia in the autumn of 1765, and after disappointment as a merchant, had bought on credit from Thomas Bosomworth, Mary Musgrove's third husband, St. Catherine's Island in St. John Parish. Elected to the Commons in 1769, Gwinnett distinguished himself most to the Messenger of the House for his absences, and in 1773 financial difficulties forced him to offer his plantation and much of his estate for sale. Not until January of 1776 did he re-emerge in Georgia politics, as a member of the Provincial Congress and the Council of Safety. His most fervent wish, though, was to lead an army, and only as a compromise did he agree to represent Georgia at the Continental Congress in Philadelphia, where on August 2 he signed the Declaration of Independence.

With the sudden death of President Bulloch in February of 1777, the Council of Safety, as the only sitting body, had appointed Gwinnett to replace him. Plans were already afoot for a second invasion of Florida, and having been frustrated in his military ambitions before, Gwinnett was determined to lead this expedition himself, without interference from his rival, the Brigadier General.

In this spirit the campaign commenced. But faced with a much smaller turnout of state militia than he had expected, Gwinnett was forced to ask McIntosh for help. The General brought his Continental troops to Gwinnett's camp in St. John Parish, but refused to take orders from him or attend his council of war. The stalemate persisted until the Council of Safety called both men back to Savannah and put Colonel Samuel Elbert in command, but the project soon collapsed under problems with transportation, supplies, and weather.

In the ensuing Assembly in May, Gwinnett lost the election for governor to John Adam Treutlen; at the same time, though, the Assembly approved his behavior in the recent debacle in the south, prompting McIntosh's charge that he was a scoundrel and lying rascal.

When Gwinnett and his second in the duel, physician George Wells, appeared at the meadow, McIntosh and Colonel Joseph Habersham had been waiting for a quarter of an hour. The seconds examined the pistols; and to avoid the eyes of gathering spectators, the four men moved to a place in the field less visible. Ground was chosen, and Gwinnett deferred to McIntosh to propose the distance. At the General's suggestion of eight to ten feet, Habersham protested, so they stood at twelve, and on the word

General Lachlan McIntosh. *(V. & J. Duncan, Antique Maps and Prints.)*

both fired. McIntosh took the ball in his thigh, but remained standing; Gwinnett fell, his leg fractured above the knee. To McIntosh's query whether he wished another shot, Gwinnett replied yes, if they would help him up, but the seconds interposed, declaring that both had behaved as gentlemen, and the two shook hands.

Three days later Gwinnett died. The heat of the season was blamed for the "Mortification" that spread from his wound, though both McIntosh and Mrs. Gwinnett ascribed his death to the "unskillfulness of his doctor," quite possibly his second George Wells, who himself would die within three years in a duel with another military officer, Major James Jackson.

The last expedition to Florida, begun in April of 1778, foundered from the same dispute of command that doomed the others. Governor John Houstoun headed the state militia and refused to take orders from General Robert Howe, the new Continental commander of the Southern Department; and Commodore Oliver Bowen refused to take orders from either of them. By the end of July they were back in Savannah.

During that year and perhaps previously, Mrs. Tondee boarded several officers at the tavern, probably quartering them as well. Receipts for rations issued to officers in the 3rd Georgia Continental Regiment were signed by her son Peter Tondee, whose regard at this time for his family's prominence, or his own, inspired him to add *Esquire* to his name. It would be a short-lived affectation.

On the morning of Tuesday, December 29, Lieutenant Colonel Archibald Campbell landed the 71st Regiment of Scotch Foot at Brewton's Hill, a rice plantation on the Savannah River about a mile and a half below town, and by mid afternoon the British had possession of Savannah. Two years later a court martial would examine General Howe's conduct in this astounding defeat, and although he was acquitted with "highest honor," his lack of preparation and gross misjudgments on that day had dazzled even the British.

Around sunset on the evening before the assault, Howe had ridden out to Brewton's Hill to view the site with several officers, among them Colonel Samuel Elbert. Though for some time it had been considered the likeliest landing place, Howe posted a picket of only fifty men at the plantation. He chose instead to draw up his troops at a bridge over a small creek on the main road southeast of town, as "the most defensible I could find." He held to that decision at his court martial, asserting that "had the enemy attacked us there, I think there was every probability that the events of that day had been determined in our favor."

But even when Howe was warned of a path through Governor Wright's old rice fields east of town by which the British might circumvent his line of defense, he failed to react decisively. Colonel Campbell, meanwhile, apprised of the path by one of the Governor's former slaves, paid him to guide the Light Infantry through the swamp, part of which was the five-acre garden lot that Tondee had sold to John Milledge, who sold it to Wright. Outflanked, Howe retreated to the southwest of Savannah, but the charge of the British trapped many of the American troops in town. With no other escape, Elbert led his men to Musgrove's Creek at Yamacraw, having been told that logs there afforded a passage, but they found the tide at flood, and those who could not swim were penned on the bank by the British. American losses were eighty-three dead—thirty drowned in the swollen creek—

eleven wounded, and thirty-eight officers and four hundred fifty men taken prisoner. British forces lost two officers and five men, with nineteen wounded.

Among those taken at Musgrove's Creek were Major John Habersham and Mordecai Sheftall, who had remained with his sixteen-year-old son Sheftall Sheftall, who could not swim. The Sheftalls were subsequently put on board the prison ship *Nancy*, where Peter Tondee Jr., evidence suggests, was held as well. Mordecai and his son spent a year on parole in Sunbury in St. John Parish, were recaptured during an escape attempt, and shipped to Antigua. By late 1780 they had been paroled again to sail to Philadelphia, where they were officially exchanged. No further record of the young Tondee, however, has been found.

Beau Geste

THE FALL OF SAVANNAH CHANGED life utterly for Lucy Tondee. Her home became quarters for British troops, and over the next three years almost all of her property, from slaves to household furniture and carpenter's tools, was sold at auction by the royal government. Colonel Campbell's regiment had brought catastrophe to the families of Whigs, and those who witnessed their rampage recalled that day with horror. Its devastation would pale, however, beside the attempt of the French and Americans to free the captive town.

Campbell reported that his men behaved with restraint after the battle. Both Loyalist and patriot accounts, though, depict their looting in detail. Mahogany tables and chairs were thrown into the streets and splintered, public records scattered in the sand, feather beds ripped open and strewn to the wind. One French volunteer in Savannah recorded, "Robbery, incendiarism, rape, and murder were the fruits of that unhappy day," and he described the savaging of fleeing American soldiers: "Plunging their bayonets into the sides of the unhappy wretches, they continued stabbing until, on withdrawing their blades, they tore out their victims' entrails."

The occupying army took up residence in the large rebel barracks, which held a thousand, in the village of Yamacraw, and in the houses of Whigs throughout town. Eventually soldiers and their wives overran the courthouse as well, where they broke up the bench and bar in the courtroom and most of the window sashes for firewood, and in time even the homes of several Tory officials were appropriated by the military.

Sir James Wright returned as royal governor the following July, with instructions to urge the Assembly, as soon as a sympathetic one could be convened, to vote a voluntary tax on the province as a gesture of good will. Finding Georgia less securely controlled by His Majesty's troops than he had expected, Wright delayed calling for elections, and by early September far more pressing concerns had arisen.

To the amazement of British and Americans alike, a French fleet appeared off Tybee, swelling over the course of a week from five to fifty-four vessels. Surrender of the town seemed inevitable, and for the Tondees and other Whig families a providential deliverance.

Under the command of Charles-Henri, Count d'Estaing, French troops landed on the night of September 12 at Bewlie, the plantation thirteen miles south of town originally granted to William Stephens when he was secretary under the Trustees. Later sold by Richard and John Milledge, as guardians for their nephew, Stephens's grandson, it was subsequently purchased by John Morel, an early Son of Liberty whose widow currently lived there. While camped around her home, French soldiers requisitioned nine horses, twenty-three cows, thirty hogs, thirteen sheep, five wagons, a carriage, candles, and crystal.

At about the same time, Polish Count Casimir Pulaski brought his cavalry across the Savannah River into Georgia upstream from town, and General Benjamin Lincoln followed not long after with the American army. On September 16, having left two thousand troops at another plantation south of Savannah, d'Estaing led a contingent of one hundred fifty grenadiers to within a mile of town and sent a summons to the British commander, General Augustine Prevost, to surrender "to the arms of His Majesty the King of France." Savannah Whigs expected liberation momentarily.

In his reply, Prevost protested that he could not be expected to consider surrender without knowing the terms. D'Estaing countered with the rejoinder that it was the role of the besieged, not the besieger, to propose terms of surrender. The protocol established, Prevost requested a truce of twenty-four hours to discuss the surrender with his officers and the civil authorities. D'Estaing courteously obliged, by which time night had fallen.

As messengers were shuttling between flags, British reinforcements arrived in small craft below the bluff. Successfully evading French ships with the help of black fishermen who showed them a cut behind Daufuskie Island, eight hundred troops from Beaufort had slogged through the marsh, dragging their boats over mud bars, until the Savannah River opened before them. On reaching the town, they were given three cheers by the sailors—a grim chorus to patriot ears—and at the end of the truce Prevost informed the Count that he had decided against surrender.

Meanwhile, the British army engineer had put four to five hundred slaves to work digging entrenchments to defend Savannah, and after the French had advanced to a camp in the pine forest a mile from town, both sides dug in. For almost two weeks the spade replaced the musket, and as the British raised redoubts and batteries behind ditches set with stakes, the French ran a fretwork of trenches toward enemy lines.

Early in the digging, the British made a sortie against the nearest trench and lured two French companies out into an ambush, inflicting close to a hundred casualties. Four days later, a French sentinel mistook battery workers at night for the enemy and shot at them, drawing return fire, and in the ensuing confusion two men were killed and seven wounded. Troops spent every second or third night in the trenches, and the weather, stormy since their debarkation, persisted cold and wet.

With the French planted squarely south of Savannah and the Americans camped to their west, the standoff continued until around midnight of Sunday, the third of October, when d'Estaing commenced a bombardment of the town. Shells fell into every quarter at a rate of more than one per minute for an hour and a half. Savannahians fled in the dark to Yamacraw, out of the line of fire.

When the shelling finally ceased, most slipped back to their homes, but another battery of cannon erupted just before dawn, inaugurating five days of continual pounding. Over one thousand shells slammed through roofs, riddled walls, and kicked up sprays of sand until the streets were pocked with craters. Explosions shook the ground, audible as far as Tybee. The barrack-master was killed in a house on Bay, and four members of a family—mother, daughter, grandmother, and niece—died at once when a shell hit their home in the middle of town. One girl was struck by a cannonball which burst through a wall and crossed the room before cutting her almost in two. Four slaves huddling in a cellar were killed by a shell, and in another house seven burned to death. Before the bombardiers had found their range, some mortars dropped into d'Estaing's own trenches, and even horses on the Common fell victim.

Some who ventured to move about the streets darted furtively from house to house, but a few Negro children, inured to the barrage, learned to rush unexploded bombs and throw sand on them to snuff the fuse. They then sold the cooled balls to the British for 7d. each. Ironically, since the shells were lofted into town from the French battery, the safest place during the bombardment was the British lines, where Governor Wright took refuge, along with many of the officers' wives.

By the third night of shelling, a throng of tearful women and children, both black and white, had assembled at the large house of Moses Nunez at the west end of Yamacraw, and eventually most of the families in town were ferried to shelter on Hutchinson's Island. There in a rice barn owned by Lachlan McGillivray, fifty-eight refugees crowded, only one male among them, old Dr. Johnston. By that time there was in Savannah "hardly a house that had not been shot through."

On Thursday, the fourth day, the French began firing incendiary bombs into the town. One American wrote his wife from camp outside Savannah that he expected "the whole will be in flames" by nightfall, but at the end of the following day only one or two houses had burned, due partly to the vigilance of the firemen, partly to the tracts of vacant space in the town—broad streets, open squares, empty lots—and not least to the recent wet weather. Throughout the day and night previous to the firebombing, a hard rain had soaked Savannah.

When five days of bombardment had failed to reduce the town, d'Estaing ordered an attack for the next morning. It was to begin no later than four, but a thick fog had shrouded the dawn, and at five the allied troops were still forming below the southwest battery when the eerie keen of bagpipes from behind British lines pierced the mist. The Count wrote later that their "mournful harmony" so dispirited him, and so deeply eroded the morale of his men, that he would have called off the offensive then had not momentum and the fear of ridicule prevented him.

Toward five thirty, musket fire announced the first of two feints against the British left, and though not all his troops were drawn up, d'Estaing ordered the vanguard of the main force to charge. The allies launched a succession of valiant assaults which stalled for lack of timely support, and like waves rebounding from a seawall, the troops in retreat ran headlong into belated reinforcements. One French captain commented wryly in his journal, "The order of attack, call it rather disorder, was so confused that M. Dillon's and Baron Steding's columns got mixed in with the vanguard."

The battle lasted barely an hour. When the fog and smoke cleared, French and American dead and wounded littered the ditch before the redoubt and hung on the sharpened stakes. Estimates of casualties varied, but the French reported roughly one hundred fifty killed and three hundred seventy wounded, and the Americans two hundred thirty either killed or wounded. The British lost eighteen men, with forty wounded. Only Bunker Hill surpassed it in casualties suffered by either side.

That afternoon d'Estaing notified General Lincoln that he was lifting the siege, and the American commander asked simply that the French remain at Savannah for twenty-four hours after his troops had left. It was an easy favor to grant; the French would take as long to dismantle their siegeworks and transport artillery to the ships as they had to land and march to town.

When they finally reembarked from Thunderbolt and Causton's Bluff, landing points much closer to Savannah than Bewlie, d'Estaing's troops left Georgia more desolate than before they had come. Rather than turning the tide for the Southern department, the failed expedition prolonged the war, costing lives not only in the assault on Savannah on October 9, but also in bitter civil bloodshed throughout Georgia and the Carolinas for the next three years.

Credit for the calamity must go to the Count. Why he did not attack the British at the first opportunity baffled everyone—the Americans, the British, his own officers. All agreed that Savannah was his to take, up to the moment that the troops arrived from Beaufort. Instead, after informing the Americans that he could devote only a week to the campaign—this was the height of the hurricane season—d'Estaing had approached at leisure and laid siege to a town replete with provisions, while his own ran dangerously low.

Other decisions of the Count show the same disregard of reason. He inflicted a heavy bombardment on neighborhoods of women and children, many of whom were the families of his allies, to force surrender from an occupying army which came under little fire. Shortly before the assault on Savannah, he replaced many of the regular officers with his own subordinates, so that troops going into battle did not know the men leading them. His plan of attack crowded his main force on the fringe of a swamp. And these decisions did not result from poor counsel; throughout the expedition, he was consistent in accepting advice from no one.

He did, however, possess bravery. One of his more equitable officers observed that the Count "conducted himself as a brave grenadier but poor general in the affair." For d'Estaing, in fact, the display of bravery, not the capture of Savannah, had been the true objective: ". . . I thought that the time was ripe to prove to the Americans by a brilliant action, although it might be a bloody one, that the King's [Louis XVI's] troops knew how to dare everything for them." It was primarily his own bravery, though, that d'Estaing was eager to prove, having been accused by an American general of deserting a previous attempt on Newport; and this goal, at least, he attained.

Wounded in his right arm soon after the first charge, he continued to command with the arm in a sling until, having seen enough confusion and carnage and taken another ball in his right leg, he ordered the retreat. He spent several days recovering at Greenwich, a plantation on the inland waterway between Thunderbolt and Causton's Bluff, and before leaving Georgia he wrote, "I even find myself happy in my situation, since my blood serves to refute bad intentions."

So he blamed the Americans for the defeat, he blamed a French officer or two, but he acquitted himself admirably, with a finesse more reminiscent of the cardroom than the battlefield. Commenting on the only significant success of the expedition—the capture of the *Experiment*, carrying not only

General Prevost's replacement and a daughter of Governor Wright, but an abundance of provisions and a payroll of £30,000—the Count had quipped, "The King of England paid the expenses of the unlucky game fate had us play."

Unlucky indeed for the dead dumped hastily in shallow pits after the battle, or the sailors who succumbed to scurvy or dysentery, at a rate of thirty a day, and were cast overboard. Responding to reports of leaking ships and a shortage of drinking water, d'Estaing had jested, "They complain of having no water; yet the ships are sinking because their holds are full of it."

In gratitude for his sacrifice, the rebel Georgia government offered the Count twenty thousand acres and the right of citizenship, and on his return to France he was hailed as a hero by the people and lionized by Versailles. He remained a favorite of Louis XVI, and was beheaded in Paris one year after his monarch.

General Benjamin Lincoln retreated to South Carolina, where he commanded the Americans at Charlestown when it fell to the British the following May. General Washington's respect for him, however, did not lessen: at the surrender of Lord Cornwallis at Yorktown, it was Lincoln who accepted his sword.

When news of the British victory in Georgia reached London, guns in the Tower were fired in celebration, and the date of the battle became the "Glorious Ninth." In Savannah, Governor Wright and his Council proclaimed a day of public thanksgiving, for nothing short of divine intervention could have delivered the town from the Americans and the French.

For Lucy Tondee and her family there was reason to give thanks as well—an end to daily terror and a return to mere destitution.

Before the Dawn

SAVANNAH SWARMED WITH His Majesty's soldiers. British, Hessian, American Loyalists—there was not a Whig house where troops were not quartered. Both Governor Wright and the Chief Justice complained that General Prevost had taken "all the Houses called Rebel's Houses, which are the most in number and the best Buildings in Town," and with the courthouse long since filled, they had to settle for an upstairs room in Lachlan McIntosh's home for holding court.

In April, over sixty government officials and loyal citizens sent an address to the King testifying their devotion and returning "most grateful Thanks for sending a Body of Your Forces here, which relieved this Colony from such a Scene of Tyranny, Fraud and Cruelty as would have disgraced any Asiatic Country." Among the signatures were those of the Reverend Zubly and two members of Unity Lodge, Lucy Oates's former brother-in-law Sinclair Waters and father-in-law John Oates. At that time Oates lived on Prince Street, across from the Governor, in a house on a half-lot which he had deeded only a few months before to a black woman named Rose, the property of Lachlan McGillivray of Vale Royal, "in consideration of the Good Will and Affection which I have and bear unto" her.

The families of rebels, meanwhile, burdened with debt and deprived of income, saw their property and possessions attached and sold at auction. In February of 1781, the *Royal Georgia Gazette* advertised for sale "Two Negro Fellows, named Joe, and Will, a good carpenter; a Negro House Wench named Cumba, a Parcel of Carpenters Tools, Household and Kitchen Furniture; seized on execution." The bidding was to begin at ten on the morning of Monday the nineteenth, at the temporary courthouse on St. James's Square. Just below that announcement was another, for a sale on Thursday, the eighth of March, of "A vacant Lot in the town of Savannah, known by No. 9 Heathcote tything Decker's Ward, . . . late the property of Peter Tondee, deceased, and seized on execution."

Joe was bought by John Morel, stepson of the Widow Morel, who shared ownership of Bewlie with his brothers. But in early June, Joe ran away. The notice for his return mentioned "his country marks upon his cheeks" and promised a reward of one guinea to whoever delivered him to Bewlie or to Peter Henry Morel in Savannah. It further warned that "If any person can prove that he is harboured by a white person he or she shall upon conviction receive ten guineas, and if by a black five guineas."

The Morel family had been active Whigs in the years before the war. John senior, now dead, had served on the committee of thirty-one who sponsored the meeting at Tondee's in August of 1774, and he represented the Sea Island District at the Provincial Congress the following summer. His widow Mary was the daughter of Jonathan Bryan. His sons, though, seem to have avoided offending either side grievously. Peter Henry was tried by the British for high treason soon after the siege, but acquitted; and no Morel appeared on either the royal list of disqualified persons or the rebel one of banishment and confiscation, unlike some Georgians who made both.

The Tondee estate remained insolvent despite the auctions, and at the end of August, Lucy advertised the sale of "A Negro Wench named Jenny and three children; also sundry Household Furniture," to be held on the ninth of October at her home. The three children may have been Cumba's Scippio, Bob, and Lucy—within six weeks after their sale Cumba had run away from her new owner David Murdoch, who offered a reward of two guineas for her return, identifying her as "formerly the property of Mrs. Tondee, and well known in town."

Also in mid October of that autumn, Cornwallis surrendered an army of over seven thousand to General Washington. Regarded at the time by Georgia rebels simply as a welcome piece of news from the far front, it would only later be recognized as the turning point of the Revolution. For Governor Wright, however, there were other alarming signs at home, familiar to his veteran eye. Since the siege, the number of British troops in the province had steadily dwindled, and with the chronic lack of cooperation between civil and military authorities, common to both Tories and Whigs, Wright's repeated pleas to London for reinforcements had produced nothing. The area of Georgia under royal control had shrunk by the end of 1781 to the town and commons of Savannah, with rebel raids approaching within a mile or two, and Wright suspected that "Since the Unfortunate affair of Lord C., . . . the Military . . . every where give *the matter up* . . . ."

The following June, for the customary celebration on the King's birthday, the Governor gave "an elegant entertainment (provided by Mr. Lewis at his own house and Mrs. Tondee's) to a more numerous company than was ever assembled on the like occasion in this place . . . . In the evening the town was illuminated, and every mark of respect shewn that is due from subjects to the best of Kings." A victualler, James Lewis supplied the food, and though Mrs. Tondee's may have been chosen out of a tender regard for her situation—or a cynical flout of the rebel sanctuary—it was just as likely the size of the Long Room.

Less than two weeks later the Governor and the Assembly learned that His Majesty's troops would be withdrawn from the province. They expressed their astonishment in a joint address to the commander of British forces in the South, protesting that Georgia was the most loyal of the British colonies in America. They were confident that merely moving the garrison at St. Augustine to Savannah would secure British control. At the same time, they scrambled to prepare for a mass evacuation.

Before he left, Wright discharged the debts of his government, among which was an entry on June 27 of £10 to Mrs. Tondee for "Rent of a House for Public Uses." Though this might refer to the King's birthday celebration, the amount implies a more extensive use of her house, perhaps as a meeting place for the General Assembly. The state of Georgia would pay her comparable sums for that purpose in the future.

By the eleventh of July, His Majesty's troops had removed to Tybee Island. Within two weeks they embarked for Charlestown and New York, the only two ports remaining to the British, and before the exodus from Georgia ended, as many as three thousand white Loyalists and thirty-five hundred blacks had left the state.

Two days after the British quit Savannah, the returned rebel Assembly met at Christ Church, elected James Habersham speaker, and resolved that the filature be "immediately fitted up and Put in order for the use of the General Assembly." They soon moved to Mrs. Tondee's, however, and on the fifth of August voted her £15 "for the use of her room which the Assembly Occupied during their Present Session." Governor John Martin—who went by Black Jack, according to Wright—was directed to give an order for that amount to her, "out of the first moneys which shall come into the Public Treasury." Over two years later she was still asking to be paid.

Goodbye To All That

AMONG SAVANNAHIANS WHO WELCOMED the returning Whig army had been a small horde of destitute widows and orphans, and soon after resuming control of the town, the Executive Council had ordered provisions issued to them from the commissary. Between mid August and mid October, Lucy Tondee received rations for herself and four children, her daughter Sally among them and possibly some grandchildren as well. Given weekly, these thirty-five allotments of food amounted to an ample forty-four pounds of beef, thirty-five of bread, and three-fourths of a pint of salt.

Also in mid August, Lucy put her name—in smooth, flowing letters—to a petition to Governor Martin and the Council praying that Doctor Andrew Johnston be released from jail and allowed to continue his practice, "so extremely necessary at this unhealthy Season of the year." Johnston had been listed among two hundred eighty Loyalists to be banished, but because of his "innofensive Life and usefull Talents," those signing the petition had pledged themselves answerable for his parole "until an Oppertunity offers of having him freed by the Legislature from his Present Penalties." The twenty-six signers included one former governor of the fugitive state; John Habersham; Lachlan McIntosh Jr.; John Milledge Jr., and his mother Ann.

The Council first responded to their petition by extending the limits of Johnston's confinement to the town of Savannah, but the following day they rescinded their order, and over the next two years vacillated between enforcing deportation—at one point he was given six months to settle his affairs—and granting him protection as a citizen. The main concern of the Council was to avoid the appearance of "a want of firmness and determination in the Executive Department," and finally it was left to the Legislature to settle matters piecemeal, a process which for some lingered into the next century. Johnston and sixteen others were removed from the List of Banishment and Confiscation in 1785, and when the doctor died in 1801, "after a tedious and severe illness," he had resided in Georgia for forty-eight years, "eminent in his profession as a physician."

The erratic treatment of Dr. Johnston was typical of the new government's attempts to sort out patriots and traitors, and in truth the line between them in Georgia was often less than distinct. In some cases, Tories were simply overlooked, perhaps out of deference to age, as with John Oates, who was not named in the List although his son William was; or to family ties, as with Inigo Jones, the younger brother of Noble Wimberly and the son of Noble. Though clearly of his father's political camp, Inigo had taken no active part in the war, and at its end had quietly resumed his life. A few, like Moses Nunez, seem to have transcended animosity by sheer strength of reputation. When he died in 1787 at eighty-two, Nunez's obituary noted he had lived his many years in Georgia "with an irreproachable character."

The state vented particular spleen on several former leaders of the liberty movement, regardless of their families' influence or their own previous contributions to the cause. Mordecai Sheftall's half-brother Levi, John Milledge's cousin William Stephens, and Noble Wimberly Jones's son-in-law John Glen were listed as enemies of the state by both the British during the occupation of Savannah and the Americans after its recapture. Sheftall and Glen had signed oaths of loyalty to the King during the dark months after the siege of Savannah and the fall of Charlestown, and neither would be exonerated until 1785; Stephens was cleared by a special act of the legislature the following February. Five years later he represented Chatham County, along with Joseph Habersham, at the convention in Augusta which ratified the U.S. Constitution, and both he and Glen served as mayor of Savannah.

Tondee's Tavern, meanwhile, saw the opening of a school within its rooms. In March of 1784, about a year after the Assembly's last session there, a clerk and teacher named Dalziel Hunter advertised a writing school "at Mrs. Tondee's large house," promising to instruct the youth of both sexes, "in the most correct method, the English Grammar, Arithmetick, and Book-Keeping, at a reasonable rate." He also held night classes from six to nine, and would arrange private attendance for "Ladies and Gentlemen who do not choose to go to a publick school . . . ." For those who lived at a distance, he added, boarding was available. Hunter concluded his announcement with the reassurance, "As the utmost attention will be given to the morals of my young pupils, particularly the female part, I flatter myself of giving general satisfaction."

Within three months, however, the venture had suffered a setback. On the last day of May, Hunter addressed a letter to the *Gazette of the State of Georgia*, which was published in the next issue:

> Be pleased to insert in your Gazette the following Declaration, which will shew the frailty and weakness of human nature, and which will I

hope set in a just and true light a much injured character, and you will oblige your most humble servant, DALZIEL HUNTER.

An unfortunate circumstance of my getting in liquor the other night (which is of a truth the second instance in my whole life) occasioned a very great and scandalous abuse given by me to my wife, and to my great shame do I now publickly acknowledge this extreme folly that I have unjustly committed against her character, for I declare before God and this world, that, for these two years and a half that I have been married to my wife, I have never found any thing unbecoming in her conduct towards me, so as to raise the least degree of jealousy within the breast of DALZIEL HUNTER.

Tell it not in Gath, publish it not in the streets of Ascalon, lest the daughters of the uncircumcised rejoice.

The teacher's subsequent success in Savannah appears limited. Six months later he announced in the *Gazette* that in order to satisfy his indulgent creditors and to prevent any more debts arising, he did "forbid and forewarn all manner of persons whatsoever from trusting or giving credit to any person or persons in my name, without my verbal or written order." He eventually moved to Augusta and acquired property, however, and by 1790 had attained the status of Esquire.

Though Hunter did not identify the event that occasioned his getting in liquor for the second time in his life, there had been in the Tondee household a cause for celebration late in April. On Thursday the twenty-second, Peter and Lucy's daughter Sally married Frederick Shick, the twenty-six-year-old son of wheelwright John Shick. Both men had fought at the siege of Savannah. As a lieutenant in the Georgia Brigade, Frederick had served under Samuel Elbert, while his fifty-three-year-old father had lost an arm defending the town. The elder Shick had applied several months afterward to Governor Wright for £25 to pay his medical bill, and Wright and the Council had granted him that and a little more, "which was allowed to be a reasonable Charge." Perhaps sensible of his situation, they also employed Shick later as overseer of public works.

The union between the Tondees and the Shicks was short-lived, though. Sally Shick had been married only a year and a half when she died in October of 1785, one month after her mother and almost exactly a decade after her father. That year saw also the passing of the two most important men in Georgia's brief history. General James Oglethorpe died in June at the age of eighty-eight, having come to respect the new nation of American states; and Sir James Wright, at sixty-nine, was buried the following November in Westminster Abbey, unreconciled to the loss of his province.

The Legatees

LUCY MOUSE TONDEE WAS BORNE to her grave in a coffin which Peter would have approved. Built by twenty-eight-year-old cabinetmaker Gabriel Leaver, who as Sally Shick's brother-in-law could not have overcharged, it had cost an even £10, one pound more than was paid in 1771 to Joseph Dunlap, Peter's partner, for a coffin made for William Gibbons, Esquire, a planter and former member of the Commons.

The other expenses of the funeral totalled almost as much as the coffin. Five and a half pounds was spent for the "Black Mode," two pounds fifteen for wine, and half a pound paid to "a Negro Wench for making of Cakes." In the vernacular of mourning, these outlays expressed "Beloved Mother," and considering her wide acquaintance from the tavern, Mrs. Tondee was likely attended to her husband's side by a train of patriots.

The end of the war had restored a substantial part of the Tondee estate—most importantly the slaves, the lot next door, and another house in town—and after Lucy's death, administration of all this fell to Elisha Elon, the husband of twenty-nine-year-old daughter Ann. The record of income and expenses which he kept for three and a half years, until the estate was finally settled, profiles both the family finances and the austere lives of the slaves.

During that span, rent from at least two houses brought in £62. One had come to Peter through John Street, and another was almost certainly the tavern, which had been emptied of much of its contents. Two months after Lucy's death Mordecai Sheftall had bought from the Tondee estate "Household furniture sold at Vendue" for £21, an amount that could have purchased half the furniture listed on Peter's inventory, including the feather beds. By 1790, when it was first advertised for sale, the old Tondee home was definitely being rented, having been "lately occupied by Mr. John Hamilton."

The accounts also confirm the result of a lawsuit Lucy filed against John Morel, Jr., just before she died. Possibly the upshot of Morel's having bought Joe under confiscation by the British in 1781, the suit sought roughly £22 "for her damages which she had sustained by the occasion of the not performing certain promises and undertakings made to the said Lucia Tondee." Unlike the other Tondee slaves sold under confiscation, who were restored to Lucy after the war, Joe was not named in the estate accounts, and the last mention of him was Morel's advertisement of his escape. The court eventually decided in Lucy's favor, and in April of 1786 Elisha entered a payment from Morel for the full amount.

By far the greatest source of revenue for the Tondee estate was the hire of the slaves, and most of the £122 earned by them came from the labor of Will and Tom. Cumba brought in £4, and Mary much less. At the same time, the amount paid out for goods for all the slaves, excluding food and medical care, came to only £11, one tenth of the income.

A skilled carpenter, Will was hired during 1786 by William Lewden, who would build the market on Ellis Square three years later. Will's subsequent activities, though, are unclear. Just before closing the accounts, Elisha entered £13 10s. from him "at sundry times," and the sole instance of any expenditure for Will was 9s. for a pair of shoes in May of 1787.

Tom and Cumba were paid by the week, with Tom averaging 7s. to 9s., and Cumba 6s. At the beginning of each winter Tom got a new pair of shoes, and about every six months a frock or shirt and trousers, or cloth and thread to make them. Slaves who worked at large in town were required to wear a badge purchased from the state; Tom's cost just over £1, his only charge aside from clothes. The single expense involving Cumba was 2s. 6d. for cloth for her child, and though her wages are recorded regularly for five months, she disappears from the accounts until July of 1787, when she and her child were sold to the Widow Finden for £90.

Settlement of the Tondee estate took Elon over five years. A few months after becoming administrator, he called in all claims against it and asked prompt payment of all debts. Two years later he repeated the notice, adding that debtors "have had sufficient indulgence." In December of 1788, resolved to close the matter, he applied to the Register of Probates for an audit of the accounts, and the following February the *Gazette* announced: "PUBLICK AUCTION. *On FRIDAY the 27th inst. at 11 o'clock precisely, will be sold, at the Exchange in Savannah,* ALL the PERSONAL ESTATE of Mr. PETER TONDEE, deceased, consisting of several valuable negroes. Conditions will be made known on the day of sale."

Final disposal of the Tondee real estate took another two years, though. Eight months after the auction, the surviving heirs signed an agreement confirming that during his lifetime Peter had given his son Charles the vacant lot next to the tavern, number nine, which he had bought from Moses Nunez. Noting that "some doubts have arisen as to the said gift," the covenant was intended to settle "all disputes which have or might hereafter arise respecting the said premises." Listed were the Elons, Mary and her husband Benjamin Jones, Elizabeth and Nicholas Champaigne, Lucy and Jean Herault, Frederick Shick, and John Peter Oates. Immediately after the release in the deed book is the purchase of number nine by Elisha, who paid Charles £200 for it.

Throughout the following October and November, the *Gazette* ran an announcement of the auction of the Tondee lot and buildings at the corner of Broughton and Whitaker. The event did not bring a sale, though, and three months later Elisha bought from the other heirs for £225 their shares of joint ownership of number ten, with its Capital Dwelling House.

The Elons took up residence there, but within eight months—in October of 1791—it was offered again: "To be sold a great bargain, For which young Negro Boys or Men will be received for greatest part of the payment." A brickmason, Elisha apparently wished to augment his work force, but when he finally sold the Tondee home early in 1792 to Matthew McAllister, an attorney from Pennsylvania who would serve as mayor at the end of the century, he was paid in cash, £325 sterling.

Missing from the heirs who signed over their joint ownership of the old home were Lucy and Jean Herault. In May of 1790, not long after the sale of number nine to Elisha, Jean had published his intention to leave the state, calling in all demands and debts. He signed his notice "John Hero," the most common Anglicized version, but he and Lucy also spelled it Hearo and Hearow, and in deeds and other documents, the variations devised by clerks ranged from Herdult and Hayrault to Airault, Ayrough, and Giro.

At least six years Lucy's junior, Herault was a native of France who had moved to Savannah by late 1787. In July of 1790 the couple moved to Fayetteville, on the Cape Fear River, and their son John was born in North Carolina in January of 1794. Lucy's second of that name, he would be baptized a Catholic four years later in St. Augustine, where the family stayed and Jean acquired property. But Lucy died by the time young John was twelve; he died unmarried at twenty-four; and in 1830 Jean Herault, between sixty and seventy years old, was living alone in a house on Marine Street.

Peter's other daughter to marry a Frenchman—Elizabeth Tondee Champaigne—remained in Savannah. In July of 1796 her husband Nicholas, a shopkeeper, was granted a license to retail liquor, but his name appears most in the lists of those defaulting payment of their taxes or neglecting jury duty, offenses common enough to put him in generous company.

Mary Tondee Jones, twenty-eight when she signed the confirmation of lot number nine to Charles, had become Mary Tondee Patterson by the time she sold her share of the tavern to Elisha a year and a half later. A schoolmaster, Henry Patterson widowed her within seven years, and before marrying again, she arranged a settlement ensuring her title to her household furniture and nine slaves. In January of 1799 her brother Charles bonded himself for the performance of the agreement, along with Thomas Robertson, who in two months would marry their niece Rebecca Lucy Elon; and Mary wed John Dews, Revolutionary Soldier. As his widow, she drew in the 1827 land lottery, and less than a year later died of decline at sixty-seven.

In Elisha Elon, Ann Tondee had married a mechanick like her father. A Savannahian by the summer of 1774, Elisha formed an early bond with bricklayer John Eppinger, and like Peter, he often worked for the city. One of his first jobs was to lathe and plaster the courtroom in the courthouse, and he served the public by digging and bricking a vault for the city necessary house. But primarily he sank wells—at least eight of them between 1790 and 1794, at intersections like Bull and Broughton and in the squares—and he kept the previous wells in repair.

When the city council determined in 1791 to enclose the old cemetery with a brick wall, they appointed Elisha, along with Joseph Clay and Noble Wimberly Jones, to inspect the bricks they had ordered. After judging a batch of one hundred fifteen thousand to be inferior, the three had recommended that fifteen thousand be demanded free to compensate for quality. About a month later, the council asked Elisha to evaluate the work completed on the wall, which was to be six feet high, with a shore every fifteen feet, and he found progress well under way, despite the recent death of the bricklayer. The man's widow and his brother, Elisha felt confident, could fulfill the contract satisfactorily. Four years afterward, an exiled peer of France praised the cemetery as Savannah's most noteworthy public place, citing "the workmanship in its brick walls" and its spacious extent, which he also deemed proof of the unhealthfulness of the town.

A lieutenant during the Revolution, Elisha had risen to captain of a company of light infantry by February of 1798. It would be his highest rank. Seven months later he died, leaving, as had Peter, a forty-two-year-old widow, two sons, and five daughters.

Likewise, he left to his family a large house, next to the site of the tavern, and as the children married and moved out, Ann Elon put the rooms to use. Some she let to friends, like seventy-three-year-old Mrs. Biddulph, widow of a Liberty Boy, who was staying at Mrs. Elon's when she died, and was buried from there. Sometimes friends or family who had died in the country were also buried from Mrs. Elon's, such as John Peter Oates's wife Frances. And occasionally her often widowed daughters returned: Ann Elon Brown was living there in 1810 when her fourteen-year-old son John succumbed after ten days to bilious fever.

But the house burned in January of 1820 in Savannah's second devastating fire, and that autumn, the city's sickly season, an epidemic of yellow fever took off twenty-seven-year-old William Elon, nineteen-year-old Jane, and Mrs. Elon, who had moved to the country. Number nine Heathcote, vacant again, was split into thirds and the Elon slaves into two groups—nothing more remained of the estate—and the five surviving heirs drew lots. Among the three slaves inherited by Mary Elon and her third husband Morris Doty was Cumba's son Bob, who as a six-year-old boy had been valued in Peter's inventory at £17; as a thirty-year-old bricklayer in Elisha's at $600; and now, as "old Bob," a returned runaway aged fifty, at $450. Within two weeks, however, the Dotys had sold him to a couple of masons for $500.

Peter's son Charles also lost property in the fire of 1820, but he no longer lived in town then. By 1807 he had moved to land on the Ogeechee River in Effingham County, where he settled for the rest of his years. Already forty-seven, Charles would outdistance all his siblings and his parents—both of whom died at fifty-two—and as the only surviving son, preserve the family name.

Fifteen at the time of his father's death and twenty-five at his mother's, Charles saw the fall of Savannah and the siege in his late teens, and at some time during the war he enlisted. When at thirty he sold number nine to Elisha, he was practicing his father's trade of carpentry, but within a few years he had taken up planting on Skidaway, the island where his mother had spent her childhood and his grandfather Thomas Mouse had broken his health. There Charles and his wife Harriet lived during the Nineties, and their household grew by three.

By 1801, however, the family had returned to Savannah and Charles had taken out a liquor license. The following year one of his daughters died at eight; the year after that his son Charles Robert was born; and in 1805, through with shopkeeping, Charles bought three hundred fifty acres on the Ogeechee River, just west of present Guyton. Within the next five years he gained and lost a daughter, buried his wife Harriet, and at fifty married again. A Justice of the Peace in Effingham in 1812, Charles aged through time into the Tondee patriarch, watching his sons and daughters marry and multiply.

Of the three young Tondees who wed in the mid 1820s, two chose spouses to whom they were already related or would soon again be. Daughter Selina married first Harmon Elkins, a neighbor down the road, whose family was so close to the Tondees that generations would share reciprocal names— Lawrence Tondee Elkins and Lawrence Elkins Tondee—and she took for her second husband postmaster Archibald Guyton, whose name became the town's. Thomas Tondee married Julia Ann Womack, whose orphaned sister Valeria would become the ward and later the second wife of his brother Charles Robert.

In 1840 Charles Robert and Valeria took their five children to Marion County in west Georgia and settled at a place called Pond Town, now Ellaville. After a decade and three more children, Valeria died, and Charles married again, a daughter of one of the first families in the county, twenty years younger than he. From their four sons, Tondees eventually dotted the countryside. At Charles's death in 1888, the Schley County *Enterprize* observed, "In the home circle his virtues shone with resplendent lustre for in all the gentle humanities of life he had the tenderness of a woman enshrined in a noble, manly heart."

Peter Tondee saw few of his grandchildren. Most knew him only from stories, and if any remembered him at all, it was in the pastels of earliest recollection. He moved through their days, though, like the breeze from the river, and of all his legatees of that generation, none was more directly touched than his namesake John Peter Oates.

He signed himself John Peter, John P., J. Peter, and J. P., but he was called simply Peter, even by his grandfather John Oates. Two months after Lucy Tondee's death in 1785, when he was no older than fourteen, Peter was taken in by the Union Society, which had begun housing and schooling poor and orphaned children in town. Third on the record of beneficiaries—his grandfather Tondee had been fifth on the list of orphans at Bethesda—he too was later bound apprentice to a carpenter.

On a Sunday evening in mid May of 1797, when he was twenty-six at most, Peter married Miss Frances Brown, twenty-one, in the Independent Presbyterian Church. The following December he became an administrator for the estate of her father, and two years later he and his brother-in-law Thomas, with whom he would play in the Cricket Challenge in 1801, sold three slaves from it. Soon after the turn of the century he also sold a lot in Yamacraw from the estate of his own father Jacob, putting his name with moderate flourish beneath that of his mother Lucy Hearo.

Like his grandfather Tondee, during his career Peter found employment with the city, and as well incurred substantial losses from one of his appointments. As jailkeeper, he confined a debtor in April of 1803, acting at the insistence of creditor Moses Sheftall, Mordecai's son and another of Peter's teammates in the Cricket Challenge. The man had remained in custody for almost ten months, until he was released as insolvent, and the city had held Peter responsible for the cost of his keep. As a consequence, Peter sued Sheftall, the city fired Peter and advertised for a new jailer, and sheriff Peter Shick—Frederick's brother—announced the sale of "Two Negroes seized as the property of John P. Oates." Peter ultimately won his suit, as well as another like it, but appeals delayed his settlement until 1811, the same year he was elected county coroner.

In the interim he had run for sheriff and lost to John Eppinger, Jr.; he had trimmed trees for the city; and he ran in 1812 for clerk of the market, again unsuccessfully. By then he had made lieutenant commander of the second company, though, and despite having lost a two-week-old daughter in 1809, he boasted a brood of sons. His fifth, Francis Jasper, was born in September of 1814. Within five months, though, the boy died from a bowel complaint, and the next year Peter's wife Frances died of consumption. Before his own death in 1817, Peter had buried two more sons, Richard and eleven-year-old Elisha, and left only a fragment of his family to survive him.

At the time of the Cricket Challenge—January of 1801—he was still in his late twenties, roughly the same age as most of the Georgia team. In the first week of the new century, Levi Sheftall had submitted to the *Columbian Museum & Savannah Advertiser* this brief notice: "A CHALLENGE. Thirteen natives of Georgia, challenge thirteen natives of any country to play a game of CRICKET, for a treat, on Thursday next at 10 o'clock a.m. near the Booths, South Common."

Thursday passed, but on the following Tuesday the answer appeared: "THE CHALLENGE ACCEPTED. Thirteen Americans or Europeans will engage any equal number of native Georgians, at the game of CRICKET, this day, at 10 a.m. near the Booths, South Common."

Sheftall's team roster for the Georgians included his thirty-year-old son Benjamin as well as his nephew Dr. Moses Sheftall, also thirty, who would join the Union Society with Peter Oates in two years, just before the lawsuit. Other team members plied more physical trades, like butcher Adam Cope and bricklayer Thomas Brown, the husband of Peter's cousin Ann Elon. Also playing for Georgia was Thomas Norton, a thirty-nine-year-old planter and sheriff of Chatham County, who had married Peter's aunt Tamer Oates Waters and whose estate Charles Tondee would administer four years later. There were two Gugels, David and Christopher, and twenty-seven-year-old merchant Henry Anderson, who would die within three years of hard drinking.

In his list of the Europeans and Americans, Sheftall adopted a more formal tone, giving only surnames—Mr. Mace, Mr. Cannavan, Mr. Turnbull. Among non-native Georgians in Savannah at the time, though, Mr. Gunn was likely forty-two-year-old Christopher Gunn from Maryland, who ran a tavern on Bryan Street under the sign of the Bear; and Mr. Wylly, probably twenty-eight-year-old Peter Wylly from New York, a carpenter who would marry Mary Elon in 1805 and leave her a widow at sixteen the next year.

Shortly before the game was to begin, Levi Sheftall turned his ankle and could not play, but he took part as judge on behalf of the Natives of Georgia. David B. Mitchell, a thirty-four-year-old Scotsman who came to Savannah at sixteen, was chosen judge on behalf of the others. Fiercely devoted to his adopted land, Mitchell would kill an opponent in a duel over republican principles the following year, and in 1809 would be elected to the first of three terms as governor of the state.

After the game, Sheftall penned the results to the editor of the paper:

"Messrs. Printers please to insert in your Gazzet that 13 Americans & Europiens met the 13 Natives of Georgia at the place appointed to play the game of Cricket & underneath is the Statement of the game—
The Natives of Georgia got ————————57
The other Party got ————————25
in favor of the Georgians ————————32"

Sheftall ended his note: "This memorandum is only done to show what 13 Natives of my country can do."

For Georgians it was a time to be proud and confident. Twenty-five years before, they had stood against an empire and prevailed. Now on the playing field they had challenged all others and won. There was every reason for faith and hope; the century lay before them full of promise.

Epilogue

WHEN THE OLD FILATURE BURNED in the spring of 1839, much of
Savannah came to the fire. There was no chance of saving the building. The
fire company and volunteers, who fought the blaze with hose and axes,
aimed their efforts at containing it, and to that end pulled down two houses
on the eastern half of the lot, to the wonder of onlookers. But this fire, like
the conflagrations of 1796 and 1820, was fanned by a strong northwest wind,
and no one questioned the measure.

For the children chasing from group to group and their parents crowd-
ing the streets, the spectacle of the old wooden structure in flames could
have signified little beyond the thrill of calamity. For their grandparents,
though, standing at the fringe of the commotion or watching from carriages
around Reynolds Square, it illumined memories of a distant time, a morning
at school or a Masonic celebration, a concert or ball or acrobatic show, a
warm May night and an introduction to George Washington.

Over its eighty years, the filature had passed through repeated cycles
of decay and repair. Its condition was the first item of business for the
returned rebel government in 1782, and throughout the next three decades it
served variously as city hall, the Lodge Room for Grand Quarterly Communications, and the main meeting place for the Union Society. The lower
rooms housed at least seven schools and academies, two simultaneously in
the fall of 1796, and during the War of 1812 the building was converted into
barracks for a corps of riflemen and a hospital for sick soldiers. By then,
though, it was in a ruinous state, and the city council ordered the structure
sold and removed by the buyer within thirty days, one of many attempts to
unload it.

The long room in the filature, which comprised the second floor, provided one of the primary halls for Savannahians' pursuit of culture, high
and low. Before 1796, the courthouse had also hosted occasional events, but
it had sustained severe damage in the fire, and though renovation of one
room permitted holding court and entertaining some groups, the building

Silk Filature—Detail from "View of Savannah, 1837" by Firmin Cerveau.
(Courtesy, Georgia Historical Society.)

as a whole was judged "unworthy of any further repair." In that state it remained until 1831, when the city council finally contracted to raze and rebuild it.

The first performance at the filature after the war was a double bill, a tragedy called *The Fair Penitent* and an entertainment titled *Miss in her Teens, or, The Medley of Lovers*, acted by A Set of Gentlemen for the benefit of the poor. Seats in the pit cost 4s. 8d., in the gallery 3s. 6d., and the curtain rose precisely at seven. Another benefit, a concert in the early Nineties, was given for the Relief of a Musician in Distress, and in 1804 both amateurs and professionals performed a program of ambitious scope to aid French refugees in Savannah from liberated Haiti. The concert began with a Grand Ouverture and ended with a Grand Simfony, both by Haydn, and included a violin concerto, a flute quartet, and five songs of love and valor.

Most performances at the filature, though, were staged for profit. On a Saturday night in June of 1784, by Permission of His Honour the Governor, Feats of Lofty Tumbling and Posturing were executed there by an acrobat who had won great applause in England; and almost twenty years later magician James Rannie paid the city $10 per night to rent the room for his show, which featured breaking and restoring watches of gentlemen in the audience, walking the slack wire, and demonstrating card tricks, ventriloquism, and imitations of hogs, chickens, and an Old Scotch Landlord.

One of the most memorable evenings at the filature, however, resulted from a performance which did not take place. Early in the summer of 1792, about three hundred people responded to a notice promising wonderful feats by one John Perry, with supporting acts by his daughter, his horse, and his pigeon. The packed house waited for an hour and a half, oppressed by the heat of the season and the stifling closeness, until some of the audience went behind the curtain, where they found on the stage only a five-year-old girl. Perry and his associates had made off with the cash by way of a ladder fixed to one of the windows. The tickets had been signed Juan Perez, the *Gazette* reported, adding that "there seems also to have been concerned in this cheat an Italian who went by the name of John Jontson, a hair dresser named Williams, and some others whose names are now unknown."

The incident sparked the wit of the paper's correspondents, one of whom directed a sardonic attack at the credulity of the crowd: "NOTICE. To compensate, in some measure, for the disappointment of a liberal Public on last Monday night, Mr. Perry gives notice, that, if the Gentlemen and Ladies then present will favor him with their company on next Monday night, Miss Perry, after performing on her head, (in tight trowsers), will exhibit several feats, to their great amusement, without a head."

Almost twenty years later, a troupe also headlined by a Mr. Perez toured Savannah with much the same show. Performances were held at the Exchange, by permission, and Perez promised tight-rope dancing, ground and lofty tumbling, and astonishing demonstrations of equilibrium while shackled or otherwise encumbered. One trick called for dancing on the tight-rope with a child clinging to his neck; another with a boy clinging to each foot. By particular request, Perez would fly over the heads of the spectators, from one end of the room to the other, with a pistol in each hand. He was assisted by his partner Mrs. Perez, who danced on the tight-rope as well, and by Mr. Rowson, who played the clown; and the evening's entertainment would conclude with a pantomime, like *The Shoemaker Deceived* or *The Clown Out-Witted*.

Perez and Company enjoyed a run of over a month at the Exchange before their performances moved to the jail. Late in January of 1812, an advertisement much smaller than previous ones announced: "At the Gaol. BY PERMISSION. Equilibriums, Tight-Rope Dancing, Leaping and Vaulting. Mr. PEREZ has the honor to inform the Ladies and Gentlemen of this City, that he will exhibit, on SATURDAY EVENING, the 1st of February, a number of admired feats. CLOWN BY MR. ROWSON." Admittance at the jail was the same as at the Exchange, and in fact the same as at the filature twenty years earlier—adults fifty cents, children half price.

When George Washington visited Savannah in mid May of 1791, the filature had been slated for repairs for four years. Unpainted, in need of new shingles, missing shutters on some windows, and sashing and glazing on most, it was a modest site for a ball for the Father of the Country. But if the building had the look of an old workhorse, at least for that evening it was a workhorse with a satin bow.

Met at Purrysburg by a citizens' committee of Noble Wimberly Jones, Joseph Habersham, Joseph Clay, John Houstoun, and Lachlan McIntosh, the President came down the river in a boat decorated for the honor, rowed by nine captains dressed in light blue silk jackets, black satin breeches, white silk stockings, and round hats with black ribbons lettered in gold, "LONG LIVE THE PRESIDENT." Ten miles from town they were joined by several other boats of gentlemen, on one of which a small chorus accompanied by a band rendered "He Comes, the Hero Comes." Hailed from the wharves as he passed and cheered by throngs on shore and in vessels in the harbor, Washington landed at the foot of the bluff to an official welcome from the mayor and a salute of twenty-six rounds from field pieces of the Artillery Company. Then, in a procession that stretched for a substantial part of the route, he was conducted to a house prepared for him on St. James's Square.

At six he dined at Brown's Coffee-house with a numerous company of civic and military leaders, among whom were Jones, the two younger Habershams, Frederick Shick, and General McIntosh, who had served under Washington during the winter at Valley Forge and who would give him a tour on Saturday morning of the remains of the British defenses of 1779. Sixteen toasts were drunk, announced to the city by rounds from the Artillery Company, and that night the town was "beautifully illuminated." One ship in the river was strung with lanterns, and the home of one alderman sported no fewer than three hundred lights, symmetrically arranged, with fifteen in front forming a W.

The rest of the citizenry were invited to dine with the President on Saturday afternoon, under a large arbor built for the banquet beneath the bluff. Supported by three rows of pillars covered with laurel and bay leaves, it offered a view of both the city and the river, extending to the rice fields above and below town. Nearly two hundred attended, and from another arbor at a small distance the Artillery Company punctuated each toast with cannonfire. Washington gave the second—"Prosperity to the citizens of Savannah and its vicinity"—and just before retiring, the thirteenth—"The present dexterous Corps of Artillery"—and when he had withdrawn, the company toasted "The President of the United States." Fireworks and a concert crowned the evening, and after divine service at Christ Church the next morning, the President resumed his journey, escorted out of Savannah by a number of gentlemen and on to Augusta by that town's dragoons.

For the ball held on Friday evening, the long room in the filature had been "lately handsomely fitted up," and was well lighted so that the President might better see the ladies presented to him. They had worn their most elegant dresses, and some "displayed infinite taste in the emblems and devices on their sashes and head-dresses, out of respect to the happy occasion."

The President appeared at half past eight. Tall, erect, long of leg, the fifty-nine-year-old Washington had grayed and sagged a bit in the jowls, but at the line where his high, white forehead met his ruddy cheeks and nose, his deepset blue eyes still inspired flutters. He was introduced to ninety-six ladies—he found them handsome and well-dressed—and after a few minuets had been moved and a country dance led down, he retired with his suite at about eleven. The company danced on until the supper room was opened at two, and afterward continued until three, when they parted "happy with the satisfaction of having generally contributed towards the hillarity and gaiety of the evening."

The fire that destroyed the filature began across the river, in an old building in the yard of the Savannah Steam Saw Mill Company on Hutchinson's Island, and from there it spread rapidly to a load of white pine lumber on a wharf nearby and a schooner lying alongside. Two men on board tried to loosen the ship from her moorings, but the flames drove them from the vessel before she could be set adrift. They escaped in one of the boats, and the schooner burned to the water's edge.

From this blaze the wind blew aloft a spark, and bore it several hundred yards across the river to the roof of the filature, which caught like tinder. No one was injured in the fire, but losses were heavy, both for one of the current owners of the building, who was not insured, and for the two housekeepers who ran separate boarding houses in it.

The plight of these ladies prompted a letter to the next issue of the *Daily Georgian*, in which the writer praised their well-known industry and resourcefulness. Though the total value of their lost possessions, he conceded, was "comparatively trifling," yet because "it was the loss of their *little all*," and of the means of their making an honest livelihood for themselves and their large families, he recommended them as worthy objects of charity, appealing especially to "the sympathetic feelings evinced by the large concourse of amiable ladies, who watched the progress of the devouring element, from their carriages, and the surrounding dwellings."

Another correspondent, musing on the fire several days later, perceived in the blazing mast of the schooner and in its topsail, which had swung out on the wind and fallen at last unscathed into the river, a metaphor for the curling flames of despotism and the victorious flag of the republic, waving unsullied "till it finally sinks, *triumphant still,* . . . like that spotless sail, into the wide ocean of eternity!" Then shifting the scene, he saw another vision of the future:

"I now turned to view the Filature, which had become a frightful mass of lurid fire, and as I looked upon the crowded panorama, again the magic wand of unfledged time, erected before me a splendid dome of 'phoenix' beauty and elegance amidst its own ashes, dedicated to benevolence, philanthropy, and medical science; the ornament of the city, and the asylum of orphan age, and neglected genius.

"So mote it be."

That June the city council advertised the sale of the entire filature lot, from Abercorn to Lincoln Street, with the express condition that no wooden buildings be constructed on it. The lot was bought within the month by Frederick Heineman, who built a block of fashionable two-story brick houses on it which he called Cassel Row, after his home of Hesse-Kassel in Germany, a region which had furnished the British with mercenaries during the Revolution.

Appendix A

List of Passengers on the *James*, Captain James Yoakley
Embarked London, 24 January 1733—Arrived Savannah, 16 May 1733

On the Charity:
Paul Cheeswright—sawyer, dead 1736.
  Rebecca, wife—"Sentenc'd 60 lashes for barborously cutting an in-
  fant down the back with a knyfe 28 July 1735 and afterwards ran
  away to England."
Henry Hows—sawyer, dead 16 September 1733.
  Anne, daughter.
Robert Hows—became a follower of Whitefield.
  Anne, wife—dead 3 October 1733 [28 October 1736 - *CRG*, XXI, 254].
  Anne [daughter—see *LES*, 79, #558]
  Mary, daughter—"Age 8, dead 1738."
Edward Johnson—sawyer.
William Savery—blacksmith, dead December 1733.
Thomas Tebbut—sawyer. "Fyn'd for assaulting an officer on duty 1 June 1734.
  . . . A roving fellow & generally absent in Carolina. He quitted on
  shutting up the stores 1739 . . . returned 1741."
  Anne, wife.
Jacob Watts—sawyer and turner.

Paid Own Passage:
Thomas Cornwall—dead 21 July 1733.
Robert Gilbert—tailor. "3d Bailiff of Savannah 30 May 1738 but at his own
  request removed 30 May 1739. . . . He returned to England, but on
  22 March 1736/7 returned again to Georgia, and gave a note to the
  Trustees to repay the expense of his passage. His wife and he turned
  Methodist, and quitted the Colony . . . 19 August 1740."
  Margaret, wife.
  Elizabeth, daughter. Married William Mears July 1733. [See Mears, *LES*,
  p. 88, #806.]
Botham Squires—"He quitted at his own desire: afterwards return'd, but could
  not obtain another grant. Quitted 14 August 1733."
Peter Tondee, Senior—dead 19 July 1733.
  Peter, son—"Servt. to Hen. Parker."
  Charles, son—"Servt. to Hen. Parker."

Appendix B

Letter of Thomas Mouse to James Oglethorpe

Savannah January 23d 1734/5

Hon'd Sir

You being well aquainted with our Settlement at Skidoway, I have made bold to Informe your Honour of the Improvement belonging to my own Lott, which I call ye House Lott, it is pailed in, and I have two large hutts built thereon one is Twenty four by Sixteen and is sett all round with upright Loggs, the other is Twenty one by fourteen with Clapboards only, which I propose as a Store House with a Yard and Conveniencys for Breed, where I keep my Fowls, of which I have about Thirty, besides what I have Sold which came Cheifly from the Fowle which your Honour was pleased to give me, but I have not had altogether such good Luck with my Sow, she has had two Litters of Piggs, the first died being nine, and the last Litter five, only two Living, which are large thriving Piggs, The Cows & Calves which we had are all run into the woods, and cannot bring them up, having so few hands that pretend they cannot Spare time to Hunt for them & theirs.

I am now to informe your Honour that the Ground brings forth plenty of Callavances [peas], Potatoes & Indian Corn, and will I dont doubt produce many other things which I intend to Try, I hope your Honour will not forget to send over some more Settlers for our Island, It being very hard for a Man (who has a Large Family) to watch continually every third or fourth Night, and for refusing one Night, I have been tied neck & heels by Mr. Dalmas our Tything Man. I am very sorry I should deserve to be Served in that manner but his being Tything Man over so few people as we are at present, he has more times to do Service for said place than he has, but must submit to an officer in power. I am informed that It is in his power to Tie me Neck and heels when he pleases, which I submit to If deserved, but If a Man is to be Governed by an officer, who will Reign Arbitrary, it is very hard to Submit to, and if it is to [continue] so, I most Humbly beg your Hon. please to permitt me and my Family to proceed for England, alltho' I like Skidoway better than any place I have seen in the Collony,

I realy declare that I think it very hard to be used as a common Soldier as I like my Place of Settlement so well, and to leave the Same after I have taken so much pains for my Family's sake is still more hard to me;

———

I take the freedome to aquaint your Honour that I do not mention out of Vanity, but I do assure you I have made ye most Improvement on my Lott of any one, in ye Settlement. am very unwilling to trouble your Honour with what Improvements others have made not Doubting but you and the Hon. Trustees will be informed therein—as to our Land which is belonging to us is lately run out ye 17th December.

I understand by Mr. Causton That The Hon. Trustees have thought Fitt, [to] Allow the People of Skidoway, another years provisions for which Great favour, your Honours have mine and my Familyes Humble Thanks.

My Spouse is in Dayly Expectation of being brought to Bed, and is now in Savanna were she Intends to Lye in. She and my Family Joins with me in Humble thanks to your Hon. and the rest of the Hon. Trustees, for all favours and am Honoured

Sir

Your most obedient
Humble Servt.
Thomas Mouse

Appendix C

Membership Roster of Unity Lodge*

Member	Occupation	Political Stance**
Peter Tondee	carpenter/tavernkeeper	Liberty Boy
John Eppinger	bricklayer	Liberty Boy
Peter Gandy	clerk/schoolmaster	
Mathias Ash	planter/tavernkeeper	
Frederick Rossberg		Liberty Boy
Sinclair Waters	tailor	Loyalist
George Ducker	butcher/tavernkeeper	
David Tubear	gunsmith/jailer	Loyalist
Thomas Hamilton	butcher/victualer	Liberty Boy
John Oates	merchant/overseer	Loyalist
Peter Pechin		Liberty Boy
Jacob Oates	clerk	Liberty Boy
Abraham Gray		Loyalist
George Johnson Turner		Liberty Boy
George Borland	tailor	Loyalist
Frederick Rhem	physician	Liberty Boy
David Saussy	planter	
Aaron Pickren	tailor	Liberty Boy
John McDougall		
Joseph Rice	sailmaker	Liberty Boy
Charles Hamilton	victualer	
Thomas Corn	jailer	Liberty Boy
Robert Gray		
Samuel Burgess		Loyalist
Malcolm Neilson	cooper	Loyalist

* Reproduced by permission of the Board of General Purposes of the United Grand Lodge of England. ** Left blank where conflicting evidence or none was found. See notes for bases of entries.

$\mathscr{A}$ppendix $\mathcal{D}$

A List & Appraisement of the Goods and Chattels Belonging to the Estate of Peter Tondee deceased taken September 17, 1776

Negroes

Will	£80.0.0	
Joe	60.0.0	
Jenny	20.0.0	
Combo & her Child Lucy	60.0.0	
Scippio	23.0.0	
} Combo's two Children		
Bob	17.0.0	£ 260.0.0
1 Round tea table	0.18.0	
1 Dineing ditto	1.5.0	
1 Square ditto	0.15.0	
2 Old Desks	1.10.0	
1 painted Beaufet	1.15.0	
1 pr. fire dogs tongs Shovel & bellows	0.15.0	
1 1/2 doz. Straw Bottom'd Chairs	2.5.0	
5 Windsor Chairs	1.0.0	
2 feather Beds with Bolsters & pillows	10.0.0	
1 pine bedstead	0.10.0	
16 Blankets Common sort @ 5/	4.0.0	
5 pr. Sheets & 5 pr. pillow Cases	2.15.0	
3 Feather Beds 3 bolsters & 6 pillows	12.0.0	
3 Old pine Bedsteads	0.12.0	£40.10.0
7 Saws	1.0.0	
3 Jointers	0.8.0	
3 Long plains	0.8.0	
3 Jack & 14 Smoothing ditto	0.17.0	
4 Raising plains	0.8.0	
1 pr. Jack hollow & round 1 plow & 3 Stricke Blocks	.10.0	
1 Cornish 2 O.G & 1 rabbitt plain	0.5.0	
143 moulding plains Including Grooving Rabbit & phillisters	7.3.0	
1 Long plain 1 Bed mould	0.4.0	
6 Augures 1 Lathing hammer 2 Chizels 1 drawbore pin	0.12.0	11.15.0
	£312.5.0	

Appraisement Continued Amt. Bro. up		£312.5.0
108 Queens Ware plates & Dishes —————————	£2.5.0	
3 Chinia & 2 delph Bowles —————————	2.5.0	
2 Large Mahogany Tables —————————	4.0.0	
1 pr. fire Dogs, Brass knobs —————————	0.5.0	
1 Brass kettle 1 Iron pott —————————	1.10.0	
6 Queens ware dishes —————————	0.12.0	
5 Iron pots 15/ 2 pr. fire dogs 5/ —————————	1.0.0	
4 pewter dishes 6/ 3 pr. flatt Irons 12/ —————————	0.18.0	
1 Brass & 5 Iron Candlesticks —————————	0.5.0	
1 doz. & 11 Scures 6/ 2 Tea kettles 25/ —————————	1.11.0	
5 Doz. knives & forks —————————	1.0.0	
1 Coffee & 1 Corn Mill —————————	1.10.0	
3 Tin Covers 1 funnel 1 pestle & Morter —————————	0.8.0	£17.9.0
1 Cart —————————	2.0.0	
1 Cow & Calf —————————	3.0.0	
300 ft. Cypress Boards —————————	1.4.0	
1500 ft. pine refuge ditto —————————	2.5.0	
Lott of Old plains —————————	0.3.0	
Lott of Sashes —————————	0.15.0	
1 Sign —————————	1.0.0	
12 Doz. Bottles —————————	1.0.0	
4 Empty Cases with Bottles —————————	1.0.0	
2 Iron bound Qtr. Casks —————————	0.5.0	
10 Lightwood posts —————————	0.10.0	
About 3m [3000] Stock Bricks —————————	3.10.0	£16.12.0
		34.1.0

Sum Total   £346.6.0

Thomas Lee
Joseph Dunlap
John Lyons
John McClure

Glossary of Names

Amatis, Paul. Italian silk expert sent on *Ann* by Trustees. Tondee boys lived with him in 1735. Died in Charleston, December 1736.

Ash, Mathias. German tavernkeeper; member of Unity Lodge. See Appendix C.

Bailey, Thomas. Blacksmith to whom Charles Tondee was apprenticed.

Barber, Jonathan. Superintendent of Spiritual Affairs at Bethesda who beat Charles Tondee in spring of 1741.

Bob. Son of Cumba; inherited from Tondee estate by Elons; bricklayer; sold to masons by Morris and Mary Elon Doty. See Appendix D.

Bosomworth, Thomas. Mary Musgrove Mathews' third husband; championed her claim to islands of Ossabaw, St. Catherine's, and Sapelo.

Bowen, Oliver. Came to Georgia in early 1770s. Delegate to Provincial Congress, July 1775; captain of *Liberty* during seizure of powder from *Philippa*; commodore of Georgia's naval forces, 1777-78.

Brooks, Francis. Anne Mouse's first husband; killed by Spaniards in 1740.

Brooks, James Thomas and John. Twin sons of Anne and Francis Brooks; born 1738. James retailed liquor during mid 1760s; ran shop on Bay with mother Anne.

Bryan, Jonathan. South Carolinian who helped Oglethorpe at founding; moved to Georgia with legalization of slavery in 1750. Acquired large tracts of land; member of Upper House and Commons. Given silver plate by Union Society for "Revolution principles" (*Georgia Gazette*). Liberty Boy; delegate to Provincial Congress, July 1775. Captured after fall of Savannah in 1778; spent two years on prison ship; exchanged and returned to Georgia August 1781; died March 1788.

Bulloch, Archibald. South Carolina lawyer; came to Georgia in 1750. President of Provincial Congress and delegate to Continental Congress, July 1775. Governor of Georgia, 1776-77. Died February 1777.

Burrington, Thomas. Savannah gentleman who owned large library; bought Tondee's forty-five-acre farm lot in 1759.

Campbell, Lieutenant Colonel Archibald. British commander who captured Savannah in December 1778.

Camuse, Mary. Volatile assistant to Amatis, later replaced him. Dead by September 1749. Daughter Mary married Richard Milledge in 1752.

Cannon, Marmaduke. Came on *Ann*; roughly Peter's age; went by "Duke." Orphaned, placed out to Thomas Causton, moved to Bethesda.

Causton, Thomas. Came on *Ann.* Keeper of the Trust's Store and later first magistrate. Removed by Trustees; died on return passage to Georgia in 1746.

Cheeswright, Paul and Rebecca. See Appendix A.

Christie, Thomas. Came on *Ann.* Court recorder (with same authority as magistrate); commanded townsmen during Red String Plot; delivered his "Bottled Beef" upriver in Trust's boat. Returned to England, June 1740.

Clay, Joseph. Nephew of James Habersham; came to Georgia in 1760 at nineteen. Partner in merchant house with Jemme and later with Joe. Liberty Boy; delegate to Provincial Congresses, 1775; Council of Safety, 1775. Died November 1804.

Coles, Joseph. Came on *Ann.* Baker; constable of Decker Ward after Samuel Parker's death on 20 July 1733. Tondee boys may have lived with him before Amatis. Died March 1735.

Corn, Thomas. Warden of Workhouse and Jailkeeper, 1774-75; member of Unity Lodge. See Appendix C.

Cox, William. Doctor with first colonists on *Ann.* First to die, 6 April 1733.

Croddy, Adam. Estate appraised and later administered by Tondee.

Cumba. Female slave bequeathed to Tondee by Margaret Pages in 1768; "well known in town" in 1781 (*Royal Georgia Gazette*). See Appendix D.

Cunningham, David. Second husband of Anne Mouse Brooks; steward of Union Society in 1760.

Cuyler, Jeanne (Mrs. Telamon). Ran lodging house on Bay where patriots lived and met. Son Henry was Liberty Boy.

Delamotte, Charles. Teacher who came to Georgia with Wesleys; stayed slightly longer.

Dunlap (Dunlop), Joseph. Tondee's partner for courthouse work.

Elbert, Samuel. Delegate to Provincial Congresses, 1775; commanded expedition against Florida in 1777 when Gwinnett and McIntosh deadlocked; assumed command of Georgia brigade on McIntosh's transfer north; governor of Georgia, 1785-86. Died November 1788.

Ellis, Henry. Second royal governor of Georgia, 1757-1760; Fellow of the Royal Society; brilliant statesman. Lauded in address by Union Society on his departure.

Elon, Elisha. Ann Tondee's husband; bricklayer; settled estate of Peter and Lucy Tondee.

Eppinger, John. Well-known Savannah bricklayer; member of Unity Lodge; wife later ran tavern. See Appendix C.

Estaing, Charles Henri d'. French count who commanded Siege and Battle of Savannah; beheaded in 1794.

Fallowfield, John. Granted middle third of Isle of Hope in 1736; appointed magistrate in 1739; left for South Carolina in 1742.

Fitzwalter, Joseph. Came on *Ann.* First gardener in Trust's garden; feuded with Amatis. Loved to hunt, fish, and ramble in the woods. Briefly married to Indian Molly. Died October 1742, "after long sickness" (Stephens).

Frink, Samuel. Contentious Anglican priest of Christ Church, 1767-1771.

Gandy, Peter. Schoolmaster and Tondee's accountant; member of Unity Lodge; witnessed Tondee's will. See Appendix C.

Glen, John. Liberty Boy. Married Noble Wimberly Jones's daughter Sarah. Lost home in fire of 6 December 1796. Mayor of Savannah, 1797.

Goddard, John. Came on *Ann*; orphaned first summer; placed with Fitzwalter.

Goldwire, Benjamin. Tondee's partner for construction of silk filature and work on Council House. Died May 1766.

Graeme, William. Attorney general of province; instigator of guardhouse incident. Died 22 June 1770.

Gwinnett, Button. Came to Savannah in 1765; soon after moved to St. Catherine's Island in St. John Parish; emerged in 1776 as leader of radicals. Signer of Declaration of Independence; governor of Georgia, 1777. Killed in duel with Lachlan McIntosh, May 1777.

Habersham, James. Came with Whitefield; managed business affairs of Bethesda; later became wealthy merchant. Married Mary Bolton; had sons James (Jemme), Joseph (Joe), and John. President of Governor's Council; Loyalist. Died in New Brunswick, N. J., August 1775.

Habersham, Joseph. Brother of James. Twice lost in swamp; died at Frederica, January 1739.

Habersham, Joseph (Joe). Middle son of James, born 1751. Liberty Boy; delegate to Provincial Congresses, 1775; promoted to colonel during Revolution; appointed United States Postmaster General by Washington in 1795. Died November 1815.

Hall, John. Partner of Robert Kirkwood in construction of courthouse.

Hall, Dr. Lyman. Delegate to Continental Congress from St. John Parish, May 1775, and from Georgia, July 1775; signer of Declaration of Independence; governor of Georgia, 1783-84. Died October 1790.

Herault, Jean (John Hero). Second husband of Lucy Tondee Oates.

Herbert, Henry. Minister with first colonists on *Ann*. Died spring 1733 en route to London to recover his health.

Holzendorf, Frederick. Saddler; friend of Tondee. Brother William later Liberty Boy.

Houstoun, John. Son of Sir Patrick Houstoun. Delegate to Provincial Congresses, 1775; delegate to Continental Congress, 1775; governor of Georgia, 1778-79, 1784-85. First mayor of Savannah, 1790. Died July 1796.

Howe, General Robert. Continental Commander of the Southern Department in 1778; credited with loss of Savannah to British in December 1778.

Hows, Robert. See Appendix A.

Jenkins, Edward. Tavernkeeper and Trustee for the Orphans before founding of Bethesda; left for South Carolina in 1740.

Jenny. Slave of Tondee; advertised for sale during British occupation; mentioned in Tondee estate records in 1786. See Appendix D.

Joe. Slave of Tondee; "has his country marks upon his cheeks" (*Royal Georgia Gazette*). See Appendix D.

Johnston, James. Printer and publisher of *Georgia Gazette, Royal Georgia Gazette,* and *Gazette of the State of Georgia.*

Jones, Noble. Came on *Ann*. Carpenter, early surveyor, constable, doctor, captain of marines, planter; granted southern third of Isle of Hope, which he named Wormslow. Children Noble Wimberly, Mary, and Inigo (born in Georgia).

Jones, Noble Wimberly. Nine at founding; roughly same age as Tondee. Physician; Speaker of Commons; delegate to Continental Congress; "Morning Star of Liberty" in Georgia. Lost extensive medical and meteorological records in fire of 1796. Died 10 January 1805 at eighty.

Jones, Thomas. Vindictive clerk who replaced Causton as Keeper of the Store.

Kemp, John and Janet. Servants to Henry Parker in 1738, while Tondee boys were living with him.

Kirkwood, Robert. Carpenter who plagiarized Tondee's courthouse plans and built courthouse with him; deponent in guardhouse incident.

Knox, William. Georgia's agent in London; removed after supporting Stamp Act in 1765.

Langworthy, Edward. Teacher at Bethesda in 1771; secretary to Council of Safety; delegate to Continental Congress, 1777-79.

Lincoln, General Benjamin. Continental Commander of the Southern Department after Howe; led American forces at Siege and Battle of Savannah; surrendered Charleston to British in May 1780; accepted Cornwallis's sword at Yorktown.

Lucy. Child of Cumba. See Appendix D.

Lyon, John. Blacksmith; tavernkeeper; deponent in guardhouse incident; Liberty Boy.

Malatchee. Cousin and supporter of Mary Musgrove; claimed to be King of the Creeks.

McGillivray, Lachlan. Wealthy Indian trader and landowner; employed John Oates as overseer on plantation Vale Royal; fond of Oates's daughter Tamer. Loyalist.

McIntosh, Lachlan. Born in Scottish Highlands in 1727; settled at Darien in 1736. Lived at Bethesda 1740-42 while his father was imprisoned by Spanish. Commanded Georgia Battalion in 1776; killed Button Gwinnett in duel in 1777. Continental Brigadier-General under Washington at Valley Forge. Died February 1806.

Milledge, John. Son of Thomas; twelve at founding. Became head of household at fourteen on death of mother. At twenty-one commissioned quartermaster by Oglethorpe; later promoted to captain. Acquired considerable property; member of Commons during Stamp Act conflict. Little known of revolutionary stance. Died October 1781, en route from Augusta to Savannah. Father of Governor John Milledge.

Milledge, Richard. Younger son of Thomas; roughly Tondee's age. Fellow orphan at Bethesda (briefly); fellow apprentice under Papot. Founded Union Society with Tondee and Benjamin Sheftall in 1750; married Mary Camuse in 1752. Died November 1768.

Milledge, Thomas. Came on *Ann*. "Our best carpenter" (Oglethorpe). Died July 1733. Father of John, Richard, Frances, Sarah, and several others.

Minis, Abraham and Abigail. German Jews who came in July 1733. Kept shop and ran tavern; acquired considerable property. Son Philip on Parochial Committee in July 1775. Abigail died in 1794 at ninety-three.

Montiano. Governor of Florida defeated by Oglethorpe at St. Simons Island in 1742.

Morel, John. Married Jonathan Bryan's daughter Mary (second wife) in 1767; bought Bewlie in 1769. Delegate to Provincial Congress, July 1775. Staunch Liberty Boy; sons John, Jr., and Peter Henry more adaptable. Died 1776.

Mouse, Anne. Oldest of Thomas and Lucy's daughters and first to marry in Georgia. Wed Francis Brooks; had twins James Thomas and John in 1738; widowed 1740. Married David Cunnningham; ran shop on Bay; mother-in-law of John Street; died 1770.

Mouse, Thomas and Lucy. Among first families on Skidaway. Thomas was shoemaker in London; planter and tavernkeeper in Georgia; died August 1742. Widow Lucy became Savannah midwife. Youngest daughter Lucy married Tondee; other daughters were Anne (Brooks Cunningham), Elizabeth (Young), Catherine (Norton), and Mary.

Musgrove, Mary (later Mathews and Bosomworth). Indian interpreter in early years of colony; keeper of trading house; later granted St. Catherine's Island.

Muter, James. Cabinetmaker taken into custody by Tondee in 1773. Bought Tondee's five-hundred-acre tract in St. Matthew Parish in 1774; signed petition of Loyalists in August 1775.

Norton, William. Grandson of Lucy Mouse, who gave him Skidaway Island tract.

Nunez, Samuel. Portuguese physician among first Jewish colonists in Georgia. Sons Daniel and Moses became Indian interpreters and traders; Moses sold Tondee adjacent lot on Broughton, number nine Heathcote Tything, Decker Ward.

Oates, Jacob. First husband of Lucy Tondee; member of Unity Lodge; Liberty Boy; killed by British pilot during skirmish at Cockspur Island in May, 1776.

Oates, John. Father of Oates clan; overseer for Lachlan McGillivray; member of Unity Lodge; salty-tongued Loyalist. Died in Savannah, 1789. See Appendix C.

Oates, John Peter. Son of Jacob Oates and Lucy Tondee Oates, named for his grandfathers. Played in Cricket Challenge in 1801. Died 1817.

Oglethorpe, James Edward. Thirty-six at founding of Georgia; only Trustee ever to come to colony. Returned to England twice for colonists and supplies; established Fort Frederica on St. Simons Island; defeated Spanish at Bloody Marsh; left Georgia permanently July 1743. Died in 1785 at eighty-eight.

Ottolenghe, Joseph. Converted Italian Jew sent to Georgia in 1751 to teach slaves and manage silk operations. Engineered passage of establishment act in 1758 and spurred religious conflict in 1769. Died 1775.

Pages, Margaret (Mrs. Anthony). French tavernkeeper who bequeathed slave Cumba to Tondee in 1768.

Papot, James. Carpenter to whom Tondee and Richard Milledge were apprenticed; "one of our best reputed Carpenters" (Stephens). Died 1752.

Parker, Henry. Linen draper in London; magistrate and later president of colony. Granted northern third of Isle of Hope. Tondee boys lived with him 1736-1740. Died 1752.

Parker, Joseph. Son of Henry; silversmith. Steward of Union Society 1769; elected to Workhouse Commission with Tondee, April 1770. Died May 1770.

Parker, William. Brother of Henry; silversmith. Split reward for capture of White.

Pickren, William. Tailor who witnessed Tondee's will and gave deposition swearing its validity.

Prevost, General Augustine. British commander during Siege and Battle of Savannah.

Price, Samuel. Part owner and pilot of *Liberty* during seizure of powder from *Philippa*; stole schooner back from Patrick Mackay after its confiscation and sale by British for debts.

Reynolds, John. First royal governor of Georgia, 1754-57; removed for incompetence.

Rice, Joseph. Sailmaker; Liberty Boy. Took part in Wells' wharf incident, seizure of powder from *Philippa*, and battle of rice boats in 1776. Member of Unity Lodge. See Appendix C.

Scippio. Child of Cumba. See Appendix D.

Sheftall, Benjamin. German Jew who came to Georgia in July 1733; lived diagonally across lane from Tondee. Successful merchant; father of Mordecai and Levi. Founded Union Society with Tondee and Richard Milledge in 1750. Died October 1765.

Sheftall, Levi. Son of Benjamin and second wife Hannah. Successful merchant and Liberty Boy; author of Cricket Challenge of 1801. Died January 1809.

Sheftall, Mordecai. Son of Benjamin and first wife Perla. Successful merchant and Liberty Boy; Deputy Commissary of Issues for Georgia in 1778. Captured at fall of Savannah in December 1778; exchanged 1780. Died July 1797.

Shick, Frederick. Son of John; patriot. Fought at Siege and Battle of Savannah; married Tondee's youngest daughter Sally (Sarah) in 1784. One of the original members of the Society of the Cincinnati in Georgia (1783). Died December 1803.

Shick, John. Wheelwright from Salzburg; Loyalist. Lost arm during Siege and Battle of Savannah. Died in Savannah, October 1797.

Smith, Haddon. Last Anglican minister of Christ Church before Revolution. Loyalist; fled in July 1775.

Squires, Botham. See Appendix A.

Stephens, Newdigate. Youngest son of William Stephens, President. Came to Georgia 1741; married Frances Milledge; inherited Bewlie; father of William Stephens, attorney; died c. 1757.

Stephens, William. Sent to Georgia in autumn of 1737 as secretary to the Trustees; kept extensive journal for them. Granted plantation Bewlie on Vernon River. President of colony, 1741-1751. Died at Bewlie, August 1753, at eighty-one.

Stephens, William. Son of Newdigate and Frances. Orphaned by 1757; ward of John and Richard Milledge. Liberty Boy; mayor of Savannah in 1793 and 1795.

Street, John. Carpenter whose estate Tondee administered; son-in-law of Anne Mouse Cunningham; John, Jr., became ward of Tondee and later of Jacob Oates.

Telfair, Edward. Came to Georgia in 1766; opened one of leading merchant houses. Liberty Boy; delegate to Continental Congress, 1778; governor of Georgia, 1786-87, 1789-93. Died September 1807.

Tomochichi. Mico (chief) of Yamacraw, small tribe on bluff where the town of Savannah was laid out. Befriended English. Died October 1739 and buried in center of Wright Square. W. W. Gordon monument now stands atop grave; boulder nearby serves as memorial.

Tondee, Charles. Brother of Peter. Baptized Huguenot, 18 January 1728. Beaten at Bethesda, May 1741; apprenticed to blacksmith Thomas Bailey; set tune for hymns in church, 1743; married, had two children, granted land in south Georgia. Disappears from records after 1765.

Tondee, Peter and Lucy. Born in London, c. 1723 and 1733; died in Savannah 22 October 1775 and 15-22 September 1785. Seven known children: Peter, Lucy, Ann, Elizabeth, Charles, Mary, Sarah (Sally).

Tondu, Pierre. Peter Tondee's father. Born in Chatillon-sur-Loire, France, c. 1684; died in Savannah, 19 July 1733.

Tooanahowi. Nephew of Tomochichi, roughly Tondee's age. Fought bravely at Bloody Marsh; killed during rescue of British marines from Spanish in 1744.

Treutlen, John Adam. Object of John Oates's invective in 1773; delegate to Provincial Congress, July 1775; governor of Georgia, May 1777-78. Murdered 1782.

Tubear, David. Gunsmith and Keeper of Common Gaol in 1773; member of Unity Lodge. See Appendix C.

Walton, George. Came to Georgia 1769. Delegate to Provincial Congresses and Secretary of July Congress, 1775; delegate to Continental Congress, 1776; youngest signer of Declaration of Independence; governor of Georgia, 1779-80, 1789. Died February 1804.

Wesley, John and Charles. Came with two companions in February 1736. Charles preached mainly at Frederica; John at Savannah and outskirts, occasionally at Frederica. Charles left after six months, John after two years, both casualties of naive piety and gossip.

Whitefield, George. Came in 1738, accompanied by James Habersham. Leading evangelist of Great Awakening; founded orphanage Bethesda in 1740. Died September 1770 at Newburyport, Massachusetts.

Will. Slave of Tondee; "good carpenter" (*Royal Georgia Gazette*). See Appendix D.

Wright, Charles and Jermyn. Brothers of Governor James Wright.

Wright, Sir James. Third and last royal governor of Georgia. Only provincial governor to succeed enforcing the Stamp Act. Died in London, November 1785.

Yoakley, James. Captain of the *James*, which brought Tondees to Georgia; won £100 for bringing ship up Savannah River to town.

Young, Isaac, Jr. Married Elizabeth Mouse; member of Commons, 1773; delegate to Provincial Congresses, 1775.

Young, William. Attorney; Steward of Union Society, 1769; Speaker of Commons, 1773; delegate to Provincial Congresses, 1775. Drew up Tondee's will. Died January 1776. Mistakenly labeled Tory in *Revolutionary Records of Georgia*.

Zouberbuhler, Bartholomew. Minister of Christ Church, 1746-1766; provided the only stable and continuous Anglican leadership in colonial Savannah. Died 1766.

Zubly, John J. Minister of Independent Presbyterian Church from 1760 through end of colonial era. Bought Tondee's one-hundred-twenty-acre tract near the glebe land. Delegate to Continental Congress in summer of 1775; returned unable to support American independence. Died July 1781.

Bibliographical Note

An excellent bibliographical essay on research sources in colonial Georgia history can be found in Harold E. Davis's *The Fledgling Province: Social and Cultural Life in Colonial Georgia.* For a brief introductory reading list, I recommend highly that volume, along with Kenneth Coleman's *Colonial Georgia: A History*; Sarah B. Gober Temple and Kenneth Coleman's *Georgia Journeys*, a colorful look at the lives of the colonists during the Trustee period; W. W. Abbot's *Royal Governors of Georgia, 1754-1775*; and Kenneth Coleman's *American Revolution in Georgia*.

Also recommended are Larry E. Ivers' *British Drums on the Southern Frontier*, a vivid account of military affairs in Trustee Georgia; Harvey H. Jackson's *Lachlan McIntosh and the Politics of Revolutionary Georgia*, an incisive analysis of the forces that led to the Gwinnett-McIntosh duel; Alan Gallay's *The Formation of a Planter Elite: Jonathan Bryan and the Southern Colonial Frontier*, an engrossing study of that remarkable man; and Alexander A. Lawrence's *Storm Over Savannah*, the authoritative work on the Siege and Battle of Savannah.

The Beehive Press has reprinted many early Georgia manuscripts in attractive editions. Most useful for my research, and interesting reading, were the collections *Our First Visit in America: Early Reports from the Colony of Georgia, 1732-1740; The Clamorous Malcontents*; and the two-volume set of letters *General Oglethorpe's Georgia*.

The early 1980s saw the publication of several books which contributed substantially to research in colonial Georgia. Savannah's Jewish community was thoroughly discussed and documented in Rabbi Saul Jacob Rubin's *Third to None: The Saga of Savannah Jewry 1733-1983* and B. H. Levy's *Savannah's Old Jewish Community Cemeteries*. Rosier and Pearson's *Grand Lodge of Georgia* chronicled Freemasonry in the colony; and Betty Wood's *Slavery in Colonial Georgia* provided a comprehensive treatment of that subject. At about the same time, Kym S. Rice detailed the business and custom of tavernkeeping in the colonies in *Early American Taverns*, and Roy Underhill championed colonial carpentry in *The Woodwright's Shop* and *The Woodwright's Companion*.

For samples of daily life in colonial Georgia, the journals of two very different men offer distinct contrasts in time and temperament. From late 1737 through 1745, William Stephens, the Trustees' Secretary in Georgia, recorded in his diary almost everything that came to his attention, with observations about almost everyone in town. He was Savannah's Samuel Pepys, with a neoclassical style and the sensibilities of a gentleman. Volume IV and its Supplement of the *Colonial Records of Georgia* contain the years 1737-1741, and the Wormsloe Foundation has published 1741-1745 in two volumes.

The other journal will be much easier to find. In 1773 William Bartram—who had accompanied his father, naturalist John Bartram, to Georgia in 1765—returned alone to explore the southeast and investigate the native flora. His narrative of the next four years epitomized the Romantic idealization of nature, with rhapsodic descriptions of plants and animals and dramatic encounters with wandering braves and bathing maidens. Popular when published in 1791, Bartram's *Travels* is still a great adventure, as well as an extensive botanical catalogue and a rich resource on Indian culture in the late 18th century.

$\mathcal{A}$bbreviation $\mathcal{K}ey$ and Sources

Sources cited only once are named in full in notes and
listed below without abbreviation.

Abstracts of Georgia Colonial Conveyance Book C-1, 1750-1761, Frances Howell Beckemeyer, R. J.
Taylor Foundation, Atlanta, 1975.
Abstracts of Wills, Chatham County, Georgia, 1773-1817, M. F. La Far and C. P. Wilson, Genealogi-
cal Publications of the National Genealogical Society, No. 6, Washington, 1936.
An Account of Money Received and Disbursed for the Orphan-House in Georgia, George Whitefield,
London, 1741.
AADH *American Archives, A Documentary History*, Fourth Series, II, Peter Force, published by M.
St. Clair Clarke and Peter Force, Washington, 1839.
ABF *Autobiography*, Benjamin Franklin, Vintage Books, New York, 1990.
ACW *Abstracts of Colonial Wills of the State of Georgia*, Georgia Department of Archives and
History, Atlanta, 1962.
AJHQ *American Jewish Historical Quarterly* (see article below).
AG *Annals of Georgia*, v. II, *Effingham County Records*, Caroline P. Wilson, Braid & Hutton, Savan-
nah, 1933.
Architecture of the Old South: Georgia, Mills Lane, Beehive Press, Savannah, 1986.
ARG *The American Revolution in Georgia, 1763-1789*, Kenneth Coleman, University of Georgia
Press, Athens, 1958.
Augusta Chronicle and Gazette of the State (newspaper).
BDSF *British Drums on the Southern Frontier, The Military Colonization of Georgia, 1733-1749*, Larry E.
Ivers, University of North Carolina Press, Chapel Hill, 1974.
A Bicentennial Festschrift for Jacob Rader Marcus, ed. Bertram Wallace Korn, American Jewish
Historical Society, KTAV Publishing House, New York, 1976.
BHS *Bethesda: A Historical Sketch*, James F. Cann, John M. Cooper & Co., Savannah, 1860.
Biographical Sketches of the Delegates from Georgia to the Continental Convention, C. C. Jones, Jr.; Houghton,
Mifflin, & Co.; Boston and New York, 1891.
Button Gwinnett, Signer of the Declaration of Independence, Charles Francis Jenkins; Doubleday, Page;
Garden City, 1926.
CB Colonial Record Book (i.e., CBE, Mortgages; CBC-1, Conveyances).
CCCH Chatham County Courthouse.
CG *Colonial Georgia: A History*, Kenneth Coleman, Scribner's, New York, 1976.
CGGD *Colonial Georgia Genealogical Data - 1748-1763*, Wm. H. Dumont, Special Publications of
the National Genealogical Society #36, Washington, 1971.
CGHS Collections of the Georgia Historical Society (see volume titles below).
CHS *Chronological History of Savannah*, A. E. Sholes, The Morning News Print, Savannah, 1900.

CJW *Captain Jones's Wormslow*, William M. Kelso, Wormsloe Foundation Publications Number Thirteen, University of Georgia Press, Athens, 1979.

CM *The Clamorous Malcontents*, ed. Trevor R. Reese, Beehive Press, Savannah, 1973 (see contents below).

CM&SA *Columbian Museum and Savannah Advertiser* (newspaper).

CM&SDG *Columbian Museum and Savannah Daily Gazette* (newspaper).

Concise Dictionary of American History, ed. Wayne Andrews, Charles Scribner's Sons, New York, 1962.

CRG *Colonial Records of the State of Georgia*, I-XIX, XXI-XXVI, ed. Allen D. Candler and Lucien Lamar Knight, Atlanta, 1904-1916; XX, XXVII-XXXII, ed. Kenneth Coleman and Milton Ready, University of Georgia Press, Athens, 1976-1989. Later volumes in typescript (MS) at GHS, Georgia Archives, and University of Georgia Library.

DG *Daily Georgian*, or *Georgian* (newspaper).

Daily Journal (London newspaper, 1733).

Daughters of the American Revolution Magazine, "The Search for Peter Tondee," Jean Federico, April, 1978, 269-72.

The Descendants of William H. Cuyler Sheftall, John M. Sheftall, 1972.

DGB *Dictionary of Georgia Biography*, 2 vols., ed. Stephen Gurr and Kenneth Coleman, University of Georgia Press, Athens, 1983.

DGW *The Diaries of George Washington, 1748-1799*, IV, Houghton Mifflin, Boston and New York, 1925.

Diary of the First Earl of Egmont, II, 1734-1738, HM Stationery Office, London, 1923.

Dictionary of American Biography, III, ed. Allen Johnson and Dumas Malone, Charles Scribner's Sons, New York, 1930.

Drugs and Pharmacy in the Life of Georgia, Robert Cumming Wilson, Atlanta, 1969.

EAT *Early American Taverns*, Kym S. Rice, pub. by Regnery Gateway, Chicago, 1983.

Family Histories, Anna Weeks Herrin, Savannah, 1980.

FP *The Fledgling Province: Social and Cultural Life in Colonial Georgia, 1733-1776*, Harold E. Davis, University of North Carolina Press, Chapel Hill, 1976.

FPE *The Formation of a Planter Elite: Jonathan Bryan and the Southern Colonial Frontier*, Alan Gallay, University of Georgia Press, Athens, 1989.

George Whitefield: Wayfaring Witness, Stuart C. Henry, Abingdon Press, New York and Nashville, 1957.

GCSAR *Georgia Citizens and Soldiers of the American Revolution*, Robert S. Davis, Jr., Southern Historical Press, Easley (SC), 1979.

GDAH Georgia Department of Archives and History, Atlanta.

GG *Georgia Gazette* (newspaper).

GG-HECS *Georgia Gentlemen: The Habershams of Eighteenth-Century Savannah*, Wallace Calvin Smith, doctoral dissertation, University of North Carolina at Chapel Hill, 1971.

GGM *Georgia Genealogical Magazine*.

GGSQ *Georgia Genealogical Society Quarterly* (see articles below).

Georgia Heritage, Documents of Georgia History, 1730-1790, GDAH, published by the Georgia Commission for the National Bicentennial Celebration, Atlanta, 1976.

GHS Georgia Historical Society, Savannah, Georgia.

GHQ *Georgia Historical Quarterly* (see articles).

GJ *Georgia Journeys*, Sarah B. Gober Temple and Kenneth Coleman, University of Georgia Press, Athens, 1961.

GL *Georgia Life*, "Georgia Family Lines," Kenneth H. Thomas, Jr., Autumn, 1979.

Georgia Military Affairs, I, Mrs. J. E. Hays, GDAH, 1940.

GRR *Georgia's Roster of the Revolution*, L. L. Knight, Genealogical Publishing Co., Baltimore, 1967.

GLG *The Grand Lodge of Georgia*, William Henry Rosier and Fred Lamar Pearson, Jr., The Educational and Historical Commission of the Grand Lodge of Georgia F. & A. M., Macon, 1983.

GOG *General Oglethorpe's Georgia*, 2 vols., ed. Mills Lane, Beehive Press, Savannah, 1975.

GSG *Gazette of the State of Georgia* (newspaper).

GWJ *George Whitefield's Journals*, The Banner of Truth Trust, London, 1960.

Great Slave Narratives, Selected and Introduced by Arna Bontemps, Beacon Press, Boston, 1969.

HCG *Historical Collections of Georgia*, George White, Pudney & Russell Publishers, New York, 1854; reprinted by Heritage Papers, Danielsville, Georgia, 1968.

HG *History of Georgia*, Hugh McCall, pub. A. B. Caldwell, Atlanta, 1909.

History of Savannah, Georgia, from Its Settlement to the Close of the Eighteenth Century, C. C. Jones, Jr., D. Mason and Co., Syracuse, 1890.

History of Schley County, Georgia, compiled by Schley County Preservation Society, W. H. Wolfe Associates, Roswell, 1982.

Holding Aloft the Torch, Lowry Exley, Pigeonhole Press, Savannah, 1958.

HTUS *The History and Topography of the United States*, Second Edition, v. I, John Howard Hinton et al., pub. Samuel Walker, Boston, 1846.

The Journal of Charles Wesley, M. A., ed. Rev. John Telford, pub. Robert Culley, London, 1909.

The Journal of John Wesley, I, ed. Nehemiah Curnock, pub. Robert Culley, London, 1909.

JAC *Journal of Lt. Colonel Archibald Campbell*, ed. Colin Campbell, Ashantilly Press, Darien, 1981.

JEE *Journal of the Earl of Egmont: Abstract of the Trustees Proceedings for Establishing the Colony of Georgia, 1732-1738*, ed. Robert G. McPherson, Wormsloe Foundation Publications, Number Five, University of Georgia Press, Athens, 1962.

JPG *The Journal of Peter Gordon, 1732-1735*, ed. E. Merton Coulter, Wormsloe Foundation Publications, Number Six, University of Georgia Press, Athens, 1963.

JWS *The Journal of William Stephens, 1741-1745*, Wormsloe Foundation Publications, Numbers Two and Three, University of Georgia Press, Athens, 1958-1959.

LES *A List of the Early Settlers of Georgia*, E. Merton Coulter and Albert B. Saye, University of Georgia Press, Athens, 1949.

LMIT *Lachlan McGillivray, Indian Trader*, Edward J. Cashin, University of Georgia Press, Athens, 1992.

LMPRG *Lachlan McIntosh and the Politics of Revolutionary Georgia*, Harvey H. Jackson, University of Georgia Press, Athens, 1979.

Lachlan McIntosh Papers in the University of Georgia Libraries, ed. Lilla Mills Hawes, University of Georgia Miscellanea Publications, No. 7, University of Georgia Press, Athens, 1968.

Lambeth Palace, Fulham Papers, II (microfilm at University of Georgia Library).

The Life and Travels of John Bartram, From Lake Ontario to the River St. John, Edmund Berkeley and Dorothy Smith Berkeley, University Presses of Florida, Tallahassee, 1982.

LSC *Loyalists of the Southern Campaign of the Revolutionary War*, I, Myrtie June Clark, Genealogical Publishing Co., Baltimore, 1981.

MAL Marion A. Levy Collection (#1414) at the Georgia Historical Society.

Memoirs of Rev. George Whitefield, John Gillies, The Reprint Company, Spartanburg, 1972.

Memoirs of the Life and Character of the Late Rev. Cornelius Winter, William Jay, Samuel Whiting & Co., New York, 1811.

MCB&B *Muskets, Cannon Balls, & Bombs*, ed. and translated by Benjamin Kennedy, Beehive Press, Savannah, 1974.

M&D *Marriages and Deaths, 1763 to 1820, Abstracted from Extant Georgia Newspapers*, Mary Bondurant Warren, Heritage Papers, Danielsville, 1968.

MUS *Minutes of the Union Society: Being an Abstract of Existing Records, from 1750-1858*, J. M. Cooper & Co., Savannah, 1860.

OA Oglethorpe in America, Phinizy Spalding, University of Chicago Press, Chicago, 1977.

OFVA Our First Visit in America: Early Reports from the Colony of Georgia, 1732-1740, Introduction by Trevor R. Reese, Beehive Press, Savannah, 1974 (see contents below).

OL Orphan-Letters, Being a Collection of Letters Wrote by the Orphans in the Hospital of Georgia To the Reverend Mr. George Whitefield, Glasgow, 1741.

The Oxford Universal Dictionary on Historical Principles, Third Edition, Oxford University Press, London, 1933.

Pennsylvania Magazine of History and Biography, "William Logan's Journal of a Journey to Georgia, 1745," XXXVI (1912).

Public Intelligencer (newspaper).

Publications of the Huguenot Society of London, XXX, Butler & Tanner Ltd., Frome, 1927.

PRO British Public Record Office, London.

The Rambler in Georgia, ed. Mills Lane, Beehive Press, Savannah, 1973.

Recollections of a Long and Satisfactory Life, William Harden, pub. 1934, reprinted by Negro University sities Press, New York, 1968.

Reconstructed 1790 Census of Georgia, Marie De Lamar and Elizabeth Rothstein, Genealogical Publishing Company, Baltimore, 1985.

Records of Effingham County, Georgia, containing *Annals of Georgia, volume II*, and Effingham Legal Records from the *Georgia Genealogical Magazine*, Southern Historical Press, 1976.

RDSG Register of Deaths in Savannah, Georgia, 6. vols., The Genealogical Committee of the Georgia Historical Society; v. I, Georgia Historical Society, Savannah, 1983; v. II-VI, R. J. Taylor Foundation, Atlanta, 1983-1989.

Roster of Revolutionary Soldiers in Georgia, III, Mrs. Howard McCall (Ettie Tidwell), Genealogical Publishing Company, Baltimore, 1969.

RGG The Royal Governors of Georgia, 1754-1775, W. W. Abbot, University of North Carolina Press, Chapel Hill, 1959.

RGGaz Royal Georgia Gazette (newspaper).

RGL Recollections of a Georgia Loyalist, Elizabeth Lichtenstein Johnston, New York, 1901.

RRG Revolutionary Records of Georgia, 3 vols., Allen D. Candler, Franklin-Turner Co., Atlanta, 1908.

R&SEL Republican and Savannah Evening Ledger (newspaper).

The Salzburger Saga, George Fenwick Jones, University of Georgia Press, Athens, 1984.

Savannah Duels and Duellists, 1733-1877, Thomas Gamble, Review Publishing and Printing Co., Savannah, 1923.

The Second or 1807 Land Lottery, Georgia Genealogical Reprints, 1968, The Reverend Silas Emmett Lucas, Jr., Vidalia.

Sheftall Papers, American Jewish Historical Society, Waltham, Massachusetts.

Some Huguenot Families of South Carolina and Georgia, Supplement No. 3, Second Edition, Revised, Harry Alexander Davis, Washington, 1940.

South Carolina and American General Gazette (newspaper).

South Carolina Chancery Court Records, 1671-1779, ed. A. K. Gregory, American Historical Association, Washington, 1950.

SCG South Carolina Gazette (newspaper).

SCG&CJ South Carolina Gazette and Country Journal (newspaper).

South Carolina Historical and Genealogical Magazine, pub. by South Carolina Historical Society.

SG The Story of Georgia, IV, Walter G. Cooper, American Historical Society, Inc., New York, 1938.

SGn Savannah Georgian (newspaper).

SiCG Slavery in Colonial Georgia, 1730-1775, Betty Wood, University of Georgia Press, Athens, 1984.

SOJCC Savannah's Old Jewish Community Cemeteries, B. H. Levy, Mercer University Press, Macon, 1983.

SOS *Storm Over Savannah*, Alexander A. Lawrence, University of Georgia Press, Athens, 1968.

SSG *Statistics of the State of Georgia*, George White, pub. W. Thorne Williams, Savannah, 1849.

Third to None: The Saga of Savannah Jewry, 1733-1983, Rabbi Saul Jacob Rubin, Savannah, 1983.

The Thirteen Colonies Cookbook, Mary Donovan, Amy Hatrak, Frances Mills, and Elizabeth Shull, Praeger Publishers, New York, 1975.

TAPS *Transactions of the American Philosophical Society*, New Series, XXXIII, pt. 1 (December, 1942), "Diary of a Journey through the Carolinas, Georgia, Florida, from July 1, 1765, to April 10, 1766," by John Bartram, annotated by Francis Harper.

Travels, William Bartram, Penguin Books, New York, 1988.

A True and Historical Narrative of the Colony of Georgia, ed. Clarence L. Ver Steeg, Wormsloe Foundation Publications, Number Four, University of Georgia Press, Athens, 1960.

"A View of Savannah on March 29, 1734", Peter Gordon (map).

The Western Pennsylvania Historical Magazine, XLIII, no. 1, "A Revolutionary Journal and Orderly Book of General Lachlan McIntosh's Expedition, 1778," ed. by Edward G. Williams.

W *Wormsloe*, E. Merton Coulter, Wormsloe Foundation Publications, Number One, University of Georgia Press, Athens, 1955.

WC *The Woodwright's Companion*, Roy Underhill, University of North Carolina Press, Chapel Hill, 1983.

The Woodwright's Shop, Roy Underhill, University of North Carolina Press, Chapel Hill, 1981.

WM *Weekly Miscellany* (London newspaper, 18th century)

Contents cited from multi-work volumes:

The Clamorous Malcontents: Criticisms & Defenses of the Colony of Georgia, 1741-1743:
I Patrick Tailfer, *A True and Historical Narrative of the Colony of Georgia in America*, 1741, pp. 23-121.

Our First Visit in America: Early Reports from the Colony of Georgia, 1732-1740:
III Francis Moore, *A Voyage to Georgia, Begun in the Year 1735* [1735-1736], 1744, pp. 81-156.
IV Journal of Benjamin Ingham [1735-1736], pp. 159-182.
V *An Extract of the Rev. Mr. John Wesley's Journal* [1735-1737], 1739, pp. 185-240.
VI Journal of Thomas Causton [1737], pp. 243-277.
VII George Whitefield, *A Journal of a Voyage from London to Savannah in Georgia* and its continuations [1738-1740], 1739-1741, pp. 281-313.

Collections of the Georgia Historical Society:

II - Selected Manuscripts; Chapter 2, "A New Voyage to Georgia," 37-67; Savannah, 1842.
III - Letters of Oglethorpe and Wright; Morning News, Savannah, 1873.
IV - The Dead Towns of Georgia, C. C. Jones, Jr.; Morning News, 1878.
VI - Letters of Honorable James Habersham; Morning News, 1904.
VII, pt. 3 - The Spanish Official Account of the Attack on the Colony of Georgia.
VIII - Letters of Joseph Clay; Morning News, 1913.
X - Proceedings and Minutes of the Governor and Council of Georgia, Oct. 4, 1774, through November 7, 1775, and September 6, 1779, through September 20, 1780; ed. Lilla M. Hawes; GHS, Savannah, 1952.
XII - The Papers of Lachlan McIntosh, 1774-1779; ed. Lilla M. Hawes; GHS, Savannah, 1957.
XVII - Jones Family Papers, 1760-1810; ed. John Eddins Simpson; GHS, Savannah, 1976.
XVIII - The Search for Georgia's Colonial Records; ed. Lilla Mills Hawes and Albert S. Britt, Jr.; GHS, Savannah, 1976.
XXI - The Journal of the Reverend John Joachim Zubly; ed. Lilla Mills Hawes; GHS, Savannah, 1989.

Articles not listed by title in Abbreviations Key and Sources:

American Jewish Historical Quarterly, LII, "New Light on the Jewish Settlement of Savannah," Malcolm H. Stern.

Georgia Historical Quarterly:

X - Notes and Documents, "Some Letters of Joseph Habersham," ed. Ulrich B. Philllips; "Peter Tondee the Carpenter," Dolores B. Colquitt.

XI - "Mary Musgrove, Queen of the Creeks," E. Merton Coulter.

XIII - "Recollections of Old Savannah, Part II," Charles Seton Henry Hardee.

XIV - "The Houses of Colonial Georgia," John P. Corry.

XXII - Notes and Documents, "The Will of Dr. John Joachim Zubly," ed. Charles G. Cordle.

XXXI - "James Jackson in the American Revolution," William O. Foster.

XXXVI - "Proceedings of the President and Assistants in Council of Georgia 1749-1751," Part II, ed. Lilla M. Hawes; "General Robert Howe and the British Capture of Savannah in 1778," Alexander A. Lawrence.

XLV - "Minute Book, Savannah Board of Police, 1779."

L - "The First List of Pew Holders of Christ-Church, Savannah."

LIV - "George Whitefield and Bethesda Orphan-House," Neil J. O'Connell; "Whitefield and the Great Awakening," David T. Morgan, Jr.; "The Society of the Cincinnati," Albert Sidney Britt, Jr.

LVIII - "The Battle of the Riceboats: Georgia Joins the Revolution," Harvey H. Jackson.

LIX - "Utopia's Last Chance? The Georgia Silk Boomlet of 1751," W. Calvin Smith.

LXIII - "Henry Ellis, Enlightened Gentleman," Tom Waller.

LXIX - "The *Philippa* Affair," Sheldon S. Cohen.

Georgia Genealogical Society Quarterly:

XIX - (Fall, 1983) "Georgia's First Settlers: Revised, Corrected, Annotated, and Cross Referenced," Robert Scott Davis, Jr.

XXI - (Spring, 1985) "The 1742 Census of Georgia and Its Critics," Robert S. Davis, Jr.

Notes

Sources are listed by chapter title and by the number and first two words of the paragraph to which they refer.

Prologue

(1) "On a" - *CM&SA*, 29 November 1796 (4) "Even the" - *LSC*, I, 561; *RRG*, III, 136, 187 (5) "One veteran" - *CM&SA*, 9 December 1796 (13) "Peter's brother" - *CRG*, IX, 395, 415.

Part One - Child of the Province

London: (1) "Peter Tondee" - *CRG*, I, 94 (2) "Born in" - *Publications of the Huguenot Society of London*, XXX, 45, 34 (3) "Five years" - *CRG*, II, 16; XXXII, 33; I, 94 (4) "Pinkerton's grant" - *JEE*, 12 (5) "As well" - *WM*, 13 January 1733 (6) "Somehow in" - *CRG*, XXXII, 20; *LES*, 99, #1183-1185; *HCG*, 332; *CRG*, I, 97, 98; *Daily Journal* (London), 31 January, 3, 5-10, 12 February 1733 (7) "Almost certainly" - *JEE*, 11; *SCG*, 26 May - 2 June 1733; *CRG*, III, 22 (8) "The Tondus'" - See Appendix A; also *CRG*, XXII, pt. 1, 263; XXIX, 6; XX, 284, 285; *LES*, 79, #588; 98, #1161; *CRG*, IV, 394 (11) "Along with" - *WM*, 13 January 1733.

Port Royal: (1) "The voyage" - *SCG*, 28 April - 5 May, 5 - 12 May 1733 (2) "That night" - *GOG*, I, 15 (3) "Early the" - *SCG*, 26 May - 2 June 1733 (6) "At that" - *GOG*, I, 7, 8, 16 (8) "Just as" - *CG*, 13, 20; *JEE*, 9 (10) "Lamentably" - *CM*, 56; *GOG*, I, 293 (11) "Perhaps most" - *JEE*, 10 (12) "On arriving" - *GOG*, I, 11; *CRG*, XXVI, 59 (13) "So the" - *GOG*, I, 13, 19 (14) "But in" - *GOG*, I, 15, 18, 20, 22, 27, 28; *A True and Historical Narrative of the Colony of Georgia*, 143.

Savannah: (1) "Around the" - *SCG*, 26 May - 2 June 1733; *JPG*, 48 (3) "On Monday" - *GOG*, I, 19 (4) "Meanwhile the" - *GOG*, I, 13; *LES*, 36, #1018, #1022-1023; 8, #210, #214; 11, #288, #291; 58, #1643, #1646; 39, #1120, #1122; 52, #1504, #1507; 18, #514; 19, #517; 10, #48, #250 (5) "Besides lead" - *GOG*, I, 21; *Drugs and Pharmacy in the Life of Georgia*, 42-43, 62; *GJ*, 22 (6) "When James" - *GOG*, I, 19-21 (7) "For the" - *JPG*, 45, 46 (9) "On the" - *SCG*, 18-25 August 1733; *GJ*, 20, 31 (10) "Much more" - *AJHQ*, LII, 174; *Third to None*, 2.

Orphans: (1) "Although the" - *JEE*, 12; *CRG*, I, 98 (2) "Oglethorpe guessed" - *DGB*, 754; *GOG*, I, 21; *AJHQ*, LII, 177 (5) "The sanguinity" - *LES*, 97, #1100; 69, #260; 23, #670; 30, #871; 55, #1585; 8, #211; 36, #1018; 99, #1183 (6) *CRG*, XX, 183-85; *LES*, 2, #22; *CRG*, XX, 93; *GOG*, I, 101 (7) "In Savannah" - *GJ*, 20, 21 (8) "A miller" - *LES*, 11, #276-278; 56, #1607; *JPG*, 30, 31 (9) "With the" - *CRG*, XX, 183-85, 301-303; XXI, 465, 466; *CGHS*, II, 136 (10) "Life with" - *CRG*, XX, 152, 186, 252, 253, 314; *GOG*, I, 88, 184, 198, 214 (11) "Fueling these" - *GOG*, I, 102; *CRG*, XX, 459, 460; *GOG*, I, 101; *JWS*, II, 83-85 (12) "But despite" - *CRG*, XX, 448 (13) "With all" - *GJ*, 68 (14) "In the" - *OFVA*, 100, 101; *CG*, 29 (15) "At this" - See "A View of Savannah on March 29, 1734" [map], by Peter Gordon; *GOG*, I, 10, 16, 29, 30 (17) "The forty-foot" - *OFVA*, 96, 97, 101 (18) "Later" - GHS, Waring Map Collection (#1018) v. 2, plates 3, 4, 5.

The Silk Man: (2) "The thirty-three-year-old" - *LES*, 16, #435; *GOG*, I, 89; *CRG*, XX, 301-303; *GJ*, 242; *LES*, 19, #517; *CRG*, XXIII, 536-37; *SCG*, 6 September 1742 (3) "Fitzwalter's affinity" - *CRG*, XX, 426-27; *CGHS*, III, 32 (4) "The incident" - *GOG*, I, 129, 133-37, 144; *CRG*, XX, 258-59 (5) "The Irish" - *GOG*, I, 29, 57 (6) "While the" - *GOG*, I, 37, 129; *CRG*, XX, 259 (8) "No attack" - *GOG*, I, 144 (9) "Later, Thomas" - *CRG*, XX, 258; *GOG*, I, 144 (10) "But the" - *GOG*, I, 132-33 (11) "The gardener" - *CRG*, XX, 314 (12) "Aside from" - *GOG*, I, 131-33, 87-88; *CRG*, XX, 426 (13) "Unfortunately, neither" - *LES*, 9, #221, #240; 39, #1113 (14) "To the" - *CRG*, XXIX, 69; *GJ*, 137-38 (15) "A year" - *JEE*, 217 (16) "Joseph Fitzwalter" - *CRG*, XXII, pt. 1, 77-78, 229; *LES*, 2, #22 (17) "Long before" - *CRG*, IV, 506.

The Parkers: (2) "From the" - *CRG*, I, 126; XXXII, 50; II, 73, 120, 123; XXXI, 235 (3) "One of" - *GOG*, I, 106-107 (5) "Richard White" - *LES*, 101, #1258; 58, #1641; *CRG*, XXIX, 20; *GJ*, 78; *GOG*, I, 71-72, 88 (7) "Alice Riley" - *LES*, 95, #1045; *GOG*, I, 137 (8) "At the" - *GOG*, I, 221; *LES*, 9, #231 (9) "The Parker" - *CRG*, II, 288; *LES*, 39, #1113, #1125; *GOG*, II, 559 (10) "When Peter" - *LES*, 39, #1115, #1116; 92, #948, #947; *OFVA*, 200.

The Wesleys: (1) "In February" - (1) BDSF, 51; JEE, 115; OFVA, 87, 185; CG, 45; FP, 15, 16 (2) "The Wesleys" - GJ, 89; OFVA, 196, 215; LES, 13, #336 (3) "John Wesley" - LES, 42, #1193; JEE, 207-208 (4) "So Savannahians" - OFVA, 197; 162, 193-94, 204-205, 212; 203; FP, 214-15 (5) "One of" - OFVA, 200, 180, 194 (9) "With the" - JEE, 107; *The Journal of John Wesley*, I, 298; LES, 90, #900-903 (10) "Since the" - OFVA, 230, 198, 200-201, 203, 214 (11) "The inland" - CG, 36-38; CJW, 172; CGHS, IV, pt. 2, 15 (12) "Returning from" - *Journal of the Reverend Charles Wesley*, 51; Egmont Papers, no. 14205, pt. 2, 160(276).

The Isle of Hope: (1) "The Indians" - CRG, IV, 613; W, 260, n.8; GOG, II, 559; LES, 73, #371 (2) "The Parkers'" - CJW, 8 (4) "It might" - GOG, I, 11 (5) "Upriver from" - Egmont Papers, no. 14205, pt. 2, 160(276); CRG, XX, 194-95; see Appendix B (7) "But Dalmas" - CRG, XX, 293 (8) "Lucy Mouse" - OFVA, 270-71 (9) "The trouble" - OFVA, 199-200, 202; GJ, 91-94; CRG, XXII, pt. 1, 32-41, 204-206 (11) "The Caustons" - OFVA, 250-51, 257 (12) "The parson" - CRG, IV, 15-21.

Rum: (1) "Almost everyone" - OA, 47 (2) "So it" - CRG, V, 222, 192, 559, 606 (4) "Like many" - GOG, I, 160-62, 483, 88, 182 (6) "But for" - JWS, I, xiii-xvii (7) "After about" - CRG, IV, 44, 21, 32-33 (8) "The final" - CRG, IV, 61 (9) "In January" - LES, 27, #770, #771 (10) "Three months" - CRG, IV, 127-28 (13) "Whatever the" - CRG, IV, 656.

Whitefield and Habersham: (1) "Early in" - LES, 57, #1617; 21, #570 (2) "Zeal incarnate" - *George Whitefield: Wayfaring Witness*, 16-19; OFVA, 285-86; GHQ, LIV, 57 (3) "His preaching" - ABF, 102; CRG, IV, 504-505; III, 21 (4) "Both the" - ABF, 104-105 (5) "Regarding the" - ABF, 103 (6) "Whitefield's impact" - CRG, IV, 490-91, 477-78 (8) "A loyal" - CGHS, VI, 236 (9) "But when" - FP, 235 (10) "From the" - CRG, IV, 145 (11) "The crux" - CRG, IV, 181-83 (15) "On his" - OFVA, 295 (16) "At the" - CRG, IV, 188-90; OFVA, 295-96 (18) "The Reverend" - CRG, IV, 487 (19) "His brother" - CRG, IV, 274.

Keeper of the Store: (1) "For the" - GGSQ, XIX, [Fall], 118 (2) "They had" - GJ, 64 (3) "At first" - GOG, I, 155-56, 168, 217, 284 (4) "In five" - CRG, IV, 13, 252 (5) "So his" - CRG, IV, 199, 206; *Diary of the Earl of Egmont*, II, 491 (6) "Around the" - CRG, IV, 287 (7) "When a" - CRG, IV, 409 (8) "Even before" - CRG, IV, 167-72 (9) "In the" - CRG, IV, 199; II, 238; XXII, pt. 2, 50 (10) "General Oglethorpe" - CRG, IV, 212-14, 223 (11) "The Trustees" - CRG, IV, 318-22; BDSF, 83-84 (12) "Along with" - CRG, IV, 214, 217 (13) "Also that" - LES, 65, #139, #140; CRG, XXII, pt. 1, 355; "Salarys and Expenses for one quarter from Christmas to Lady Day 1751," Force Transcripts, Bevan Collection, 7E, Box 3, (Manuscript Division) Library of Congress; Egmont Papers, no. 14205, pt. 2, 160(276); CRG, IV, 520-21.

Parker's Fall: (1) "After the" - CRG, IV, 242, 251, 252-53; 224; III, 422-26 (3) "Christmas in" - CRG, IV, 251-52 (4) "Jones was" - GOG, II, 394 (6) "William Stephens" - CRG, XXII, pt. 2, 140-43 (7) "Whether or" - CRG, IV, 270; 248-50; 261; XXII, pt. 2, 495-97; XXV, 321 (8) "Meanwhile" - WM, 10 February 1739 (9) "In March" - CRG, IV, 294-95, 298, 318-22, 331-33 (10) "The tension" - CRG, IV, 324, 355-56, 359, 363, 353, 406, 420 (11) "On a" - CRG, IV, 396-97 (13) "Two Saturdays" - CRG, IV, 406-407; BDSF, 104; CG, 63 (14) "Less than" - CRG, IV, 412-13, 416, 427 (15) "Early in" - CRG, IV, 428; GOG, II, 379 (16) "The smoke" - CRG, IV, 428-30.

Orphans Again: (1) "Henry Parker's" - CRG, IV, 509 (2) "What Oglethorpe" - CRG, IV, 430-32 (3) "So in" - GOG, II, 420; CRG, 433-34 (5) "On Christmas" - CRG, IV, 477-78; GHQ, LIV, 54-56 (6) "Just before" - HCG, 335; LES, 70, #275; CRG, XXI, 249 (7) "The Reverend" - CRG, IV, 487-91; HCG, 332, 333 (8) "The Tondee" - CRG, IV, 505-506 (12) "At that" - CRG, IV, 508-509 (13) "Egregiously" - CRG, IV, 509; V, 360; GOG, I, 281 (14) "William Stephens" - CRG, XXX, 269; IV, Supplement, 57-58.

Bethesda: (1) "In his" - CRG, XXII, pt. 2, 359 (2) "Nothing else" - CGHS, IV, pt. 2, 16-17; FP, 246-47; GG, 21 March 1770 (3) "In any" - GOG, II, 437-40 (5) "On reading" - CRG, V, 359; 382; IV, Supplement, 64; GWJ, 500 (6) "Before work" - HCG, 334; OFVA, 300-302; LES, 86, #749, #744; CRG, IV, 615; BDSF, 193; *Lachlan McIntosh Papers in the University of Georgia Libraries*, 5 (7) "Even as" - CGHS, III, 110 (9) "To be" - CRG, IV, 539-41; OFVA, 302 (10) "Instead, John" - CRG, IV, 546, 548, 551; HCG, 332-33 (11) "When he" - CRG, XXII, pt. 2, 373-74; XXX, 269; IV, Supplement, 57-58; HCG, 332; JWS, II, 187; *Architecture of the Old South*, 21.

The Great House: (1) "Not long" - CRG, IV, 612-14 (2) "In March" - Egmont Papers, no. 14205, pt. 2, 160(276); HCG, 335; CRG, I, 505 (3) "In May" - CRG, IV, 573-74 (4) "Concerning" - CRG, IV, 608-609, 627 (5) "The Spanish" - CRG, IV, 612-14 (7) "In mid" - CRG, IV, 615, 619, 635; BDSF, 131 (8) "The August" - CRG, IV, 639, 644, 650, 660; IV, Supplement, 11, 17 (9) "But at" - CRG, IV, Supplement, 15, 21 (10) "The magnitude" - "View of the Orphan House" [frontispiece], *An Account of Money Received and Disbursed for the Orphan-House in Georgia*; OFVA, 299; CRG, IV, Supplement, 53 (11) "A week" - CRG, IV, Supplement, 23, 27-28; IV, 656-57, 661; LES, 48-9, #1401; CRG, XXII, pt. 2, 43; "Sketch of the Northern Frontiers of Georgia" (Campbell), in CGHS, VIII, facing p. 32 (12) "On the" - CRG, IV, Supplement, 36 (13) "When the" - IV, Supplement, 52; *Memoirs of Reverend George Whitefield*, 55; CRG, IV, Supplement, 57-58, 61; HCG, 332 (14) "Papot also" - HCG, 332; CRG, IV, Supplement, 166-68.

House of Mercy: (2) "The Reverend" - OL, 3, 4 (3) "With spring" - OL, 9-20; GJ, 229-33 (4) "Most of" - GWJ, 500 (8) "There was" - CRG, IV, Supplement, 166-68 (11) "The magistrates" - JWS, I, 41-42 (12) "Charles they" - HCG, 332; CRG, IV, Supplement, 119-20.

Bloody Marsh: (2) "With about" - *BDSF*, 151-53 (4) "The first" - *JWS*, I, 91; *GOG*, II, 614; *BDSF*, 157, 155; *JWS*, I, 106, 110 (5) "A cadet" - *HCG*, 334; *W*, 109; *GGSQ*, XXI, no. 1, 5; *BDSF*, 146, 148; *JWS*, I, 70, 110; *GOG*, II, 635 (6) "From the" - *BDSF*, 152-53, 156 (7) "The initial" - *BDSF*, 161; 162-66; *GOG*, II, 620-21; *CRG*, XXXV, 535 (8) "Another encounter" - *CRG*, XXXV, 535-36; *BDSF*, 167-68; *GOG*, II, 621; *CGHS*, VII, pt. 3, 73 (9) "That evening" - *BDSF*, 167, 168; *GOG*, II, 622, 634; *CRG*, XXXV, 537 (10) "The next" - *BDSF*, 169; *GOG*, II, 622-23; 634-35; *CRG*, XXXV, 538 (11) "But there" - *GOG*, II, 623; *CRG*, XXXV, 538 (12) "By a stroke" - *BDSF*, 170; *CGHS*, VII, pt. 3, 79 (13) "Two weeks" - *BDSF*, 171 (14) "The Spanish" - *BDSF*, 183, 184.

Apprentices: (1) "Volunteers" - *JWS*, I, 112, 114, 117, 119, 121, 131, 132; *LES*, 103, #1298 (2) "A more" - *CRG*, XXII, pt. 2, 394 (3) "Stasis reigned" - *CRG*, IV, Supplement, 254; XXXI, 190 (4) "When at" - *JWS*, I, xxvii; *CRG*, XXXI, 235; *CG*, 174-75 (5) "For a few" - *GGSQ*, XXI, no. 1, 5; *BDSF*, 206, 214 (6) "As Thomas" - *CRG*, VI, 60 (7) "A year" - *CRG*, VI, 101 (8) "Early in" - *JWS*, II, 87; *CG*, 155 (9) "About a year" - *JWS*, II, 187 (10) "Another event" - *CRG*, I, 495 (11) "Savannahians" - *CG*, 84-86; *GHQ*, XI, 15 (12) "For group" - *GHQ*, XI, 18, 19, 22; *CRG*, VI, 262, 265, 276, 328 (13) "The Bosomworths'" - *GHQ*, XI, 3; 16, 19, 21-22 (14) "But fresh" - *GHQ*, XI, 18-19, 21-23; *CRG*, VI, 262, 263, 271, 274, 279 (15) "But Mary"- *JWS*, II, 129; I, 149 (16) "As the Forties" - *FP*, 221-22; *CRG*, XXV, 94 (17) "And at least" - *FP*, 53; *CG*, 132 (18) "For amusement" - *CRG*, IV, Supplement, 117, 147; IV, 257; *JWS*, I, 67, 145; II, 86-87, 136.

Part Two - House Carpenter

Changing Times: (1) "The colonists" - *FP*, 97 (3) "As membership" - GHS, MAL, r. 1; *LES*, 96, #1071; *GGM*, April, 1965, 102, 104 (4) "Change came" - CBC-1, Conveyances, 21; *DGB*, 777-78; *JWS*, II, xxvii; *GL*, 38 (5) "Also in 1752" - CBC-1, Conveyances, 22; *GGM*, July, 1967, 1669-70 (6) "On December" - *CRG*, VI, 378; *CG*, 205 (7) "It is certain" - CBC-1, Conveyances, 106; *CRG*, I, 505; XXV, 319 (8) "During this" - CBC-1, Conveyances, 25; *Abstracts of Georgia Colonial Conveyance Book C-1*, 64/71, 110/111, 112/113, 161/161, 317/316; *GG*, 16 November 1768, 31 May 1769 (9) "Within a year" - *GL*, 38; *CRG*, VI, 251 (10) "One other" - See entry for Style, sense IV, *Oxford Universal Dictionary*.

Royal Omens: (3) "When the" - *DGB*, 835-36; *SCG*, 31 October 1754; *CRG*, VII, 174; XXII, pt. 2, 470; *JWS*, I, 99; *CRG*, XXVII, 33 (4) "But Savannahians" - *SCG*, 31 October, 7 November 1754 (5) "Less than" - *CRG*, VII, 21 (6) "They reconvened" - *CRG*, VII, 22; XXVII, 33 (7) "Nine days" - *CRG*, VII, 35; IV, 285-86 (8) "Without entering" - *CRG*, VII, 35-36; IV, 83 (9) "Papot's apprentices" - CBK, Marks and Brands, 5; CBA, Wills, 294-95; *GG*, 11 January 1769.

Ominous Endings: (2) "Foremost" - *RGG*, 5-6; 36-37 (3) "As would" - *RGG*, 37 (4) "But even" - *CRG*, VII, 19-20, 23-25, 33-34 (5) "But a full" - *RGG*, 47-48; *OA*, 90-91; *CG*, 83 (6) "Even the Board" - *CRG*, XXXIV, 170 (7) "In his" - *RGG*, 44-45; *CRG*, VII, 22-23 (8) "Even when" - *CRG*, VI, 423-26; 436 (9) "On touring" - *CGHS*, IV, 224; *CRG*, XXVII, 62 (10) "Consequently" - *CRG*, VII, 200; 515 (11) "The lack" - *CRG*, XXVII, 63; *CGHS*, IV, 225, 226n (12) "He galled" - *RGG*, 45-46; *CG*, 181-82 (13) "Early on" - *CRG*, XXVII, 35; VII, 101, 204 (14) "Only at" - *CG*, 183; *RGG*, 51-52 (15) "By the end" - *RGG*, 52, 53, 64 (16) "Reynolds' career" - *CG*, 184; *DGB*, 836 (17) "Perhaps the" - *RGG*, 56; *CRG*, VIII, 29; XVIII, 48-64 (18) "To Peter" - CBE, Mortgages, 70-71

Money's Worth: (2) "In colonial" - *SCG*, 22 November 1760 (note beneath Price Current list) (3) "The price" - CBJ, Miscellaneous Bonds, 259; CBC-1, Conveyances, 786-87; *OFVA*, 98 (4) "Slaves comprised" - GDAH, Whitefield's Estate Inventory, Loose Deeds and Bonds; CBFF, Inventories of Estates, 1-2; *FP*, 135 (5) "Household furniture" - CBFF, 1-2; CBHH, Store Account of Richard Milledge, 9 February, 5 September 1762 (for Johnson & Wylly, see *GGSQ*, IV, 1044) (6) "By contrast" - CBFF, 1 (7) "Clothes were" - *CGHS*, VI, 61; Whitefield's Estate Inventory; CBHH, Store Account of Richard Milledge, 30 June, 5 September, 27 May 1762; Estate Inventory of Thomas Tripp, James Wright Papers, Telamon Cuyler Collection, University of Georgia Library (8) "At the standard" - *GOG*, II, 476-77, (9) "Despite the" - *OFVA*, 97; *GOG*, II, 393 (11) "To discourage" - *CRG*, XVIII, 57; CBE, Mortgages, 62.

Rule of Reason: (1) "A more dramatic" - *GHQ*, LXIII, 374; *RGG*, 82; *FP*, 32 (2) "Born into" - *DGB*, 291-92; *GHQ*, LXIII, 364-66 (3) "When he" - *SCG*, 28 April 1757; Henry Ellis Papers, University of Georgia Library, Accession #708 (4) "Even before" - *RGG*, 59-60, 56 (5) "Once in Savannah" - *CG*, 189; *GHQ*, LXIII, 368 (6) "First, Ellis" - *RGG*, 61-62; *CG*, 189 (7) "With deft" - *RGG*, 62-64, 52-53 (8) "Ellis had" - *RGG*, 56, 69; *CG*, 190 (9) "By the time" - *CG*, 190 (10) "To bolster" - *RGG*, 68-69; *CG*, 190 (11) "To attract" - *CG*, 191; *RGG*, 72 (12) "To encourage" - *RGG*, 71 (13) "Having set" - *RGG*, 73 (14) "The chiefs" - *CRG*, VII, 643-48 (16) "Cordial addresses" - *CRG*, VII, 657-59 (17) "Ellis then" - *CRG*, VII, 664, 667.

Establishmentarianism: (1) "That Georgia" - *CG*, 230; *FP*, 205-212 (2) "Its sponsor" - *DGB*, 770-72 (3) "The establishment" - *FP*, 212 (5) "Where Peter" - *FP*, 203; *CG*, 273, 275 (6) "During his" - *GHQ*, L, 86, 79, 80; *CRG*, VII, 183; *FP*, 222n; *CRG*, XX, 420 (7) "For Peter" - Ottolenghe to Waring, 12 July 1758, MSS of Dr. Bray's Associates, Pt. H (LC reel 11, 335/211-212); *CRG*, XXVIII, pt. 1, 162.

The Filature: (1) "For many" - *CG*, 114-15; *CRG*, XXVIII, pt. 2, 168 (2) "But the French" - *GHQ*, LIX, 26-27; *CRG*, XXXI, 184-85 (3) "The first public" - *CRG*, XXVI, 143-44, 145, 190, 202, 228; *GHQ*, XXXVI, 68;

CRG, IV, Supplement, 136 (4) "The first filature" - *CRG*, XXVI, 228-29, 231; II, 519; XXXI, 261 (6) "The fire that" - Ottolenghe to Waring, 12 July 1758, MSS of Dr. Bray's Associates, Pt. H (LC reel 11, 335/211-212); *CRG*, XXVIII, pt. 1, 162 (7) "In less than" - *CRG*, VII, 792-93; 802 (8) "The Governor" - *TAPS*, XXXIII, pt. 1, 28 (9) "Preparing" - *CRG*, XXVI, 433; XXVIII, pt. 2, 168; see also "Epilogue" and notes (11) "Tondee and Goldwire" - *CRG*, VIII, 82; 55; IX, 182; VII, 863-64; IX, 553 (12) "Tondee's family" - *CRG*, VIII, 55 (13) "Like Tondee" - *GL*, 38; *CRG*, VII, 447; 173-74; XVIII, 213 (14) "At the close" - *SCG*, 15-22 November 1760 (15) "It concluded" - *CRG*, XXVIII, pt. 1, 214; *HTUS*, 463 (16) "Accompanying" - *SCG*, 15-22 November 1760.

Halcyon Days: (1) "It is" - *RGG*, 182-83 (2) "If, amid" - *RGG*, 87-89; *DGB*, 1097; *FP*, 254, 32; *CG*, 226-27 (3) "Early in" - *RGG*, 84, 100-101 (4) "After the" - *RGG*, 95-96; *CRG*, XVIII, 774, 798-99; XIX, pt. 1, 154, 434; *CG*, 197-98 (5) "The wharves" - *FP*, 107, 123-24, 72; GHS, John Ettwein Papers, Collection #235, item 1; *GG*, 7 April 1763 (Savannah Price Current); 1 June 1768; 15 February 1769; 18, 25 April 1765; 10 September 1766, 13 May 1767, 29 January 1768 (6) "To treat" - *GG*, 13 May 1767, 29 January 1768 (7) "At the office" - *GG*, 7 April 1763; 17 October 1765; *FP*, 189; CBHH, Tondee Account, 9 October 1762; see also *GGSQ*, IV, 1044 (8) "The price" - GHS, John Ettwein Papers, Collection 235, item 1; *GHQ*, XIV, 195 and n (9) "Houses were" - *FP*, 36-37; *DGW*, IV, 178 (10) "What the" - *GG*, 25 January 1775, p. 2, c. 2 (12) "In 1760" - *AG*, II, 100; *RDSG*, IV, 240 (13) "Just over" - *GL*, 38; CBHH, Richard Milledge's Account, 30 June 1762; *CRG*, VII, 924 (14) "John and his" - *LES*, 96, #1089; *GL*, 38; *GG-HECS*, 176; *W*, 177 (15) "The small" - *DGB*, 882-85; *SOJCC*, 53-54; CBC-2, Conveyances, 731-32 (16) "Since Lucy" - *LES*, 65, #139, #140; *JWS*, I, 132; *CRG*, X, 605-606; IX, 415 (17) "With the increase" - CBP, Mortgages, 142-44 (18) "When Tondee" - *CGHS*, XVII, 8 (19) "Savannahians also" - *FP*, 172-74 (21) "Centers of" - *GG*, 22 December 1763; 7 November 1765; 21 May 1766; 22 June 1768 (22) "State occasions" - *FP*, 166-67 (23) "During her" - *CRG*, VIII, 490-94; *GHQ*, XIV, 186 and n (24) "Despite the" - *GG*, 7 June 1775.

Number Nine Heathcote: (1) "The lot" - CBC-2, Conveyances, 786-87 (2) "One setback" - *Concise Dictionary of American History*, 906-907; *CGHS*, VI, 30-32 (4) "When Tondee" - *CRG*, VIII, 411-12; *LES*, 89, #846 (5) "Moses Nunez's" - *SSG*, 619-20; *DGB*, 754-55 (8) "The Nunez family" - *AJHQ*, LII, 174-75 (9) "In Georgia" - GHS, Hartridge Collection,, #1349, 130/237; *CRG*, XXI, 384; XXVI, 42; VIII, 285, 427; *GG*, 20 and 27 October 1763 (10) "At the height" - *A Bicentennial Festschrift for Jacob Rader Marcus*, 54; *LES*, 91, #917-922; *CRG*, IV, 656; *JWS*, I, 78, 122; *BDSF*, 146 (11) "When he sold" - *CRG*, XI, 204; *GG*, 6 September 1787; *DGB*, 755 (12) "Peter intended" - CCCH, Book H, pt. 1, 61-63.

1765: (1) "When American" - *TAPS*, XXXIII, pt. 1, 29; *Travels*, 369-70; *The Life and Travels of John Bartram*, 246 (2) "The Bartrams" - *RGG*, 103-104, 122 (3) "Parliament had" - *ARG*, 18-19; *CG*, 247 (4) "To the Tondees" - *GG*, 7 February 1765 (5) "His career" - *CRG*, XIV, 231; IX, 295 (6) "As far back" - *CRG*, XVIII, 577-80; *GG*, 18 July 1765 (7) "The previous" - *CRG*, XIV, 337; IX, 478; 30, 143, 230 (8) "What is apparent" - *CRG*, XIV, 357 (9) "Oddly enough" - *CRG*, XIV, 337-38 (10) "By that time" - *CRG*, XV, 252; XVIII, 743; XIX, pt. 1, 48; 496 (11) "When completed" - GHS, Minutes of Council, 1794-1796, p. 165; *CGHS*, X, 84 (12) "Though no" - *FP*, 40; *CGHS*, VI, 207 (13) "Usually owners" - *CGHS*, VI, 39; *FP*, 71 (14) "During the summer" - *GG*, 11 July 1765 (15) "Summer's end" - CBA, Wills, 434-36; GHS, MAL, r. 1 (16) "Also during" - *CRG*, IX, 395, 415; GDAH, Georgia Surveyor General, Land Warrants, 1761-1766.

Chagrin: (2) "Few were" - *DGB*, 713; *GG*, 7 November 1765 (3) "Two months" - *DGB*, 713 (4) "For his part" - *RGG*, 114-15; *CRG*, XXVIII, pt. 2, 132 (5) "When the royal" - *ARG*, 21-22; *CRG*, XXVIII, pt.2, 135-37 (6) "For their part" - *ARG*, 21; *CG*, 248 (7) "But even" - *CRG*, XXVIII, 135-37 (8) "His success" - *CG*, 250; *CRG*, XXXVII, 123 (9) "The most biting" - *RGG*, 121; *CRG*, XXXVII, 126 (10) "At this time" - *GG-HECS*, 267 (11) "A different kind" - *CRG*, XVIII, 751; 219; *GG*, 21 January 1767.

Friends and Family: (1) "The amendment" - *CRG*, XVIII, 751-52 (2) "This was" - *GG*, 19 January 1764; 24 January 1765; 21 January 1767; *RGGaz*, 4 January 1781; 24 January 1782 (4) "The taverns" - *GG*, 21 January 1767; *FP*, 75 (5) "This ready" - *CRG*, XXXVIII, pt. 1, 140, 143; *EAT*, 94-95, 98 (6) "For the most" - *EAT*, 96-97; *CRG*, IV, 433-34; *Pennsylvania Magazine of History and Biography*, XXXVI, 3, 5 (7) "But public" - *EAT*, 100; *FP*, 75; *GG*, 27 January 1768 (8) "In May" - *GG*, 4 June 1766; CBA, Wills, 161-63; CBF, Inventories of Estates, 217-18 (9) "One of" - *GG*, 7 July 1766; see Appendix C; *GG*, 23 February 1774; Estate Appraisaer of Thomas Tripp, Wright Papers, Telamon Cuyler Collection, University of Georgia Library (10) "A clerk" - *GHQ*, L, 77, 83; *GG*, 25 May, 8 June, 22 June 1768 (12) "As well as" - *GG*, 26 September 1765 (13) "Gentlemen desiring" - *GG*, 13 July 1768 (14) "For the Tondees" - *CRG*, XXVIII, 798-99 (15) "But 1767" - *GG*, 10 June 1767; *CRG*, X, 282, 605-606, 751 (16) "And another" - *CRG*, XIX, pt. 1, 49.

Slavery: (1) "Tondee's slave" - *FP*, 129, 82; *SiCG*, 193; *GG*, 6 June 1765 (2) "Georgians went" - *FP*, 129; *CRG*, XVIII, 109 (3) "In estimating" - *CRG*, XIII, 514, 645; XIV, 36, 101; XXXVII, 198; XXXVIII, 145; *FP*, 129n (4) "But the *Georgia*" - *SiCG*, 125-26 (5) "In the case" - *CRG*, X, 245-46; 45; *GG*, 3 September 1766; *SiCG*, 243, n. 7 (6) "Other developments" - *FP*, 131-32; *GG*, 22 October 1766; *SiCG*, 58 (7) "To regulate" - *CRG*, XVIII, 102-38; *FP*, 127 (9) "But reality" - *FP*, 127-28; 192 (10) "Even the colony's" - *DGB*, 771; *FP*, 142-43; Ottolenghe to Waring, 12 July 1758, MSS of Dr. Bray's Associates, Pt. H (LC reel 11, 335/206) (11)

"Likewise" - *FP*, 143; *CGHS*, VI, 241 (12) "In each case" - *FP*, 142-43; Ottolenghe to Associates of Dr. Bray, 18 November 1754, MSS of Dr. Bray's Associates, Pt. H (LC reel 11, 335/223) (13) "Meanwhile" - *CRG*, XIV, 292-93; Grand Jury Presentments, *GG*, 24 December 1766 (14) "The Grand Jury" - *GG*, 6 July 1768; *CG*, 230; *SiCG*, 123 (16) "The memoirs" - *Great Slave Narratives*, 96-97; 105-107, 122-24 (17) "Doubtless" - *RGGaz*, 28 June 1781, 6 February 1781 (18) "What they" - *RGGaz*, 28 June 1781, 22 November 1781 (20) "At least" - CBA, Wills, 280-82.

Estates: (1) "Anthony and" - *CRG*, XXXI, 199, 204; VI, 351; *FP*, 102; "Salarys and Expenses for one quarter from Christmas to Lady Day 1751," Force Transcripts, Bevan Collection 7E, Box 3 (Manuscript Division), Library of Congress; *GG*, 19 January 1764 (2) "The following" - *GG*, 19 January 1765; 16 February 1764; *CGHS*, XVIII, 23; VI, 20-21, 27; *GG*, 21 March 1765; CBF, Inventories, 147-49 (3) "The Widow" - CBA, Wills, 280-82; *SiCG*, 164, 239; CBR, Miscellaneous Bonds, 94, 527-28 (5) "Tradesmen whose" - Estate Appraisals of Matthias Kugle, Thomas Tripp, Frederick Holzendorf; Bond to Administer Estate of Thomas Lee, Senior; Wright Papers, Telamon Cuyler Collection, University of Georgia Library (6) "During the summer" - PRO, America and West Indies, XIX, 54; *South Carolina Historical and Genealogical Magazine*, X, 216; *GGSQ*, XXI, 11, 15; *CRG*, XXIV, 402 (7) "At his death" - *CRG*, VIII, 610; *GG*, 7 March, 25 April, 25 July 1765 (8) "In April" - Bond of Frederick Holzendorf, Wright Papers, Telamon Cuyler Collection, University of Georgia Library; *FP*, 107-108; Hollingsworth Genealogical Card File (microfilm), University of Georgia Library; Appraisal of Estate of Frederick Holzendorf, Wright Papers, Telamon Cuyler Collection, University of Georgia Library; CBR, Miscellaneous Bonds, 469; *HCG*, 103 (9) "Perhaps the best" - CBF, Inventories of Estates, 348-49; *FP*, 44 (10) "Croddy's will" - *GG*, 13 July 1768; 26 April 1769; CBA, Wills, 403-404; 360 (11) "Four years" - Bond for the Estate Appraisal of Jane Oates, wife of George Strobhart, Wright Papers, Telamon Cuyler Collection, University of Georgia Library; Papers Attached to Will of Peter Tondee, Chatham County Courthouse (12) "Finally" - *The Salzburger Saga*, 14; *SG*, IV, 559; *FP*, 209 and n; see Appendix C (13) "The purpose" - CBF, 1-2; *WC*, 121-22, 124, 128-29, 134-36, 131; *WS*, 158-64 (14) "By far" - *WC*, 129-31 (15) "One carpenter's" - *CRG*, X, 28; *GG*, 16 November 1768; *GL*, 38; CBA, Wills, 294-95 (17) "Six months" - *GG*, 31 May 1769.

The Guardhouse Incident: (1) "According to" - *GG*, 27 June 1770 and Supplement; 3 January 1770 (2) "The general" - *CRG*, XVIII, 212 (3) "But two" - *CRG*, XVIII, 225, 290, 462; 212-15; *GG*, 22 July 1767 (4) "So when" - *CRG*, XV, 75, 112-13; XIX, pt. 1, 147 (5) "Graeme's career" - *CRG*, XIV, 599; X, 646, 913; *GG*, 20 April 1768 (6) "Though the Governor's" - *SCG* 25 October-1 November 1760; *South Carolina Chancery Court Records, 1671-1779*, ed. A. K. Gregory, American Historical Association, Washington, 1950, p. 390, 533, 537, 539; *CRG*, IX, 506, 511, 607 (7) "But Wright's" - CBF, Inventories of Estates, 479-87 (12) "The depositions" - *GG*, 27 June, 11 July 1760 and Supplement (26) "In this last" - (MS)*CRG*, XXVIII, pt. 2, 723; *GG*, 11 July 1770, Supplement (27) "But the Grand" - *GG*, 27 June 1770, Supplement (28) "Subsequent issues" - *GG*, 4, 11 July 1770 and Supplement (29) "For when" - *GG*, 27 June 1770, Supplement (30) "As for the issue" - *CRG*, XV, 95, 211; XIX, pt. 1, 147; *CGHS*, III, 171; *CRG*, XV, 510, 530-31; XVII, 763-64 (31) "As for Tondee's" - *GG*, 18 April 1770.

Part Three - The Tavern

Politics and Religion: (1) "Tondee's election" - *FP*, 154; *GG*, 6 April 1768, 29 March 1769, 18 April 1770, 6 April 1774, 19 April 1775; *SCG&CJ*, 16 April 1771, 5 May 1772; *CGHS*, III, 228 (2) "It was" - *CRG*, XVIII, 558, 799; XIX, pt. 1, 436 (3) "The same" - *FPE*, 79, 117, 119; *RGG*, 151-52; *GG*, 14, 21, 28 March 1770 (4) "The ensuing" - *GG*, 11, 25 April 1770 (5) "As gratifying" - *GG*, 4 April 1770 (6) "The Oateses" - *CRG*, VIII, 444; CBO, Miscellaneous Bonds, 152 (7) "In late" - *GG*, 22 November 1764; 4 April 1765; Hollingsworth Genealogical Card File (Microfilm), University of Georgia Library (8) "Oates stayed" - *GG*, 16 December 1772; 7 June 1775; CBR, Miscellaneous Bonds, 141-2; *LMIT*, 256-57 (9) "Jacob Oates" - Telfair Family Papers, Box 1, 4/38, entry #10; *GG*, 21 December 1774; 22 March, 5 July 1775 (10) "The wedding" - *GG*, 4 April 1770; *CM&SA*, 16 May 1797 (11) "With the death" - *FP*, 224-28; *CG*, 233-34 (12) "It was finally" - *FP*, 198 (13) "The judge" - *GG*, 10 May 1769 (15) "Frink's contempt" - *FP*, 78 (16) "The first" - *GG*, 31 January, 21 March 1770 (18) "The second" - *Memoirs of the Life and Character of the Late Rev. Cornelius Winter*, 80-81 (20) "In the spring" - *CRG*, XV, 252.

Limbo: (1) "At the end" - *CRG*, XV, 252 (2) "The Governor" - *RGG*, 153-56; *ARG*, 32-35 (3) "When the next" - *CRG*, XV, 300 (6) "To begin with" - *GG-HECS*, 264; *CGHS*, VI, 39, 122, 145-47, 152, 160; *DGB*, 1097 (7) "Habersham also" - *CGHS*, VI, 145-48, 162, 168-69; 159 (8) "In addition" - *CRG*, VI, 163-64; *CRG*, XII, 217-18 (9) "During this" - *CGHS*, VI, 157, 167, 171 (10) "By the time" - *CGHS*, VI, 171; *RGG*, 156 (11) "When the House" - *ARG*, 35-36; *RGG*, 156-57; *CRG*, XV, 332; *CGHS*, VI, 179, 215-16, 221 (12) "Only after" - *CRG*, XVII, 655-57; *CGHS*, VI, 174-80 (13) "When he finally" - *RGG*, 157-58; *CRG*, XV, 334-39; XIX, pt. 1, 486; *GG*, 16 December 1772.

Custody: (1) "At the end" - *CRG*, XIX, pt. 1, 486; *CG*, 178; *CRG*, XV, 422 (2) "The ten days" - *CRG*, XV, 334-42; XII, 666-71 (3) "Within a week" - *CRG*, XV, 363, 375 (4) "Governor Wright" - *CRG*, XV, 388,

381, 384-85, 389-90, 394 (5) "Wright had" - *RGG*, 158-59; *FP*, 29-30; *CRG*, XXXVIII, pt. 1, 96 (6) "With so much" - *CRG*, XIV, 616; XIX, pt 1, 360-61, 369-70; XV, 505 (7) "Among the members" - *CRG*, XV, 355, 358; 471; 445; *FP*, 190 (8) "Ironically" - *CRG*, XV, 471, 474; *FPE*, 128-34 (9) "The Commons" - Hollingsworth Genealogical Card File (Microfilm), University of Georgia Library; *CRG*, XV, 400-401 (10) "Without doubt" - *CRG*, XV, 510-12, 512-13, 516-17; *FP*, 101 (11) "Livid" - *CRG*, XV, 516 (12) "Though Tondee" - CBCC-1, Conveyances, 508.

Lightning Rods: (2) "Late in" - *GG*, 16 December 1772 (3) "The following" - *SCG&CJ*, 6 April 1773; *FP*, 23-25; *CG*, 226-27; *CRG*, XVII, 401 (4) "Tondee's Tavern" - *CRG*, XIX, pt. 1, 488; XV, 358-60, 370; XVII, 676 (5) "The catering" - *CGHS*, VI, 184, 219; *SOJCC*, 75 (6) "Tondee and Minis" - *CRG*, XIX, pt. 1, 488, 486, 496 (7) "The very next" - *CRG*, XIX, pt. 1, 497; *GG*, 27 June 1770; *South Carolina and American General Gazette*, 18-25 July 1770 (8) "Though the tax" - *GG*, 16 June 1773; *CGHS*, VI, 228-31.

Unity: (1) "What is most" - Unity Lodge, No. 2, Savannah, Georgia, No. 465, [Membership] "Register for America & All the British Settlements / Commencing Octr. 28 A.L. 5768 A.D. 1768 / No. 3"; *GLG*, 21 (2) "Among the members" - *GG*, 18 April 1770; 16 June 1773, Supplement; *CRG*, XV, 466; *GG*, 5 January 1774, 17 May 1775; see Appendix C; *GSG*, 16 June, 15 December 1785 (3) "Surely the central" - See Appendix C; *GG*, 7 September 1774; *HCG*, 49; *GLG*, 22; *GG*, 7 February 1776; *CRG*, XXXVIII, pt. 1, 20; *RRG*, I, 329 (4) "Besides Tondee" - *CRG*, XXXVIII, pt. 1, 402-406, 632; *RRG*, I, 199; *GHQ*, XXXI, 251 (5) "Of the Unity" - *CRG*, XXXVIII, pt. 2, 314; 21; *RRG*, I, 329; *GG*, 7 September 1774; *GHQ*, XLV, 254, 246; PRO, Audit Office, 3/119, Accounts of The Right Honorable the Lords Commissioners of His Majesty's Treasury, Colonial Expenses in Georgia, West Florida, and the Carolinas from c. 173_-178_ ; *RGGaz*, 6 June 1782; *RRG*, II, 355, 376 (6) "For whatever" - *RRG*, III, 85, 118, 400; *GCSAR*, 56-62 (10) "The House" - *CGHS*, XXI, xiii; *GHQ*, XXII, 387.

Resolution and Dissent: (1) "As Tondee's" - *GG*, 23 February 1774 (2) "The genial" - *EAT*, 66-68; *GG*, 25 January 1775 (3) "Bad debts" - *GG*, 13, 20, 27 April 1774 (4) "Though Wright" - *BHS*, 9; *CRG*, XII, 188; XVII, 739; XV, 602; *GG*, 21 March 1770 (5) "To Mistress" - *EAT*, 90-92; *The Thirteen Colonies Cookbook*, 224-25, 237-44; *FP*, 72; *CRG*, XXXVIII, pt. 1, 141-42 (6) "Guests at" - CBFF, Inventories of Estates, 1-2 (7) "The rift" - *GG*, 13 July 1774 (8) "The following day" - *GG*, 7 September 1774 (9) "Meanwhile" - *CRG*, XXXVIII, pt. 1, 307; *RRG*, I, 11; *Georgia Heritage, Documents of Georgia History, 1730-1790*, plate 46 (10) "The meeting, however" - *GG*, 7 September 1774 (11) "The following *Gazette*" - *GG*, 3 August 1774 (12) "Two days" - *GG*, 10 August 1774; *RRG*, I, 13-14 (13) "Wright's edict" - *GG*, 7 September 1774 (14) "The meeting accomplished" - *GG*, 17 August 1774 (15) "With his proclamation" - *ARG*, 42; *GG*, 7 September, 12 October 1774 (16) "In response" - *GG*, 21 September, 19 October 1774 (17) "Four days" - *GG*, 9, 16, 23 November 1774 (18) "Accordingly" - *GG*, 14 December 1774 (19) "Departing" - *FP*, 186; *GG*, 14 December 1774 (20) "Ironically" - *DGB*, 539-41.

Sons of Liberty: (2) "The first" - *GG*, 14, 21 December 1774 (3) "Two days" - *GG*, 4, 11 January 1775 (4) "The next issue" - *GG*, 11 January 1775 (5) "Though anonymous" - *HCG*, 52, 61 (6) "The simultaneous" - *ARG*, 46; *GG*, 30 November, 21 December 1774 (7) "Governor Wright's" - *HCG*, 50-51 (8) "For Wright" - *GG*, 18 January 1775 (9) "Although the answer" - *HCG*, 52-54 (10) "While the Whigs" - *CRG*, XXXVIII, pt. 1, 474; *W*, 104; *CRG*, XXXIX, 41 (11) "Ironically" - *GG-HECS*, 122, 207, 212-13, 225; *HCG*, 44, 60, 65 (12) "Like their" - *GG*, 18 January 1775 (15) "Assured of" - *HCG*, 58-61 (16) "The resolutions" - *GG*, 1 October 1766, 7 March 1770; *SCG&CJ*, 16 April 1771 (17) "Forty-five" - *GG*, 1 February 1770; *HCG*, 60-61, 61-63; *ARG*, 49-50 (18) "Aware of" - *HCG*, 62; *CGHS*, III, 197-98; *RRG*, I, 53; *ARG*, 48-49.

First Blood: (1) "If the" - *ARG*, 50; *CRG*, XXXVIII, pt. 1, 395-409 (13) "Governor Wright" - *Georgia Heritage, Documents of Georgia History, 1730-1790*, plate 49; *CRG*, XXXVIII, pt. 1., 395.

Opposition Party: (1) "Report of" - *ARG*, 52; *HG*, 286-87 (2) "The day" - *GG*, 17 May 1775; *CRG*, XXXVIII, pt. 1, 439; GHS, Joseph Clay to Bright and Pechin, 16 May 1775, Letterbook of Joseph Clay & Co. (3) "The next three" - *ARG*, 52; *HG*, 287 (4) "But on Friday" - *GG*, 7 June 1775 (5) "On Monday" - *CRG*, XXXVIII, pt. 1, 458-59 (6) "The *Gazette* reported" - *GG*, 7 June 1775 (8) "These represent" - *Dictionary of American Biography*, III, 299-300 (9) "The *Gazette* had" - *GG*, 14 September 1774; 31 May, 17 May 1775 (10) "Among members" - *GG*, 26 April, 7 June 1775 (11) "In the House" - *HCG*, 461, 681; *SSG*, 607 (12) "After the Liberty" - *CRG*, XXXVIII, pt. 1, 450-51, 456-59; *GG*, 31 May 1775 (13) "By the time" - *CRG*, XXXVIII, 452-53 (14) "The Sons" - *Ibid.*, 454-55 (16) "Captain Matthew" - *Ibid.*, 460-62 (19) "By six" - *GG*, 7 June 1775; *CRG*, XXXVIII, pt. 1, 61 (20) "Two days later" - *Ibid.*, 456-58 (21) "To Habersham's" - *Ibid.*, 463-65 (23) "Late in May" - *CGHS*, III, 187-88, 185.

Shining Moment: (2) "They met" - *GG*, 14, 21 June 1775 (3) "This last" - *CGHS*, III, 183 (4) "William Tongue" - *GG*, 14, 21 June 1775; *CGHS*, III, 183 (7) "The next issue" - *GG*, 28 June 1775 (8) "Though a lodging" - *GG*, 19 April 1775, p. 3, c. 1; 26 April 1775; *RRG*, I, 375; *HCG*, 65 (9) "The proprietress" - *GG*, 10 August 1768; 7, 21 March; 4, 11 April 1770; 16 December 1772; 16 June 1773; *ACW*, 35; *GCSAR*, 98; *CRG*, XII, 492 (10) "So it is" - *GG*, 12 July 1775 (11) "As before" - *HCG*, 66-67, 71 (12) "By the time" - *Ibid.*, 65-66; *AADH*, Fourth Series, II, 1557-1568 (13) "Several members" - *CRG*, XXXVIII, pt. 1,

493-500.

The *Liberty*: (1) "At Tondee's" - *HCG*, 66, 70; *CGHS*, III, 192-93 (2) "Meanwhile work" - *GG*, 8, 15, 29 November 1775 (3) "She was" - *CRG*, XXXVIII, pt. 1, 614-15; *GG, ibid.* (4) "The goal" - *CGHS*, III, 189-91, 194, 199; *GG*, 19 October 1774 (5) "The South Carolinians" - *GHQ*, LXIX, 340-45 (6) "So the South" - *CGHS*, III. 189; *AADH*, Fourth Series, II, 1109-1111 (7) "On July 7" - *HCG*, 70-71; *CRG*, XXXVIII, pt. 1, 606-16, 632 (15) "On that same" - *Ibid.*, 631-38 (19) "Two days" - *Ibid.*, 613-14; *GG*, 13 September, 2 August 1775 (20) "James Habersham" - *GG*, 12 July 1775; *Biographical Sketches of the Delegates from Georgia to the Continental Congress*, 82 and n.

Boys of Summer: (1) "When Henry" - *HTUS*, 463-64 (2) "Unlike the former" - CBFF, Inventories of Estates, 1-2 (3) "From the published" - *HCG*, 65-85 (5) "The Reverend Smith" - *CGHS*, III, 200-201, 203-204; Lambeth Palace, Fulham Papers, II, 44-45 (7) "On the next" - *CRG*, XXXVIII, pt. 1, 532-33 (8) "The next evening" - *Ibid.*, 536-38; *GG*, 26 July, 2 August 1775; *CGHS*, III, 200 (10) "During his ordeal" - Lambeth Palace, Fulham Papers, II, 45; *RRG*, I, 69; *GG*, 23 August; 13, 20 September; 25 October 1775 (11) "On the first" - *GG*, 2 August 1775; *W*, 104, 153.

Last Days: (1) "All this" - *GG*, 17 May 1775 (2) "The source" - *CRG*, XXXVIII, pt. 1, 548 (3) "Being ashore" - *GG*, 21 June, 5 July 1775 (4) "The two" - *CRG*, XXXVIII, pt. 1, 548-61 (8) "Of this last" - *CGHS*, III, 204-205; *CRG*, XXXVIII, pt. 2, 19-21 (9) "The chairman" - *CRG*, XXXVIII, pt. 1, 625-27; *SOJCC*, 54; *CGHS*, III, 212 (10) "The vessel" - *GG*, 13 September, 4 October 1775 (11) "Around eleven" - *GG*, 8, 15, 29 November 1775 (12) "As autumn" - *ARG*, 61-62; *CRG*, XXXVIII, pt. 2, 32-35 (13) "The Sheftalls" - *GG*, 15 November 1775.

Notices: (1) "*Savannah*, October 25" - *GG*, 25 October 1775 (2) "In the odd" - CBAA, Wills, 227-32; 232-46 (3) "Joseph Habersham sent" - *Biographical Sketches of the Delegates from Georgia to the Continental Congress*, 82; *GG*, 8 November 1775; *GHQ*, X, 145-46; *CGHS*, III, 220; *W*, 104 (4) "Two weeks" - Papers Attached to Tondee's Will, CBAA, Wills, 227-32 (7) "William Young" - *GG*, 24 January 1776 (8) "Joseph Habersham had arrested" - *GG-HECS*, 267; *CGHS*, III, 234; *RRG*, I, 94, 98, 100-101; *History of Savannah, Georgia, from Its Settlement to the Close of the Eighteenth Century*, 220-21; *ARG*, 68 (9) "Early in March" - *GHQ*, LVIII, 235-41; *CGHS*, III, 233-34; XII, 1-4; *RRG*, I, 86, 94; *HCG*, 88-89; *CRG*, XXXVIII, pt. 2, 79 (10) "Meanwhile" - *HCG*, 87-88; *LMIT*, 262 (11) "Both sides" - *CGHS*, XII, 3-4; *CRG*, XXXVIII, pt. 2, 119-21; *HG*, 304 (12) "Lieutenant Oates" - CCCH, Will of John Oates, #9, 17 June 1789; Deed Book 2H, 177-78.

Discord and Debacle: (1) "One of" - *GHQ*, X, 314-15; *RRG*, I, 98, 145; *GG*, 10 January 1776 (2) "The Declaration" - *RRG*, I, 174; *CGHS*, 200-201 and n (4) "Less than" - CBAA, Wills, 227-32; GDAH, Colonial Loose Wills, #366 (5) "In mid September" - CBFF, Inventories of Estates, 1-2; *CRG*, XXXVIII, pt. 1, 529-30; "The Search for Peter Tondee," *Daughters of the American Revolution Magazine*, April, 1978, pp. 269-72 (10) "About the time" - *ARG*, 84, 86, 95, 97, 101-102 (11) "All these" - *LMPRG*, 47; *Button Gwinnett, Signer of the Declaration of Independence*, 152-55 (12) "Button Gwinnett" - *DGB*, 374-76; *LMPRG*, 30-34; *Savannah Duels and Duellists, 1733-1877*, 11-16 (14) "In this spirit" - *LMPRG*, 60-64 (16) "When Gwinnett" - *LMPRG*, 64-66; *The Western Pennsylvania Historical Magazine*, XLIII, 3-4 (17) "Three days" - *DGB*, 1044 (18) "The last" - *ARG*, 107-108 (19) "During that year" - Sheftall Papers, American Jewish Historical Society; *GCSAR*, 130 (20) "On the morning" - *GHQ*, XXXVI, 308-22; *JAC*, 26 (23) "Among those" - *HCG*, 340-42; *DGB*, 885; *Some Huguenot Families of South Carolina and Georgia*, 29.

Beau Geste: (2) "Campbell reported" - *JAC*, 28-29; 110-11, n. 64 and 69; *RGL*, 48-49; *GHQ*, XXXVI, 323-24 (quotation from "Memoirs of a Revolutionary Soldier," *The Collector*, LXIII, 224-25) (3) "The occupying" - *JAC*, 30, 41; *CGHS*, III, 275, 298; X, 84-86 (4) "Sir James Wright" - *ARG*, 125 (5) "To the amazement" - *CGHS*, III, 262; *MCB&B*, 93-94 (6) "Under the command" - *CGHS*, III, 263; *CRG*, IX, 90; CBU, Conveyances, 519-21, 528; *SOS*, 31-32 (7) "At about" - *SOS*, 30, 32, 51; *MCB&B*, 122-23; *HCG*, 349 (8) "In his reply" - *HCG*, 348-51; *SOS*, 32-33 (9) "As messengers" - *SOS*, 41-47; *CGHS*, III, 264; *MCB&B*, 51, 97; *HCG*, 351 (10) "Meanwhile" - *SOS*, 39; *MCB&B*, 52, 54-59 (11) "Early in" - *SOS*, 60, 57; *MCB&B*, 10, 15-16, 18, 21 (12) "With the French" - *Ibid.*, 11-12, 109-10; *CGHS*, III, 265; *SOS*, 68-69 (13) "When the shelling" - *SOS*, 69-70; *CGHS*, III, 265; *MCB&B*, 18-19; 99; 112 (14) "Some who ventured" - *RGL*, 57-58; *SOS*, 70, 74; *MCB&B*, 112-13 (15) "By the third" - *Ibid.*; *RGL*, 58 (16) "On Thursday" - *SOS*, 70-71; *MCB&B*, 132, 114, 19, 52, 63; *RGL*, 59 (17) "When five days" - *SOS*, 88, 92-94; *MCB&B*, 100-101, 73 (18) "Toward five thirty" - *SOS*, 94-96; *MCB&B*, 20-21 (19) "The battle" - *Ibid.*, 37, 68; *SOS*, 106-107 (20) "That afternoon" - *MCB&B*, 74 (21) "When they finally" - *Ibid.*, 73; *SOS*, 105-106, 119-20 (22) "Credit for" - *Ibid.*, 52-53, 81, 78-79 (23) "Other decisions" - *MCB&B*, 32, 20-21, 36-37; *SOS*, 84-86 (24) "He did" - *MCB&B*, 21, 39-40; *SOS*, 85; 164, n. 17 [quotation from Joachim Merlant, *Soldiers and Sailors of France in the American War for Independence (1776-1783)*, translated from the French by Mary Bushnell Coleman (New York, 1920), 89f]; *MCB&B*, viii-ix (25) "Wounded" - *SOS*, 96, 99-101; 113-15, 117 (quotation from Thomas Gamble Scrapbooks, v. I, p. 1, Savannah Public Library) (26) "So he blamed" - *SOS*, 116-17; 77-78; *MCB&B*, 60 (27) "Unlucky indeed" - *HCG*, 537; *SOS*, 105, 79, 80, 163 n. 7 [quotation from *Observations sur l'Expedition de la Georgie, et les evenements qui ont suivi la prise de la Grenade*, Memoires Historiques, (Carton 248/2) Library of Ministere de la Guerre,

Chateau de Vincennes] (28) "In gratitude" - *SOS*, 117, 126-27 (29) "General Benjamin" - *ARG*, 131; *SOS*, 136 (30) "When news" - *Ibid.*, 104-105; *CRG*, XII, 449-50.

Before the Dawn: (1) "Savannah swarmed" - *ARG*, 301; *JAC*, 30, 41; *CGHS*, III, 275, 298-99; X, 84-86 (2) "In April" - *CGHS*, III, 300-303; CBJJ, Conveyances, 124; CBV, Conveyances, 231 (3) "The families" - *CGHS*, III, 289, 298-99; *RGGaz*, 8 February 1781 (4) "Joe was" - *RGGaz*, 28 June 1781; *ACW*, 97-98 (5) "The Morel" - *HCG*, 44, 65, 102-105; *FPE*, 108; *CGHS*, III, 273; *RRG*, I, 374-87 (6) "The Tondee" - *RGGaz*, 19 April, 30 August, 22 November 1781 (7) "Also in mid" - *CGHS*, III, 349-52, 360-61, 364, 369-71 (8) "The following June" - *RGGaz*, 6 June 82; *LSC*, I, 560 (9) "Less than two" - *CRG*, XV, 660-65 (10) "Before he left" - *LSC*, I, Appendix A; PRO, Audit Office, 3/119, Colonial Expenses in Georgia, West Florida, and the Carolinas from c. 173_-178_ (11) "By the eleventh" - *ARG*, 144-45 (12) "Two days" - *RRG*, III, 122, 136, 187; II, 742; *CGHS*, III, 367.

Goodbye to All That: (1) "Among Savannahians" - *RRG*, II, 356, 377; *Georgia Military Affairs*, I, 56-57 (2) "Also in mid" - MS 1170, Georgia Governors/Martin, Folder 29, Telamon Cuyler Collection, University of Georgia Library; *RRG*, I, 387 (3) "The Council" - *RRG*, II, 361-63; III, 367, 384, 409, 500, 563; I, 612; *CM&SA*, 1 December 1801 (4) "The erratic" - *RRG*, I, 386; *CRG*, XIX, pt. 2, 574; *W*, 100-102; *DGB*, 754-55; *HCG*, 49; *CRG*, XXXVIII, pt. 2, 20; *GG*, 6 September 1787 (5) "The state" - *HCG*, 102-104, 620; *RRG*, I, 375-77, 610-11, 616-17; *CRG*, XII, 476-77; XIX, pt. 2, 154, 178; *CGHS*, III, 312-13; *DGB*, 883; *CHS*, 66-67; *W*, 272, n. 1 (6) "Tondee's Tavern" - *GG*, 26 February 1784; *RRG*, III, 544 (7) "Within three" - *GSG*, 3 June 1784 (8) "The teacher's" - *GSG*, 23 December 1784; *Reconstructed 1790 Census of Georgia*, 65, 92, 143, 150; *GG*, 11 February 1790 (9) "Though Hunter" - *GG*, 29 April 1784; GHS, Hartridge Collection, #1349, Box 142, Folder 2563; *RRG*, II, 187-88; *GG*, 25 January 1769; *SG*, IV, 559; *Roster of Revolutionary Soldiers in Georgia*, III, 205; *CGHS*, X, 82, 99; *LSC*, I, 556 (10) "The union" - *GG*, 27 October, 22 September 1785; *DGB*, 761-62; 1097-98; *ARG*, 307.

The Legatees: (1) "Lucy" - CCCH, "An Account Current of the Estate of Mr. Peter Tondee & Wife, Deced, with Elisha Elon," Papers Attached to Tondee's Will; Epitaph of Gabriel Leaver, Colonial Cemetery, Savannah; GHS, Hartridge Collection, #1349, Box 142, Folder 2563; Telfair Family Papers, Collection #793, Box 13, Folder 106, "Account of the Estate of William Gibbons," entry for 8 May 1771; *ACW*, 60; *CRG*, XIII, 417, 728 (4) "During that" - *GG*, 7 October 1790 (5) "The accounts" - GHS, Superior Court Judgments, 1782-1868, Collection #5125 SP-45, Location 41-I-6, #2423 (7) "A skilled" - *GG*, 4 March 1790 (8) "Tom and Cumba" - *CRG*, XIX, pt. 2, 23-26 (9) "Settlement" - *GSG*, 26 January 1786; *GG*, 4, 18 December 1788; 12 February 1789 (10) "Final disposal" - CCCH, Book H, pt. 1, 61-66 (11) "Throughout the" - *GG*, 7 October-25 November 1790; CCCH, Book H, pt. 1, 585-88 (12) "The Elons" - *GG*, 13 October 1791; CCCH, Book I, 167-71; *CRG*, XIX, pt. 2, 454; *CHS*, 67 (13) "Missing from" - *GG*, 20 May 1790 (14) "At least" - *GG*, 27 December 1787; *1790 Census of North Carolina*; *Roman Catholic Records, St. Augustine Parish, White Baptisms, 1792-1799*, Historical Records Survey, Tallahassee, 1941; *Spanish Land Grants In Florida*, Claims Confirmed: Vol. III, D-J, Historical Records Survey, Tallahassee, 1941; Death Certificate of Juan Herault, 3 April 1819, Catholic Parish Records, St. Augustine Parish; 1830 Census of Florida; *El Escribano*, II, no. 2, p. 7, (pub. by St. Augustine Historical Society) (15) "Peter's other" - GHS, Minutes of City Council, 1794-1796, p. 163; *GG*, 16 August 1787, 10 July 1788, 19 June 1794, 27 September 1799 (16) "Mary Tondee Jones" - CCCH, Book W, 125-27; *GG*, 5 March 1799; *GGM*, 1986, p. 309; *RDSG*, IV, 240 (17) "In Elisha" - *ACW*, 26; *GG*, 4 March, 1 July, 28 October 1790; GHS, Minutes of City Council, 1794-1796, pp. 138, 145; *ibid.*, 1790-1796, pp. 63, 108 (18) "When the city" - GHS, Minutes of City Council, 1790-1796, pp. 24, 61, 108, 156; *The Rambler in Georgia*, 3 (19) "A lieutenant" - *GRR*, 414; *CM&SA*, 9 March 1798; *GG*, 13 September 1798; CCCH, Book 2K, pp. 165, 180-81; *RDSG*, IV, 72 (20) "Likewise" - *Ibid.*, III, 126; *CRG*, XXXVIII, pt. 1, 626; *RDSG*, III, 148; II, 93-94 (21) "But the house" - *CM&SDG*, 15 January 1820; *RDSG*, IV, 72, 76, 92; CCCH, Book 2K, 180-81, 191; GHS, Inventories and Appraisements, 1794-1805, 221-222 (Microfilm X-5125-18); *R&SEL*, 30 June, 6 August 1807; 9 July 1808 (22) "Peter's son Charles" - *The Second or 1807 Land Lottery of Georgia*, 188 (23) "Fifteen at" - *SGn*, 29 May 1827; *GG*, 5 September 1793; CCCH, Book Q, 128; Book T, 24-29; Bible Records of Thomas Elkins, Jr., of Effingham County; Thomas Tundee [sic], 1830 Census of Georgia; *M&D*, 115; *AG*, II, 100 (24) "By 1801" - *CM&SA*, 17 July 1801; *M&D*, 115; *Records of Effingham County, Georgia*, 86; GDAH, *Justices of the Peace, 1799-1812*, 887 (25) "Of the three" - Bible Records of Thomas Elkins, Jr.; Effingham County Records, Deed Book O, 329; *SGn*, 24 October 1826; *AG*, II, 100, 108, 145 (26) "In 1840" - C.R. Tundee [sic], 1840 and 1850 Georgia Censuses; *History of Schley County, Georgia*, 390-93; Schley County *Enterprize*, 4 October 1888 (28) "He signed" - CCCH, Will of John Oates, #9, 17 June 1789; *MUS*, 1 (facing 206) (29) "On a Sunday" - *Holding Aloft the Torch*, 21; *CM&SA*, 16 May, 5 December 1797; *GG*, 2 May 1799; CCCH, Book W, 127 (30) "Like his grandfather" - GHS, Judgment Rolls, Collection #5125, Box 30, Folders 2830 and 2832; Minutes of City Council, 1800-1804, 31 December 1804; *CM&SA*, 8 December, 17 October 1804; 17 October 1811 (31) "In the interim" - *Public Intelligencer*, 16 October 1807; GHS, Minutes of City Council, 20 December 1811, 417; *R&SEL*, 27 August, 5 December 1812; *RDSG*, II, 61; III, 113, 148, 153, 156 (32) "At the time" - *CM&SA*, 6 January 1801

(33) "Thursday passed" - *Ibid.*, 13 January 1801 (34) "Sheftall's team" - GHS, MAL, r. 1; *RDSG*, V, 26; *The Descendants of William H. Cuyler Sheftall*, John M. Sheftall, 1972; *BHS*, 14, 16; *RDSG*, (Cope) V, 219; (Brown) II, 72; (Norton) I, 19; CCCH, Book H, 325; GHS, Index of Estates, 1733-1838, entry for Norton, Thomas (Microfilm X-5125-22); *RDSG*, I, 1 (35) "In his list" - *RDSG*, III, 165; *CM&SA*, 23 September 1796; *RDSG*, I, 52; *Family Histories*, 17 (36) "Shortly before" - GHS, Description of Collection #569, David Brydie Mitchell Paper; *DGB*, 722. (37) "After the game" - GHS, MAL, r. 1; *CM&SA*, 16 January 1801.

Epilogue: (1) "When the old" - *DG*, 26 March 1839; *GHQ*, XIII, 42. (3) "Over its eighty" - *RRG*, I, 123; II, 612; *GSG*, 16 October 1783; GHS, Minutes of Clerk of City Council, 1790-1796, 61, 69-71, 119, 156; (Masons) *GG*, 17 May, 23 August, 15 November, 20 December 1792; 8 December 1797; 3 June 1802; *CM&SA*, 2 March 1799, 15 February 1804; 31 May, 11 November 1808; 14 November, 23 December 1811; *R&SEL*, 23 February 1811; (Union Society) *MUS*, 21-24; *GG*, 21 March 1799, 20 March 1800; 15 April 1802; *CM&SA*, 22 March 1808, 20 March 1809; *R&SEL*, 20 April 1809, 3 January 1811, 12 June 1812; (schools and academies) *GG*, 23 December 1790, 28 April 1791, 24 May 1792, 28 November 1800; *CM&SA*, 14 June, 23 September [p. 3, c. 4 and p. 4, c. 2] 1796; 3 April 1801; 11 October 1808; *R&SEL*, 13 January 1810; (barracks) GHS, Minutes of City Council, 1812-1817, 82, 103, 118, 135 (4) "The long room" - *GSG*, 19 January 1786; GHS, Minutes of City Council, 1805-1808, 24 February and 10 March 1806; *ibid.*, 1828-1831, pp. 166, 170; *CM&SDG*, 16 May, 2 December 1818; 25 November 1819; *CHS*, 71 (5) "The first performance" - *GSG*, 2 October 1783; *GG*, 22 March 1792; *CM&SA*, 14, 18 January 1804 (6) "Most performances" - *GSG*, 10 June 1784; GHS, Minutes of City Council, 1800-1804, 296; *CM&SA*, 1, 8 April 1803 (7) "One of the" - *GG*, 7 June 1792 (8) "The incident" - *Ibid.* (9) "Almost twenty" - *R&SEL*, 3, 7, 10, 14, 19 December 1811; 4, 7 January 1812 (10) "Perez and Company" - *R&SEL*, 28, 30 January 1812 (11) "When George" - GHS, Minutes of Clerk of City Council, 1790-1796, 69-71 (12) "Met at Purrysburg" - *The Augusta Chronicle and Gazette of the State*, 4 June 1791; *DGW*, 175-78 (13) "At six" - *MUS*, 1; *GHQ*, LIV, 559-60 (17) "The fire" - *DG*, 26, 27, 30 March 1839 (23) "That June" - *DG*, 4 June 1839; GHS, Travis Index, Reynolds Ward, Trust Lot S; *Recollections of a Long and Satisfactory Life*, 8.

Appendix A. List of Passengers on the *James*: Names of those who embarked at London 24 January 1733 and arrived at Savannah 16 May 1733 were culled from *A List of the Early Settlers of Georgia*, E. Merton Coulter and Albert B. Saye, eds., University of Georgia Press, Athens, 1949. (The *South Carolina Gazette* of 26 May 1733 puts the *James*'s arrival at Savannah on 14 May, however, which is the date used in the text.)

Appendix B. Letter of Thomas Mouse to James Oglethorpe: PRO, Colonial Office, 5/636, 158-59; published in *Colonial Records of Georgia*, XX, 194-95, and *General Oglethorpe's Georgia*, I, 113-14.

Appendix C. Membership Roster of Unity Lodge: Reproduced by permission of the Board of General Purposes of the United Grand Lodge of England. Sources for Occupations and Political Stances - (2) John Eppinger - *ACW*, 45; *RGGaz*, 16 August 1781 (3) Peter Gandy - *GG*, 25 May 1768, 18 January 1775 (4) Mathias Ash - *CRG*, X, 522; XII, 128; *GG*, 19 January 1764, 4 February 1767 (5) Frederick Rossberg - *RRG*, I, 132, 145 (6) Sinclair Waters - *GG*, 14 September 1774; *CGHS*, III, 302 (7) George Ducker - GHS, Waring Map Collection, #1018, v. I, plate 34; *GG*, 19 January 1764; 10 January 1765 (8) David Tubear - *CGGD*, 35; *CRG* XV, 466; *GG*, 16 June 1773; 7 September 1774 (9) Thomas Hamilton - *GG*, 6 September 1775; *CGHS*, III, 202; *GHQ*, XXXI, 251, 269 (10) John Oates - *GG*, 22 November 1764, 12 August 1767; *CGHS*, III, 302 (11) Peter Pechin - *GCSAR*, 25 (12) Jacob Oates - *CRG*, XXXVIII, pt. 1, 632; pt. 2, 120 (13) Abraham Gray - *HCG*, 49; *LSC*, 10 (14) George Johnson Turner - *GRR*, 173 (15) George Borland - *CGGD*, 7; *RRG*, I, 329 (16) Frederick Rhem - *GCSAR*, 56-62; *RRG*, II, 481; III, 85, 153, 400 (17) David Saussy - *Abstracts of Wills, Chatham County, Georgia, 1773-1817*, 62 (18) Aaron Pickren - CBA, Wills, 360-61; *RRG*, I, 199 (20) Joseph Rice - *CRG*, XXXVIII, pt. 1, 403-406; 632 (21) Charles Hamilton - *GG*, 6 September 1775 (22) Thomas Corn - *GG*, 5 January 1774, 17 May 1775; *RRG*, II, 19; *GCSAR*, 129 (24) Samuel Burgess - *GHQ*, XLV, 254; *HCG*, 102 (O'Bryan) (25) Malcolm Neilson - *GG*, 2 March 1774; *CRG*, XXXVIII, pt. 2, 21.

Appendix D. Estate Inventory of Peter Tondee: CBFF, Inventories of Estates, 1-2.

Index

Page numbers in bold indicate illustrations; bold italic indicates places on maps.

Carl Solana Weeks is a native Savannahian and a direct descendant of Peter Tondee. He graduated from Emory University and received his MFA from the University of Iowa in Creative Writing. He makes his home in Savannah.

Descendants of Peter Tondee are invited to write:
Martha H. McCorkle
903 Prospect Way
Dalton, GA 30720